Favela Resistance

Urban Periphery, Pacification, and the Struggle for Food Sovereignty

**Timo Bartholl, Christos Filippidis,
Antonis Vradis, and Minhocas Urbanas**

Preface by Raj Patel

Favela Resistance: Urban Periphery, Pacification, and the Struggle for Food Sovereignty
Timo Bartholl, Christos Filippidis, Antonis Vradis, and Minhocas Urbanas

This work is licensed under CC BY-NC-SA 4.0. To view a copy of this license, visit
https://creativecommons.org/licenses/by-nc-sa/4.0/

ISBN: 979–8–88744–038–5 (paperback)
ISBN: 979–8–88744–048–4 (ebook)
Library of Congress Control Number: 2023944255
Cover by John Yates / www.stealworks.com
Interior design by briandesign

10 9 8 7 6 5 4 3 2 1

PM Press
PO Box 23912
Oakland, CA 94623
www.pmpress.org

Printed in the USA.

Contents

Acknowledgments and Credits

The authors would like to thank Raj Patel for his kind support throughout, and his preface to this book; Alda Lima for her decisive translation assistance throughout the project; Cara Hoffman, Joey Paxman, and Claude Misukiewicz for their kind and attentive editing of the manuscript; PM Press for the care with which they surrounded this book; Museum of Maré for hosting the Week for Food Sovereignty in Maré in December 2018; the Department of Geography at Loughborough University for creating the necessary research space; and finally the self-managed community space Roça! in the favela Morro do Timbau, Rio de Janeiro, for providing this research project with the conditions of possibility.

Antonis Vradis would like to thank Eleni, Roy, Alekos, Stella, Ben, and Kiran for their unconditional support from near and far; Dan and Johnny for their hospitality and tolerance; and comrades and colleagues at the Radical Urban Lab at St Andrews who have taught him, in practice, another way in which to exist in academia today.

Minhocas Urbanas would like to thank Carolina Niemeyer for supporting the group research at the local level, all the Maré residents who contributed to the research process, and the agroecological movement of Rio de Janeiro for their sharing and openness regarding the action research carried out by the group.

Timo Bartholl would like to sincerely thank Rogério Haesbaert and all colleagues of NUREG/UFF (Núcleo de Pesquisa Território e Resistência na Globalização / Research Group on Territory and Resistance in Globalization) for the continuous exchange of ideas and reflections and for the mutual support that is common practice within NUREG.

Finally, Christos Filippidis would like to thank Oliver Belcher for his genuine interest, hospitality, and support during his stay at the Department of Geography of Durham University; the Institute of Advanced Study and the Department of Geography at Durham University for their decisive support, which allowed the development and deepening of this research; Roussa for her constant presence and her lifesaving advice; Ioanna for being an unexpected motivation during the writing process so that his chapter could be completed on time; and finally Vidraki for that persistent gaze that points beyond the human.

Credits

- The chapter entitled "Food Sovereignty Action and Research" was translated from Portuguese to English by Alda Lima and edited by Timo Bartholl and Antonis Vradis.
- The chapter entitled "Pacifying Hunger: Lessons from/for Rio's Urban Periphery" was translated from Greek to English by Alexandros Vagenas and edited by Antonis Vradis.

A Portuguese version of this book was published by Consequência Editora (*Favela, Resistência e a Luta Pela Soberania Alimentar*, 2021), while a Greek version was published by Futura Books (*Seeds and Concrete: Counterinsurgency, Resistance, and the Struggle for Food Sovereignty in the Favelas of Rio de Janeiro*, 2021).

On Movement Time

Raj Patel

This short collection is the fruit of a long collaboration and a longer history of food sovereignty. The term "food sovereignty" was coined by La Via Campesina, in opposition to "food security." Liberalism's codes—food security, nutritional adequacy, caloric balance—are terms not for the cessation of hunger but for its permanent management. It is difficult to parse the permanent condition of two billion people in food insecurity, or the rising number of malnourished people even before COVID-19 and its recessions, in any other way. Rather than defer the promise of hunger's end as "food security" does, "food sovereignty" refers to the political preconditions required for everyone to eat with dignity.

One way to parse food sovereignty is as "a right to have sovereignty over the food system." For any rights to be effective, they need a state willing to enforce them. In the Maré neighborhood in Rio de Janeiro, rights are a deferred promise. Favelas are places to which the state has promised development, but nothing has been done. They are, to redeploy Dipesh Chakrabarty's phrase, a waiting room of history. It would, however, be a mistake to assume that just because the state summons patience from its citizens, citizens willingly offer it. In order to enforce this patience, the state has deployed a suite of violence, of which food insecurity is a part.

How might citizens have the right to have rights when the state is the enemy? In this excellent series of essays, you can learn about the movements to achieve food sovereignty. In particular, you can also learn about the singular constitutive difference between movement outcome and movement process: movement time.

Thinking of the capitalist prison complex in California, initially created to manage the economic crises attending neoliberal policies, Ruth Wilson Gilmore observes: "Today's prisons are extractive. What does that mean? It means prisons enable money to move because of the enforced inactivity of people locked in them. It means people extracted from communities, and people returned to communities but not entitled to be of them, enable the circulation of money on rapid cycles. What's extracted from the extracted is the resource of life—time."[1]

Social movements, by definition, understand the resource of life, its flows and appropriations. Resistance is always in counterpoint to the rhythms of bourgeois history, which erases the activities that happen in movement time. To bourgeois history, movement time is invisible. To its participants, it's regenerative and necessary. It is not merely a moment of social reproduction, of food and care, but a time of political reinvigoration.

Movement meetings stretch into the night with homework, and childcare, and encounter, and the energy of peer-to-peer education as sustenance. Pleasure and joy are an intimate part of making movements work. You'll see bursts of this joy in street protests, in the spilling out of movement time into bourgeois time and space. If you found yourself exhilarated to the point of forgetting what time it was on a Black Lives Matter march recently, you experienced a moment of movement time. The fount of this energy is, however, structurally less visible to the state because it happens both as political and social reproduction, off the clock.

In movement time, the evening yields only reluctantly to morning. Meetings end as people leave to clock in to the jobs that rediscipline time and value through the wage form. In movement time, meals are shared over theory and vice versa. In that time, the materialism of food, pleasure, and commensality are intrinsic to transformative and constitutive praxis. In movement time, dance and song and poetry are practices of self-defense. In movement time, children aren't left at home.

Food sovereignty's procedures involve the complex synchronizations of temporalities, perhaps most visibly when they have to mesh with the sites in which they mesh with the bourgeois world. La Via Campesina, for instance, is the cause of much angst in certain philanthropic circles. Grant-makers have their own rhythms of funding, reportable activity, and evaluations. Foundations claim that such disciplines are forced upon them by the tax code, and they reluctantly but necessarily transmit similar discipline to their grantees in turn. These rhythms are not matched to the needs of subaltern-led research.

More than once, I've heard my comrade bourgeois scholars acknowledge that "the process" of articulating international deliberations with translation, the scheduling of national and local meetings, retranslation, and then reconvention is both interminable and requires lightning-fast response. This is as it should be. It's only in an academy where all demands of social reproduction are independent of the production of knowledge that academic time can be measured out to the tempo of semesters and funding cycles.

When social movements meet the tempo of grant-makers, there's friction. When movement time meets capitalist acceleration, there is fire. To achieve food sovereignty under fascism (what else are we to call Bolsonaro's Brazil?) requires the complex management of movement resources. Stealth, mendacity, subterfuge, and collaboration with local gangs are all part of processes that remain invisible to the state.

When movements produce leaders who are ready to demand transformation from the state, to raise their voices and fists, and to demand that the state change its pace, there must be danger. This is how movement leaders become targets. Marielle Franco, a city council representative for the Socialism and Liberty Party, was born and spent most of her life in Maré. She was executed in March 2018 by two former police officers. Wherever there are shack dwellers, she was mourned. An exhibition in the Museu da Maré in December 2018 showed quite how many lives, in quite how many continents, she had touched.

It is, as Boaventura de Sousa Santos noted on his visit to the Museu da Maré, deeply unusual for movements to curate their own history, to organize it with their own chronology, and to represent it to one another, and to visitors. The state's long history of oppression against Black anarchists means that there are few traces of those in whose footsteps Marielle marched (Domingos Passos, for instance, couldn't be more relevant today). But it is from the autonomous libraries that such spaces constitute that we can and must draw our visions of the future. The collectivities that produce food sovereignty must also make museums.

Marx was coy on this, noting in the *German Ideology* that a communist society would allow him "to hunt in the morning, to fish in the afternoon, rear cattle in the evening, criticize after dinner."[2] Marx describes a solitary life, a fantasy of a cabin in the woods in which a bearded man reads books and eats a fully Paleo Diet®. This future is one stripped of the enchantments and pleasures that sustain human communities in the web of life. Any future unalienated postcapitalist world must make time for dancing and eating and cooking and cleaning and public theorizing in a museum that doubles as a canteen. In this book, you can see the extent to which that communism already exists, must exist today, in order for humans to thrive tomorrow.

As I write these words in lockdown, in the waiting room for a better world, I pine for a joyous and sensuous poetry of the world back together. Andrew Marvell's poem of love, lust, and hunger seems about right for this moment, for dreaming of a time when communist movement time subverts capitalist time. For

> "though we cannot make our sun
> Stand still, yet we will make him run."

Austin, Occupied Texas, July 2020

NOTES

1   Ruth Wilson Gilmore, *Abolition Geography and the Problem of Innocence* (New York: Verso, 2017), 301–26.
2   Karl Marx and Frederick Engels, *The German Ideology*, ed. C.J. Arhur (New York: International Publishers, 2004), 53, https://www.google.com/books/edition/_/DujYWG8TPMMC?gbpv=1.

CHAPTER ONE

Thinking About the Favela Through Food and Through Time

Antonis Vradis

—

This book is an experiment. It was initially born out of NutriCities, our collective research project in Rio de Janeiro, Brazil, which lasted between 2017 and 2019, and was funded under the British Academy's Cities and Infrastructure Programme. In NutriCities, two of us, researchers from the European periphery with an institutional base in the UK, came to collaborate with a Rio-based researcher and soon enough an entire group of community members and researchers from the favelas of Maré in Rio de Janeiro's North Zone. Later on, one of our researchers further elaborated some questions in another research project entitled "Urban Fragility as Military Object: The Case of Rio de Janeiro." This research was to a large extent conducted in conversation with the NutriCities project, and the fruit of this conversation is presented in the last chapter of this book. What you will find here are reflections from all of us, especially from the field researchers in Maré, on which we focused when trying to answer the swarm of questions around food and the favela, which is what had ignited our curiosity and this peculiar and exciting research journey in the first place. You will also find reflections from us three, the Rio-based researcher and the two Europeans who spent time in Maré, trying to answer these very same questions.

In the time of COVID-19, little can appear more reminiscent of our previous world, the world of the previous chapter of capitalist normalcy, than the sheer density that has come to be associated with the favelas, similarly with any residential area for the poor, for the working classes, for the many the world over. The calculation of the capitalist city had been simple enough: the many should occupy as little space as possible, the many should be cramped as much as possible. This is the territori-alization of the logic of profit at its most unashamed, some would call it sincere: you may only occupy as much space as is physically required for your physical survival, the absolute minimum that guarantees the working classes remain in the city, but only just enough to keep the cogs of the urban machine turning. Now, in the COVID-19 outbreak moment, we have come to rethink what this presence in the city means, what this ever-abstract right to the city might entail. Finally doing away with the shiny nothingness of consumption in the capitalist city, we have the shockingly unique opportunity to think, more clearly than ever, of the compartments that make up our urban existence daily: here is the produce we need access to, and here is how easy or difficult it is for us to get hold of, depending on personal circumstances, or how fortunately near or unfortunately distant we happen to be from that particular circuit of produce circulation. Here is what we need for our daily survival; here is what we need in terms of maintaining our home and safeguarding our shelter; here is what we need to entertain ourselves; here is what we need to be productive—those of us, that is, who happened to be in a line of work that allowed for productivity from inside the home, even with whatever restrictions that may come along. Here, here, and here, the COVID-19 crisis has laid bare, in the most painfully evident of ways, how fragile the capitalist systems of produc-tion and circulation really are. And this shines the most ironic of lights upon the high priests of policy (and recently, academia even) who had the nerve to talk of the fragility of marginal populations, and the seem-ing need to make them resilient to crisis. The table has entirely and fully turned: the ever-resilient populations look on as the capitalist system of production and circulation crumbles in the face of a medium-sized threat. It crumbles in face of sheer probability. But putting food on the table is not a matter for equations, chance, or probability. It materializes, in the most dramatic of ways, the certainty of biological necessity, the certainty that life needs this basic fuel if it is to maintain itself.

But even specifically in the Brazilian context, and COVID-19 aside, this may have felt like a strange moment for a book on food and the favela to come out. Surely, having settled into an era with the far-right Bolsonaro in power, and with his authority coming into question amidst the global pandemic, Brazil must have more pressing things to worry about? But perhaps what the world is eager to hear is the resistance explicitly against this humanity-hating regime. Maybe a bunch of people coming together to study, understand, and perhaps even change dietary habits in a settlement in Rio's North Zone is not exactly hot stuff right now. In one sense, Bolsonaro's election changes everything. Here is a right-wing extremist, a fascist coming out of the fringes of Brazil's political landscape, sweeping away all sense of reality or normalcy as we had known it so far. What value is there in delving into the past? But dig a little bit deeper and the continuities are there. Cast aside the smoke screens of mainstream politics, and their irrelevance and detachment from the everyday in the peripheries becomes glaringly obvious. In a sense, the favelas might have been the territories least able to be swayed to the right by shifts and swings of the national political pendulum, no matter how dramatic. The communities vilified by Bolsonaro and his cronies as fostering crime would be expected, one would think, to rally around the social-democrat flavor of power, which at the very least offered the tangible help of alleviation programs aiding millions out of poverty, and the warm words of a fatherly, and then a motherly, figure that promised to be the driving force behind Brazil's social-democratic turn, what ended up being its brief respite from authoritarianism (2002–16). After all, on the other side of the political spectrum stood the figure spitting out hatred and even putting vile death plans into practice, the figure that vilified the favelas the most in his ascendance to power. Bolsonaro was elected on a program granting the police a license to kill, and there is nowhere that this license applies more directly than in the favela territories. By winter 2019, the Bolsonaro family was being directly linked to the murder of Marielle Franco, a Rio native and beloved favela activist—the most notorious assassination in the country's recent history. So why, then, decide to talk about food of all issues in the midst of Brazil's feverish social and political crisis? A crisis that has been, furthermore, a crisis of representation, of trust: a crisis that has broken down, it would seem, even the most rudimentary of principles. A fascist is in power, and the police now kill, more than ever, more indiscriminately than ever. Where does food in the favela fit into this macabre landscape? Allow me a brief perambulation that might begin to answer some of these questions.

The favelas in Rio partially owe their existence to the city's very morphology, with its grand mountains sliding into the sea, making the hard-to-reach slopes a safe haven for perennial newcomers, away from and above those who previously settled in the plains below. But in the strangest of ways, the Rio favelas also owe their continued existence to time. It was the victorious soldiers coming back from the Canudos War in Bahia in the 1880s that first gave birth to the favela. It was them arriving here, and then waiting along the hillsides overlooking the city for the government to hand them the money promised after the victorious war. The money never arrived, and the soldiers never left. In a way, the favela was born as a waiting place, and remains so.

There is a seemingly strange obsession with time, not only in the favelas or in Rio, but in Brazil as a whole, the "country of the future," no less. The present historical moment, whichever that happens to be, is always read as a precursor for the opening to the next episode, but this next episode is always waiting, suspended. This is in a sense, a common feature across most countries that do not quite belong to the so-called developed world, countries where the argument in favor of development has been repeatedly built upon the narrative of a need to "modernize" things. In the case of Greece, from which two of us originate, the word that has been used time and again was slightly (but crucially) different: *eksynchronismos*, which translates not just as modernization, but as a bringing up to speed, the act of synchronizing something that was asynchronous before. In the Greek case, this was an act of synchronizing and bringing up to speed the local state of affairs, presumed to be backward, with the Northern European and Western/Anglophone world, presumed to be the modern, the contemporary speeding ahead. This is of course the perennial reading of the periphery as backward, and the ensuing certainty that all it would take for development to successfully arrive would be a change of gear, a change of speed, the turning of a page that would land us upon a new chapter, a fast-forward move that would rid us of these anomalies of the past and usher us into a perfectly functioning present. To look at the state of the world today and doubt whether this linear narrative still makes any sense would be something of an understatement. But this makes all the more staggering the fact that so many have put so much faith in the exercise of waiting as a means of overcoming the bleakness of the present, this perennial in-between where we are and where we should, or could be.

And in a sense, no place represents the faith put into moving beyond this in-between moment better than the favela. Here there is an assumption of temporariness on all parts. Some favela residents dream of their stay as a passage en route to their settling in the city proper, a mere temporary stopover. The local authorities had for quite some time assumed the favela was an urban form, soon to be tamed, controlled, and integrated. There would be a moment when the city below would swallow its unruly higher-altitude neighbor. The police and the army coming in with their heavy artillery had also presumed it was only a matter of time before this strange, informal territorial formation was pacified and normalized, conforming to the image of the city proper. They all thought it was a matter of time; but the favela is not a matter *of* time, but quite literally a matter *over* time with its consecutive layers of constructions, improvements, and expansions. Each is a small admission that things are not so temporary after all, that their creator is there to stay a tiny bit longer. In the meantime, they might as well seek to improve their daily conditions by that tiny bit further.

What separates the Rio favela from the city proper is not the altitude, the urban form, or infrastructure—or at least, it is none of these alone. What separates the favela from the city proper is also the time and effort that it takes for the favela resident to reach the rest of the urban form, and vice versa, the time it takes the outsider to arrive here. There is something of a historical irony in this, given that the prime attracting factor of the favela was exactly its proximity to the city proper. Its proximity to the wealthy middle-class households that favela residents could work for, and to the services and public spaces the city had to offer. But this proximity was also read, from the outset, as a potential threat by the powers that be, residing on the more prosperous urban lowlands below. The favela was always perceived as a threat to order and power. And therefore its residents should be allowed to come down from their rugged dwellings only to the extent that their presence in the city facilitated its otherwise unhindered function. After all, favela residents were only to be tolerated up until the moment when the authorities could devise a way to do away with them, to rationalize them, to transform them to the liking of the city proper.

To begin with, the lack of nearly all formal infrastructure that could facilitate access to the favela hilltops meant that the higher up you were geographically, the lower you were in social or economic terms. Swap the tropical mountain masses for the sunlit concrete blocks of southern European cities during their own rapid urbanization phase, and the image becomes strangely familiar: we only have to think of so-called vertical segregation in the post–World War II apartment blocks that were emerging at the time in Greek cities. Before the rise of these apartment blocks, the affluent middle classes occupied ground floor villas, enjoying their direct access to the street level, which in turn allowed them an unfettered passage to civic life. As for the workers and the servants who toiled for these middle classes, they had to settle for small spaces away from the street in the basements or the attics. These *domatia ypiresias* (service rooms) were, quite literally, reserved for those who served. Yet once the building frenzy got going, the ensuing noise and pollution became too much for the sensitive noses and ears of the middle class. These affluent urbanites would now move to the very top of newly built condominiums, to enjoy their distance from the hustle and bustle of the streets below. In this sense, the arrival of blocks of flats as a material manifestation of modernity, together with elevator technology, were enough to entirely reverse the city's vertical social order: to turn it, quite literally, on its head. Almost overnight, the presence of the elevator now meant upper-level apartments were for the most privileged, combining their newly found ease of access with the relative quiet and clean air allowed by their elevation above the nuisance and pollution of the street below. The highest floor of the dwelling was once the humble attic, the hidden abode of those that were there to serve their masters below. Now, all of a sudden, the building's top tier belongs instead to those in the social top tier.

But in Rio things were a little bit more complicated. Here the populations arriving to serve the city's middle classes were also residing up above. But unlike the built environment, the formidable mountain masses dominating the city's landscape would take an equally formidable infrastructure network to provide for the mobility and access needed for the favelas to become truly and fully a part of the city proper, for this up-down inversion to happen here as well, and for the tops of the city's marvellous hills to become a material manifestation of social stratification, as had their Mediterranean counterparts. In this way, lack of access and limited mobility became the very essence, the state of being, of the favela: it is what has inadvertently permitted it to come into being in the first place, and what continues to allow for its existence despite the talk of, and attempts at, pacification, gentrification, or normalization in whatever shape or form. The favela is and continues to be part of the urban precisely because of its lack of access, exactly because it is difficult for people to go in or out, up or down, to the city proper. If the problem of access could be resolved, the favelas on the hills could presumably become indistinguishable from the "city of the asphalt" down below overnight.

There is already abundant literature on favela integration, favela pacification, or even the favela as a parallel state, as well as on the favela as a solid state of being that might one day be brought back into the city whole, as something that can somehow and sometime be quelled, or that can exist along and in parallel with the city proper. But next to this, we also ought to think of the favela as this inadvertent outcome of the constant struggle over mobility and access, as the inadvertent witness of a fight over controlling who gets to move and who gets to stay. Not only broadly and abstractly as a right to the city, then, but as a right to get in and around the city. In this way, before infrastructure and before urban planning, what defines the favela is the question of access. Access defines what can come in, what stays in the favela, who can come out, and on what terms. Access, in this way, works both ways: access into the favela determines the degree and type of control authorities may impose on this territory while access out of the favela determines what kind of freedoms its residents have in terms of moving around, of reaching the rest of the city, and under what terms. Maré, in particular, lies at the junction of three of the most important thoroughfares in Rio's metropolitan area. First, there is Linha Amarela, the "yellow line" expressway strategically connecting the university island and the airport to the east with Barra da Tijuca, the sprawling US-like suburb anchored by the long stretch of Barra beach by the city's western edge. Barra hosted the 2016 Olympics, its Olympic Park having once stood as a testament to the city's ambition of joining an imagined global elite. Today, it stands as a testament of failure: in early 2020 a judge ordered the site to close down, citing poor maintenance and an inadequate safety record. Second, there is Avenida Brazil which, with its twelve lanes in total, is the busiest road in and out of Rio. And third, there is Linha Vermelha, the "red line" ushering the city's northern residents, and visitors flown into the international airport, down to the riches and seductive beaches of the South Zone. In terms of its location, then, Maré occupies one of the most strategic sites in the city. Yet the infrastructure built along and around Maré does not facilitate access to the rest of the city, instead it excludes the neighborhood from it. Even though Maré neighbors one of the biggest water treatment stations in Latin America, it is not served by it, because of an impasse with the government. On the eve of the 2016 Olympics, the number of buses connecting Maré to the South Zone was reduced drastically in an ostensible attempt to limit and control the access of its residents to the city proper. The story of Maré has continuously been a story of struggle for access to the city proper.

But what happens inside Maré? What forces bring the favela into being? Trying to think through these forces, I would be tempted—at the risk of oversimplifying a much more complicated dynamic—to think of three sides in the favela formation. First, there are those living in the favela: its original inhabitants, the ones who have been arriving in the time since, those who continue to move to settle here, and those who make their home in the favela, while they might be striving to get jobs elsewhere. Second, there are the authorities: municipal or national, military or police, and local or international NGOs with their soft power, their prudent and eloquent Western-educated planners with their sophisticated technical skills meticulously applied to this fascinating, if macabre, urban laboratory. In short, there are the people who make the favela what it is, those who gave birth to it and who continue to keep it breathtakingly alive, this incredible hub of a vibrant community that celebrates life every day, despite it being—or maybe exactly because it is—so fragile and precarious. And then there are the authorities, those who ensure that life in the favela is and continues to be fragile and precarious, and who often end it altogether. But this is not all. A third actor comes in the form of ideas that travel to and through the favela without being grounded here, without being favela-specific. Let me go back to an example from Greece, once again, to help explain what I mean here.

When the far-right party Golden Dawn went up from polling at around 0.3 to over 7.0 percent in the country's 2012 elections, people were shocked and tried to find an explanation. How could these Nazis possibly reach these—astronomical, it felt at the time!—figures? One of the things people tried to do was to look for traces of any local features and characteristics explaining this astronomic rise. They tried to identify anything that might have been particular to any specific neighborhoods, cities, or regions, anything that could explain something about the rise of the party locally. Maybe there was a particular, semi-hidden story of local far-right presence after the country's Civil War (1945–49)? Maybe there were larger-than-average migrant communities that would help local far-right thugs vilify them, to use them as targets, and to rally the local population against them? Maybe there was a particularly charismatic figure who would help propel the party to some kind of unusually high levels of success? But to their disappointment, people quickly found out there was nothing of the kind. If anything, we quickly found out that Golden Dawn had scored one of the most consistent percentages among all parties across the country; their electoral performance in nearly every region was stunningly similar. Of course, there were some areas that were traditional far-right strongholds, and Golden Dawn performed better there. Clearly, there were others, where they are traditionally weak and the left is strong, and they underperformed in those too. No surprises either way. But in general terms, Golden Dawn scored one of—if not the most—geographically even percentages among all parties that entered parliament that year, and went on to perform in a stunningly similar manner in the elections that followed in 2016. What was the lesson there? Many in Greece think that, simply enough, the role of the media and the role of key institutions that exist and are active across the country's entire territory (read the police and the Greek Orthodox Church) were key. We know a great number of police support Golden Dawn, and we know the same goes for some of the church leaders. And more than anything, we know that mainstream media vilified, and continue to vilify, migrants and their plight as they escape war-torn areas. Bombarded with stories that target and dehumanize, that foster hatred for the other, many people in areas that hardly recorded any newcoming migrant populations at all voted with this media construction in mind. They voted while thinking of a reality elsewhere, one certain reality that existed only in the sickening, vile, and poisonous antimigrant propaganda spewed by news anchors and mainstream journalists—an invented reality that, through the power of discourse, came to be a hellish reality for those it had targeted in the first place.

Something similar can most probably be told about the favelas in Rio's North Zone, and elsewhere in the city and in the country as a whole. After all, many were shocked to find Bolsonaro had a pretty much even number of supporters over here as he had in the affluent neighborhoods of the South Zone. But these votes were not the same. In the case of the favela, the powers that were influential, but not grounded there, became painfully apparent. The power of a hate-spewing candidate to portray entire communities and territories as little other than reserves of criminals that must be neutralized, the power of the church to promote this hate-spewing figure as a viable and respectable candidate, and the power of fake news distributed through well-dressed news anchors and mobile phone apps alike. These are all powers that are not grounded in the physical geography of the favela but nevertheless come to shape it. They are extraterritorial forces that originate outside these given places but that still seep through it and change these communities, just like they do with every other community in this city, in this country, and this world. That is where the frightening de-territorial reach of these powers lies. There are three forces, then: One is the force of the people that make the favela what it is. Two, the powers that be that allow the favela to exist, that tolerate and even facilitate its unruly presence as long as things are not to move too much, as long as their populations are not to move too quickly, as long as they are not to get out of control. And three, there are the extraterritorial forces, like the church or media, that quell and that soothe, that blur the divisions only to then divide communities further in return. The favela is the end result of this constant, if sometimes unspoken, negotiation among these forces. An unspoken agreement that rests on questions of mobility and access. The mobility and access of people in the first case, of authorities in the second, and of the immaterial powers of ideas and (dis)information in the third. This is the favela's undeclared and unsigned contract. It is the unspoken understanding that you are allowed to exist up here, here and there—as long as you can sort out even basic amenities yourself, and as long as you do not aspire to move over there, to the rest of the city, too frequently or too quickly. The informal physical settlement up on the hill can only exist if this equally informal yet equally rigid arrangement among these forces exists in return. This unsigned contract then exposes the ingenuity of "integration," "pacification," and all sorts of programs launched by the powers that be in the name of quelling the untamed force of the favela and making it more to their liking. Even the flagship integration programs that reach near the favela bypass it; this is, in the eyes of authorities, the obstacle to connecting the key hubs and flows that make the city proper. To make the favela in the image of the city proper is never going to be the end target, as the target is precisely not to have an end. The target is for this state of flux to continue, for this perpetual struggle and the tension between competing forces to lead toward, but never resolve into, a solid state of affairs. A state of affairs that is never quite settled. The favela was, and can only continue to be, an in-between space.

To think of the favela as a struggle over time, mobility, and access might also help move the conversation forward from what have been some tired understandings. First there are those who argue that favela communities are entirely independent, and perhaps emancipated even, from the long arm of the Brazilian state—thanks, in part, to the state's own apparent admission that things are not entirely under control in these bizarre territories lying at the hillsides and up above from the city proper. Then, there is often this understanding of a "parallel state" that thrives in the favelas: an entire constellation of *traficantes* and militias that build, whether together with, or despite, official security personnel, a separate entity that teeters on the edge of legitimacy—if not lying beyond it. There is a third understanding of the favelas as gray zones, zones that are formed not by an absolute, clear-cut distinction between the formal and informal economy, but that instead spring up in the space of tolerance of the former toward the latter. While drug dealing and all sorts of activities that come with it are, strictly speaking, outside the remit of the law, the state is still seen as a shadowy partner here, as an accomplice and as a stakeholder with a genuine interest in tolerating—if not outright facilitating—these very activities.

In all three cases, the favela has thrived in the middle-class imagination as this Near Other, this nearly-within-reach territory: an always-never-quite-urban space. From the "favela chic" boom of the South Zone, complete with celebrities allegedly snapping up "prime" properties with unobstructed, glorious views of the middle-class wealth at their feet, all the way to the hip bars, safari tourism—but also, to the police raids on favelas broadcast live on national TV, the scorn and the hatred of politicians capitalizing on a discourse that dehumanizes and hounds. Whether seemingly positive or negative, the favela image has been conceptualized and consumed through these portrayals precisely as a distant representation, and one that is easily digestible at that: something that is within sight but out of reach, and for this reason can be talked about from a safe distance. The safety of installing scores of police before coming to "celebrate" the vibrancy of the communities these police displace, to "celebrate" by enjoying a view of the wealthy plains down from the hills, or better even, from behind the TV glass that stands in between those doing the talking about the favela and those who live it.

When the favela meets the rest of the city, things get a little bit more complicated. Talk to many in the South Zone about favelas and their residents, and, more often than not, something like the *arrastões* will quickly spring to their mind. These are the media-popularized "dragnets" of youths, sometimes dozens at a time, running through the most popular spots (such as the South Zone's renowned beaches) in the hope of causing enough havoc to get away with their loot from petrified tourists. Or they might have a word of praise for the militarized police operations, or a huffing despair at their apparent halting as of recent years. Or again, although admittedly not as often, it might be a word of sympathy for the mind-blowing high number of people killed by police in Rio. In the first half of 2019, police killings in the state of Rio alone averaged five a day (2,964 between January and June that year), a rapid increase of about 15 percent from 2018, and a tendency that has accelerated since, but still much precedes the rise of Bolsonaro to power. There is a common thread running along these otherwise disparate responses. In every single case—from the outright negative to the less frequently positive—the talk about the favela from the safety of the South Zone is akin to talk about the plight of a different, impoverished world. Another "world" that needs to be "saved," that is, annihilated through normalization of some kind, before it's too late. It has to happen for its own benefit, but also for the benefit of the wealthier urban areas that are engulfed by this strange world, and which it threatens by its very existence.

So is the Brazilian state on a mission to save the favelas from themselves? In a way—a macabre, but nevertheless fascinating way—the Brazilian authorities have developed a two-pronged approach when it comes to handling the favela question. First, there is the idea of making the rest of the city safe from the favela. Here the asphalt and the dirt are not only separated as two distinct entities, but one is understood to be threatened by the other. The role of the state security forces is therefore to ease the fear of the asphalt by locking up the dirt. But in another sense, the security forces have come into the favelas portraying themselves as liberators, as those who will free the favelados from the murderous grip of the gangs, who will restore peace and usher the favelas into progress. The state weapons will force the favelas into the time of the asphalt.

One of the reasons why the favela territory is so important is because it allows us to rethink some more fundamental questions around the institutions made by humans, set up in the name of serving them, but which end up repressing or otherwise disadvantaging humans over history's long course. In *Against the Grain*, James C. Scott traverses the depths of history to bring a counterargument to the narrative that has prevailed, up to the present day, around state formation and the subservience of populations to these newly established forms of human organization. As Scott explains, the mainstream argument so far had been that humanity gearing toward permanent and agriculture-dependent societies was what paved the way for the arrival of the state onto the stage of world history: the permanence of settlement and the dependence on crops became the two prongs of the fork that early states used to pin down populations they may have otherwise been unable to contain and control. And ironically enough, these populations were pinned to the very land they had used and depended upon for their survival. But the argument that Scott is pushing through is that the time sequence we had assumed regarding sedentism, pacification, and state formation was all wrong. We thought that domestication led to sedentism and fixed-field agriculture. But instead, sedentism and domestication preceded all these. As for state formation, it only follows much later, more than four millennia after the first crop domestication and sedentism.[1] The first states appeared only a long time after fixed-field agriculture had already made an entry onto history's stage. This is a problem, Scott goes on to explain, because such a considerable lag means it should not be a given for us to assume that once crops and sedentism were established, this would directly lead to state formation.

Why is this important, and how do crops and sedentism relate to the intimidating guns pointed and fired daily by the hands of those representing the state in Rio's favelas today? The lag that Scott has identified, this gap between the historical moment when crops and sedentism and the moment when the state would fall into place, under-mines our assumption that agriculture was the ever-formidable force to replace "the savage, wild, primitive, lawless and violent world of hunter-gatherers and nomads."[2] And overturning this assumption is no small feat. This is exactly what we have relied on to build our imaginary of a linear reading of humankind's history, which in return naturalizes the state and glorifies the narratives of progress and civilization. Of course, anyone following political and social developments around the world—or even if they were to confound themselves to the Global West—in the past decade, would certainly have some doubt about this assumption of ever-continuous, linearly progressive prosperity and growth. But what Scott lays out here goes a little bit deeper than that. If we are to really question and untie settlement from progress, the result is more than unsettling for some of our key assumptions. We have held these assumptions to such a degree that they have become entirely normalized. Think of this for a second: in UK media, a person suspected of having committed a crime is often described to be "of no fixed abode"; they have no permanent address. A vagabond, homeless, a financially unstable person, all of which presumably make for someone more likely to (re)lapse into crime. And vice versa, if we are to read about someone being "of no fixed abode," we would be very likely to expect the story to relate to a crime of some kind. To be mobile is to be out of bounds. And conversely, to lay claim to a dwelling insinuates not only a certain level of social security but also acceptance. In the wake of the COVID-19 crisis, this inextricable connection between dwelling and social acceptance became all the more painfully evident: "stay at home," came the order from the high priests of normalcy, with little regard as to what this "home" might consist of for the many, and what staying there indefinitely could entail.

We have so far assumed that "progress" denotes a positive idea, a desirable standing. As Scott so eloquently shows, this positivity follows from settling down. This very expression, this assumption that to settle is the pinnacle of success, is yet another indicator of how deeply ingrained this equation lies in our collective psyche. Settlement equals success. But why is Scott's endeavor so important? It is because we have come to accept the idea of a state as a necessary evil. Moreover, we have come to agree—not even to agree, as agreement presumes debate—we have come to accept, unequivocally, that we owe what we are to where we are, and to the fact that, more or less, we do not move. This is despite and against the painfully obvious fact that progress is a retrogressive wave: that for every step forward there is another (or more) step(s) back. Despite and against the fact that successes are more often than not borne on the back of the gruesome reality of people on the move; that the most inspiring of ideas have time and again come from explorers, not settlers; despite and against the fact that what gets the world moving is, well, people who move: people who move their bodies, people who move about, and in so doing, move our ways of thinking along with them.

The great irony in contemporary history is that the moment when people move to and settle in new cities, these growing mega-settlements around the world, is also the moment when they cut the umbilical cord to the vast agricultural peripheries, the backlands (*Os Sertões*) that Euclides da Cunha famously immortalized as the remote regions of the Brazilian periphery. The regions that are struggling against poverty, lawlessness, and corruption—and of course, the combination of the three. Sure enough, Canudos, the setting of da Cunha's novel, happens to be one of the country's most arid regions; but the overarching narrative, which claims that the lawless peripheries are unable to sustain themselves, is still strongly ingrained in the national consciousness. And when the population from the peripheries comes to settle in the big cities, it is equally incapable of sustaining itself, or so the imaginary goes. The moment it cuts off its ties to the resources the agriculture-oriented "home" had been able to provide, this population becomes, truly, a surplus.

There is a great paradox here, but this does not lie in the desire of populations to move from the "periphery" to the "center," from the rural to the urban. The paradox lies precisely in our understanding of the two as separate and even opposite; it lies in this teleological understanding of human movement as a perennial perambulation with a nevertheless finite and set endpoint. The paradox lies, most importantly, in our belief that human settlement will somewhat settle social ills and will usher us all into some kind of trouble-free future. This is a paradox because we assume both that the people will, that indeed they must, settle into cities if they are to prosper; and meanwhile we lament this very settlement as the mother of all the ills that make the city what it is in the first place. It is a paradox because we recognize roots and authenticity in culture, in high taste, yet we disapprovingly reject the same roots and authenticity as preposterous when they come from below. At a time when the unsustainability of our way of being has become painfully clear, when everything from killer pandemics to the changing weather to glaring inequality or simply the vulgarity of semi-lunatic autocratic politicians that have taken center stage the world over, everything screams: "things can no longer go on like this." This is the perfect time to question both what "no longer" and "like this" mean right now, in the present: this is the perfect time to explore our sense of direction in history so far, and our assumption about what it really means to achieve "progress" in the first place.

The core argument in Scott's book is that we need to expand our understanding of domestication as control over reproduction. This applies, he argues, not just to plants or fire, but goes all the way to "slaves, state subjects, and women in the patriarchal family." The convenient dichotomy, in our minds, of the domestic and the public as being two separate domains is far from true. The successfully executed domestic allows for a subservient public. How does this ring in our COVID-19 moment? "Stay at home," bark the priests of high authority, and a successfully executed domestication order guarantees a subservient public in return. Even better, it guarantees that public space, the public realm, and public consciousness vanish and are replaced by the sad spectacle of units, individuals waving through zoom panels. But a virtual sum of individuals does not make a "public"; the individual parts are never going to equal the public sum.

Fast-forward a few thousand years and not only have these issues not been resolved, they have this strange tendency of getting even more complicated. Where do the semi-peripheries stand in the dichotomy between the rural and the urban? Where do the spaces of the favelas stand between the domestic and the public? The favela, in its essence, is a gray zone. Not in terms of its legality or state regulations—though this is also the case—but in terms of its conceptualization and being along this divide. No space is quite entirely private, and no space is quite public, either. The luxury of the divide rests with the affluent middle classes. But is this really a luxury? Favela homes open up to the back alleys that become extensions of otherwise small living rooms. In a positive reading, these hybrid spaces extend the living spaces of favela inhabitants, strengthen their bonds, broaden and lighten the community spirit. But on the negative side, the alleyways (and the homes themselves) become prey to whatever police or army operation occurs. Cries for a warrant would sound like a bad joke. Equally, at the time when the affluent countries and cities of the world were urgently calling for social distancing in face of the COVID-19 pandemic, this "distancing" sounded again out of context in an urban fabric built precisely on density, proximity, and movement. How could people possibly now be asked to stand still and apart?

Density, proximity, and movement: perhaps three of the most important ingredients that make up the favela. And there exists, in my mind, a wonderful if perhaps mistaken metaphor concerning the particular favela complex where our research took place, Maré. Visitors here have the opportunity to visit its brilliant and informative, community-led museum. If they seize this opportunity, what they will discover is that this proud and amazing neighborhood has one of the most poetically moving names I have come across in a long time: Maré, the tide. What better word to signal this longing for movement, what more apt of way in which to capture and reflect the dream of mobility than the soothingly slow retrogression of the sea water, constantly swinging between highs and lows. The people that came here made land out of water. They ended up not in the heights of the favelas in the surrounding mountains, but at the water's edge, with its high and low tides instead. I like to think of this as an excellent reflection of this faith in time: the faith that things will always turn around, and that the lows will turn to highs. We don't know when, but this will surely happen, sometime.

But let me now go beyond these slightly obscure reflections on the history of the place, to talk more about our present moment. If the favela was built on waiting, this waiting has long given its place to a realization of permanence. The centrifugal force has settled. The community is here to stay, and it has been so for a long time. Bold, proud, and determined to carve out this urban space for its own. Much like what happens to the individual migrant at the moment when they realize they are never going back to where they started their journey. I think there is a moment when a community similarly also comes to realize it is not as temporary as it had imagined itself to be. That is a crucial, transformative moment—a threshold of sorts, after which the person's and the community's mentalities alike change; yet they do continue, of course, to hold onto fragments of their past identity. In Maré, the community here has brought with it the tide of another place—that of the Brazilian northeastern heartlands—and the pride of existing and coping, striving against the difficulties, what the academics of my kind, from their high offices and distant campuses would somewhat patronizingly call "making do." This has brought about a sense of place that the plains of the South Zone are no longer able even to dream of, swamped as they are by the millions of temporary beachgoers, blinded by the affluence of centuries of amassing predatory capital through historical relationships of the utmost exploitation ingrained into every inch even of the sidewalks in Leblon's mind-boggling affluence—a place, as I was told from my very first day in Rio, directly comparable in its riches to the affluent metropolises far away in the northern hemisphere. But the near north—Rio's North Zone—has held onto a sense of place, and the living testament is this museum. Not just its existence, but the fact that only here, in Maré, can a museum feel so much alive and such an organic part of the community hosting it. How would a museum in the South Zone fare compared to its immediate and contemporary surroundings? What would a Leblon museum look like? It would be a gross mismatch in place and in time. In Maré, this line of continuity is uninterrupted. Here history is still alive: it never really died away in the first place.

In a way, this sense of place, or living history, or whatever we may want to call it, merely describes the repeated fascination of urbanists and social scientists looking at the city and dividing it between "formal" and "informal," "center" and "periphery," "ville" and "cité." The divide, broadly speaking, is between what was meant to be there, what the authorities had wished for and planned for on the one side, and then what actually sprang up inadvertently on the other. The city that happened organically, despite and beyond the plans and the control of the powers that be. The city that is versus the city that was meant to be—if authorities fully had it their way.

The question now, for the wonderfully and organically developed "informal" spaces of the urban peripheries, is how to improve life as it is at the moment. To go beyond just "making do" and to claim a right to something better, bolder, and bigger. There is another obscure, even beautiful-sounding expression that academics have used in describing laying claim to another type of life in the city: they called it the right to the city. But just like that, as an abstract and all-encompassing term, it stays void of meaning, and useless in its otherwise elusive beauty. What we had in mind when starting NutriCities was to understand what a right to the city could mean in terms of one specific realm of our daily lives. It is not difficult to imagine what is one of the most important aspects of our lives as humans, the one thing we cannot do without: food. Without food, we are all dead! Yet we take it all for granted: the quality or quantity of what we eat, where it comes from, and at what cost. And we fail to realize, except for the tiniest moments of panic when food shortages loom on the horizon, how fragile the food chain is in the big cities where we all live now. In the wake of the COVID-19 pandemic, the fear of this fragility became painfully clear: even though the food supply systems were strained but did not collapse, people still went on panic-buying sprees anticipating that the supply chain would, sooner or later, snap. Those of us who were in Athens at the height of the economic crisis remember the scenes in supermarkets that emptied out in hours and the days after capital controls were announced, limiting the amount of money people could withdraw from ATMs. Big cities like New York or London only have enough food supplies to get them through a few days, should the supply chain be halted for whatever reason. If access to and from any of these cities was halted, it would be a matter of a few hours or days before the businessman in the pristine suit joined the homeless, searching for scraps of food from a trash can, in being equally unable to get anything to eat any longer. It is impossible to even comprehend how important this truth is, fixed as it is in our minds that the global food chain works and will continue to work apace, for ever and ever: a food chain that is so fragile, and ironically, poses as being so strong.

This is why we felt it was so important for us to conduct this exercise: the exercise of understanding not only what it is that we eat in the city, not only what the foods that we currently consume do to us, but also what our location in the city determines in terms of what we can access—and at what price. And then, in a learning exercise led by our wonderful Minhocas Urbanas collective on the ground in Rio, we want to explore what new ways there are of growing our own food and strengthening current agroecological networks in the national peripheries or urban peripheries. What ways there are, in short, of making more viable the path toward food sovereignty, toward taking back control over the substance that gives us life. Not just any right to the city, but a right to food in the city, a right to life in the city. The experiment of this book then comes at a critical moment: this critical moment when life and cities as we knew them come under an unprecedented attack.

NOTES

1   James C. Scott, *Against the Grain: A Deep History of the Earliest States* (New Haven: Yale University Press, 2017), 7.
2   Scott, *Against the Grain*, 7.

CHAPTER TWO

Food Sovereignty Action and Research

Minhocas Urbanas

▬

From late 2017 to mid-2019 the group Minhocas Urbanas (Urban Earthworms) formed an active part of the NutriCities research project. We carry this experience and its teachings with us and keep on struggling for the causes of the urban peripheries—in our case, the causes of the favelas of Maré, in Rio de Janeiro. We came from community struggles that had already been related to food sovereignty in some way, and which we spoke of in this research and within this group's work.

Before being, or seeing ourselves as, researchers, we are residents of this territory of experiences and resistances called Maré. In a political-communitarian sense, we act in various groups and small grassroots movements. We represent many subjects and subjectivities—residents, researchers, militants, farmers, public health specialists—who act and try to fight for our community by distributing agroecological products, engaging in media activism, organizing cultural activities, mobilizing to maintain the few green areas in Maré's favelas, and creating urban gardens, such as the Parque Ecológico. Except for farmer Juliana Medeiros, all of our local researchers live, work, and act in Maré. Some of us have graduated in fields such as nutrition, public health, social services, geography, social sciences, and communication.

Research and community action do not need to be separate, nor should we think of them as such. As subjects, we are many, and we can live together, be activists, and do research in an integrated way. In the words of Orlando Fals Borda, our concern is "how to investigate reality in order to transform it."[1] The urban earthworm spirit still lives in us, and the experiences we had during this research and intervention process continue to feed our work, our struggles, and to strengthen the groups and movements we are part of. We are urban earthworms, and our wormholes make up the city. The urban periphery is the place where we struggle for self-emancipatory transformation of our (so)ci(e)ty.

Which Maré Are We Talking About? A Little Bit About Our Territory

"Maré's development originated in people's struggles and resistance—the people who resided above Baía de Guanabara's waters and still live on its margins—against removal processes and their social demands' invisibility, throughout [ninety] years of history."[2]

Along with Rio de Janeiro's industrial development around the 1940s, there was considerable mobility of people around our area, known as the city's North Zone. From that time on, the city received a high flow of northeastern migrants in search of work and better living conditions. When these people arrived, for lack of better opportunities, they settled in areas despised by the real estate sector—such as hillsides and marshland areas. At this time, the Leopoldina region of our city had already become an industrial core. And as the suburbs' "good lands" had started to become less accessible to the newly arrived migrants, they were forced to find ways to live in areas with difficult access, like the one around Guanabara Bay. Our Maré (which translates as "tide") was named like this because the houses founded here at the time were built on stilts, literally occupying mangrove areas amidst the tides, in a dispute over land where there wasn't even proper land: only the waters of the Guanabara Bay. In a visit to Parque Ecológico, a park in a favela of the same name here in the Maré, our group's member Geandra Nobre summarized, "Maré, as a whole, had only two dry spots, which were Morro do Timbau, a rock, and the woods here in [Parque Ecológico], which is more forested. The rest was mangrove marshland."[3]

At the time of the first occupations, stilt houses or simply wooden shacks were built on mud and water, serving as the primary form of housing and resulting in large-scale human settlement areas in the Maré. The construction of the Avenida Brasil, Rio's main highway connecting the northern and western parts of the metropolitan area to the center, was completed in 1946, and the demand for construction labor was

26

decisive for the area's occupation, which continued in the 1950s and resulted in new favelas taking form in the Maré area.

Parallel to a new influx of people into the Maré, Carlos Lacerda's state government (1961–65) carried out modernization projects in the city's South Zone, resulting in the eradication of slums and removal of their populations to distant regions in the municipality. From then on, residents of several South Zone's favelas and homeless people from the banks of the Faria-Timbó River were transferred to "provisional" dwellings built in the Maré, leading to the emergence of new communities.

Until the early 1980s, the Maré das Palafitas (Maré of stilts) was known as a symbol of misery all over Brazil as portrayed in the famous 1986 song, "Alagados" (Flooded), by the band Os Paralamas do Sucesso:

> And the city
> With its postcard open arms
> Its real-life closed fists lacking charm
> Refuses them opportunities
> Shows the harsh face of evil
> Alagados, Trenchtown, Favela da Maré
> Hope is not found in the sea
> Nor from the antennas of the TV

The small carnival street band, Se Benze Que Dá, which celebrated fifteen years of existence and resistance in 2020, and which members of our group are part of, also portrays Maré's history in its lyrics. It highlights "the struggle" as crucial to Maré residents' survival in the great metropolis. In 2006, the group paraded in an "undeterred" fashion through Maré's alleys and lanes with this song:

> The Mareense in the sea
> Where instead of ground he chose to be
> Rooted the stilt house, his way of living
> Keeps strong in his struggles
> Undeterred,
> Tables were turned,
> He'd never allow
> To be walled around
> Bring down walls of day-to-day
> The tide's always high, night and day

With the end of the twentieth century nearing, land reclamation began in a self-organized way on a small scale—in late-night mobilizations bringing trucks of debris from nearby large construction sites to at least fill the access roads to the houses on stilts. This then gave way to a large-scale state intervention, the federal government's first major intervention in the area: Projeto Rio (Rio Project), which provided for the filling of flooded areas and transferred stilt house residents to prefabricated popular housing. In 1988, the Thirtieth Administrative Region was created, covering the entire Maré area and becoming the city's first to be located in a favela area, followed by the formal recognition of our favelas as Bairro Maré (Maré Neighborhood) in 1996.

What used to be water ended up becoming land, and with it, a land and a territory on which to live and resist. By becoming residents of these areas, Mareenses made Maré their own. The entire landfilled area we now know as Maré served to build popular housing in various formats in different urban projects—some earning international awards for their architects irrespective of how low the quality of life they would provide. Rio de Janeiro as a whole seems to be a landfilled capital, from the artificially expanded beaches to the extensive park of the Aterro do Flamengo and the Estácio-Manguinhos axis from the west and the northwest of the city center. Many of these were created so that Rio spread itself amid mountains, (former) mangroves, and (former) rivers, which became canals and ditches. This socially and territorially complex and diverse history led to what we know today as Conjunto de Favelas da Maré (Favela Neighborhood Maré), at present made up of sixteen favelas.

Landmarks tell the story of this dwelling process between the tides. A former island, for example, was integrated into the landfills that became the base for the favelas Vila do Pinheiro, Parque Ecológico, Salsa and Merengue, Vila do João, and Conjunto Esperança. The landfill surrounded the island and left behind a green hill that became the Parque Ecológico (Ecological Park), commonly also known as Mata do Pinheiro (Pinheiro Forest), the largest green area of Maré. According to Naldinho Lourenço, "What used to be an island turned into an un-island."[4]

This story is vividly told by the Museu da Maré, located in a shed previously used by the region's maritime industry. The museum offers an illustrative portrait of Maré's history, and it also housed the Food Sovereignty Week's activities in 2018. The programing included a visit to the museum.[5] In one of his visits there, Portuguese sociologist Boaventura de Sousa Santos emphasized that one of the reasons he enjoyed visiting the museum was that, unlike the vast majority of museums (especially the famous ones in the Global North), it did not consist of stolen objects. On a guided tour during the Food Sovereignty Week, our group's Geandra Nobre revealed that the residents themselves collaborated with the museum's construction. "After the proposition to build the museum, Maré's residents were invited to donate items. Therefore, aside from the printed photographs, the objects seen here are personal, memory-filled objects."

In the same visit, Lourenço highlighted the importance of the museum for those that come from Maré themselves: "That's because it makes us remember a lot of what we've lived through.... The most interesting thing about reclaiming all this, in a community museum, is having access to this memory and passing it on to younger people, right?"[6]

The museum tells countless stories of struggle, suffocation, hopes, frustrations, pain, creation, and collective forms of defense and resistance. They highlight the favela's becoming and the favelados' becoming part of Rio's urban reality.

Maré is located between the city's three main access highways. Air pollution is one of the factors that make our daily lives difficult, in addition to the lack of proper infrastructure such as sanitation and sewage, problems with the electrical grid, few high schools, precarious healthcare, and so forth. But sadly, Maré's greatest fame is one of urban violence, often making headlines in national mainstream media and beyond. There are constant incursions by state agents that violate our rights and kill our youth. Nonetheless, the state allows the illicit activities of drug trafficking groups that divide our favelas' territory among themselves, even though they contend with them for territorial power.

In this territory with all its problems, we also find many opportunities for a daily life with dignity. In November 2017, the Roça! Collective invited us to participate in their research. Their case study would be the favelas of Maré. We became part of a locally rooted research and intervention group that could develop methods and conduct research in dialogue with the leading researchers. While learning about the issue, we research it, and, while researching it, we also learn, looking for ways to intervene, even if only minimally.

We tried to work with a bottom-up approach, at least as much as possible. Authors like James C. Scott have shown that in trying to understand behaviors and social patterns, social scientists typically accept the opinions and views elite groups hold of their own actions.[7] However, when it comes to non-elite groups, statistics, consumption patterns, electoral behavior, and all other indicators are employed to explain them in an abstract, de-individualized way, as objects of study and never as subjects of social intervention or change, never as agents to their actions.

In a collective approach to community research, we talked to ordinary people and gave great importance to what they think and do, but we were also part of this group of people. We are part of the people who live, work, and eat in the favelas, people who benefit from better insight into how food security or sovereignty and the urban periphery relate. It is in this sense that NutriCities is based on an action research approach as discussed by geographers such as Rachel Pain, Duncan Fuller and Rob Kitchin, and Kathryn Herr and Gary L. Anderson, but which, before that, derives from a genuine Global South militant research tradition, such as that of Colombian social scientist Orlando Fals Borda, or Indian social scientist Muhammad Anisur Ramnath.[8] Approaches that Timo Bartholl has referred to in previous works as "research as a tool for struggle."[9]

Our approach allowed us two things: first, to empirically obtain data and field experience in one of Rio de Janeiro's most populated favela areas. Second, by being in touch with international researchers, we gained a different perspective from studying the bigger picture— that is, the international debates and policies on food matters. The exchange and conversations among our local and global community researchers helped us identify key thematic areas for research and action, and develop focused working groups such as one devoted to "urban agriculture and the right to the city" (Working Group 1), another concentrating on "agroecological fairs and networks of distribution and access to organic and agroecological food" (Working Group 2), and one focused on "food habits in the favela, food sovereignty, and agroecology" (Working Group 3).

Working Group 1 visited urban gardens and urban agriculture initiatives and was actively involved in a larger-scale community garden in the area known as Mata do Pinheiro, in favela Parque Ecológico, in the southeast part of Maré. This gave us firsthand experience of the challenges in trying to transform the favela into a more agroecological, food-sovereign territory.

Working Group 2 visited street fairs in different parts of the city. It then mapped and discussed spatial patterns in the distribution of agroecological and organic food in Rio de Janeiro's metropolitan area. At the same time, we studied the possibilities and limitations of commercialization of agroecological products in the favelas of Maré.

Through Working Group 3, we coordinated empirical research in its most classical sense, through short and long interviews and a photo diary. It was also through this group that we intervened directly in the territory's activities with workshops on food, health, and land offered in previously existing spaces and groups that we knew about as professionals or had participated in as members.

Thinking About Food Sovereignty in the Urban Periphery

"We began to realize that food sovereignty is crucial if we want a more democratic, sovereign, egalitarian society."
—Beto Ribeiro, Small Farmers' Movement (MPA)[10]

During NutriCities' research, our debates on the relationship of the urban periphery and the question of food sovereignty brought up a set of key questions:

- How do we access food in the favela, and how do we eat?
- What interventions are possible to spread knowledge and practices toward a periphery that is less dependent on supermarkets, agro-industry, and conventional food distribution networks, which are based on food that is often genetically modified and poisoned with agrotoxins?
- How do we connect with resistances in the countryside that seek to advance toward food sovereignty?

Our Access to Food and Our Eating Routines

The Brazilian population has experienced significant social transformations in the last decades, which have resulted in changes in food consumption patterns. The decrease in hunger and malnutrition was followed by an increase in obesity in all social strata. Food and nutrition security is established in Brazil as a public policy horizon, viewed as everyone's right to regular and permanent access to quality food in sufficient amounts, without compromising access to other essential needs. It is based on health-promoting food practices that respect cultural diversity and that are environmentally, culturally, economically, and socially sustainable.[11] In addition, it is crucial to guarantee people's autonomy regarding food choices—while considering social inequalities and aspects such as housing, infrastructure, and general living conditions, locally available types of food, and the need for sufficient purchasing power.

Rio de Janeiro's main food arrival and redistribution hub is the Supply Center of Rio de Janeiro, known as CEASA-RJ.[12] Numerous trucks reach CEASA-RJ, in the North Zone neighborhood of Irajá, and thousands of resellers buy from the distributors daily. Anyone can become an informal reseller as no documentation is needed to purchase food items at the CEASA-RJ. In this way, a supermarket chain or an independent supermarket might buy from the same source as a small individual market vendor. Retailers' demands, whether small or large in scale, are met at CEASA-RJ. Of course, the leading supermarket chains have their own distribution networks beyond this hub. But what is essential here for the favelas' residents, in regard to the products they have access to, is that it is nearly impossible for them to know their food's origin and means of production, except in the case of one specific area at the CEASA reserved for family agriculture, where sometimes the resellers might know where the food they offer comes from. Not knowing the origin of the food you buy makes it impossible to choose between different sources or modes of production.

A tomato bought at the weekly market in one of the favelas of Maré could have come from a family farm or an agro-industry production complex. This information is not disclosed to the end consumer, often not even the seller has it. The use of pesticides is intense in Brazilian agriculture, be it at an industrial or a family production scale. As a consequence, no matter where Maré's consumers buy their food, they do not know where it comes from or how it was grown. Yet the chances are high that pesticide and GMO-based conventional production methods were used for most of the food they have access to.

In general, and from what we have seen when analyzing our interviews on food habits with Maré's residents, most buy much of their food either in local supermarkets or in one of the big supermarkets in nearby neighborhoods such as Bonsucesso. Many residents also buy fruit and vegetables at the weekly street fairs, local *hortifrúti* shops, or in permanent stalls in the main access streets to the different favelas.

In their daily routines, the vast majority of residents have hardly any access to any type of alternatively produced food, be it agroecological or certified organic food. The nearest weekly fairs that supply such food are the Federal University's fair (although at relatively high prices) and a weekly fair in the Olaria neighborhood (at slightly more moderate prices, comparatively speaking) or at the Fiocruz Health Center–based Josué de Castro Fair (see figure 1). However, Maré's residents hardly ever purchase food items at either of these as they lie beyond the reach of their daily routines and routes (and during the pandemic lockdown these fairs have been closed).

In terms of particular eating habits and routines, most people in Maré have a rather light breakfast consisting of white bread, either with margarine or butter, cheese or mortadella, and some coffee with a reasonable amount of refined, white sugar. Lunch is an important meal. It nearly always contains rice and black beans, potatoes (often french fries), *farinha* (a manioc flour), noodles (spaghetti), and meat (beef, pork, chicken) or less frequently, fish. Often, but not always, it can include some kind of vegetable and salad. Families who cook at home either by choice or necessity (to cut down on their spending) will always have rice and beans as their base; their meals vary only in what accompanies it.

At the same time, however, it is also common to have lunch in one of the numerous street restaurants—either by ordering an individual dish from the menu, or choosing from a buffet that tends to vary little, yet always contains an assortment of vegetables, salad, carbohydrate sources, meat, and eggs. Lunch is the main meal for people in Maré, and the time it is taken can vary from late morning to late afternoon. After lunch, their routine is less regular and differs from one individual to another. It is not unusual for people to have the same food they had for lunch by heating up the leftovers. Another common way to satisfy hunger at night or any time of day, though, is to have a *lanche*, or snack. There are four main types of *lanches*. The first is a hamburger and its variants (with added eggs, bacon, cheese, etc.). Then come *salgados* (wheat flour–based savoury pastries filled with meat), and *pastéis* (a deep-fried, flour-based envelope pastry filled with meat or cheese).

Finally, there is meat and chicken on a stick, fried on a grill, sometimes with rice and a chopped tomato and onion sauce (*molho a campanha*, similar to *pico de gallo*), which, in this case, can be considered the most complete fast-food option available.

Many of Maré's numerous street restaurants offer one or more of these four main types of snacks or lunches exclusively. At night there are very few restaurants offering meals compared to what is available at lunchtime, and especially as affordably as during lunchtime (five to fifteen reais for a full dish). Most snack places also offer fruit juices or açaí bowls (a sorbet-like sweet snack of frozen açaí berry pulp) to be eaten either along the savory snacks or separately. There are also several different ice cream shops, many offering low-quality ice cream with high levels of hydrogenated fat.

A fifth category worth mentioning are pizzerias, which are also quite numerous. Motorcycle couriers can also deliver all these *lanches* and meals to residents' homes for a small service charge. At lunchtime, it is also very common to pick up or ask for a meal delivery in an aluminum or styrofoam container, called a *quentinha*.

In general, we can observe that many of those food items are low in nutritional value and represent a particular set of urbanized eating habits. These habits take up more and more space in daily menus when compared to traditional habits that older generations (many of whom are migrants from northeast Brazil) may still maintain to a degree, but that younger generations increasingly leave behind. New types of food that come to be part of the routine, at least for some of the residents, usually show up as trends. One example is yakisoba, a noodle dish with some vegetables and fried meats, inspired by Asian cuisine, or, to a lesser extent, sushi.

It is finally worth mentioning that on most social occasions, families and friends organize *churrascos* (barbecues). This once again means that meat is the main ingredient in social events' menus. Last but not least, beer is also widely consumed on these occasions and is also consumed regularly by a significant portion of Maré's residents.

Through this brief summary of food habits and food consumption patterns in the favelas of Maré, we can notice two main characteristics when it comes to food sovereignty. First, regarding primary resources, Maré's residents have little to no choice over where their food comes from or how it is produced, as well as very limited means, in terms of scale, to produce food on their own. We can say that there is a high degree of nonsovereignty when it comes to primary food production in the favelas of Maré, even though urban agriculture's role has its importance, which we will discuss more extensively below. On the other hand, we can confirm that many types of food offered in the favelas have been handled and processed locally in small-scale production units. With no access to organized data in this regard, we can say with a degree of certainty that a considerable proportion of the workforce in Maré is employed—mostly informally—in food-related activities, often in small family businesses such as lunch and dinner restaurants, snack bars, fast-food stalls, bakeries, markets, and street vendors.

Given this setting, we ask ourselves how we can improve our eating habits in Maré. And furthermore, what motivates us to make certain eating choices? First of all, we know that there is a media appeal with its offer of practical, palatable, durable, and attractive food that significantly affects food choices, especially when it comes to children and adolescents. This widely advertised food, however, is usually ultraprocessed, has a high energy density, is rich in sugar and fat, and contains many chemical additives. This type of food is massively and widely distributed by major players in the food industry, such as Nestlé. These companies seem to dream that one day we will all eat exclusively from aluminium bags, cans, plastic boxes, or any packaging whatsoever, in which items such as glutamate and preservatives prevail among countless ingredients blended into a design that promises much and nourishes little.

When expanding their markets to the last corners of the vast Brazilian territory, food sector multinationals use sales and resale strategies that take advantage of the labor market's precarious nature, setting up marketing networks for small individual entrepreneurs. The *New York Times Magazine* goes straight to the point when it discusses "how the big industry has managed to get Brazil hooked on junk food."[13] It is worth noting that these types of food are the preferred choices for children's school meals as well, perhaps because of practicality or price, or even because parents have limited information on healthier options. This fact not only affects children and adolescents but also most of the population across different social strata.

There are predominant paradigms in the field of nutritional care that relate "well-being" to a diet focused on weight loss—a fitness logic that boils the matter of food down to what to eat and how to exercise in order to lose or maintain weight. Jamylle Andrade, our group's nutritionist, has trouble finding alternative spaces to follow up on people with food and health issues with a more integrated perspective. People who look for a nutritionist often reproduce the fitness logic they expect the nutritionist to guide them through. According to Andrade, "That's what bothers me regarding [nutritional] care. People look at us and want to lose weight, [they want you] to write a prescription [and that's it]."

What needs to be critically discussed is how to put the relationship to food at the periphery on the communitarian agenda and rethink it in a context of struggle for food sovereignty.

- Besides only consuming and influencing food policy through campaigns, elections, or support for rural social movements, what needs to be done for residents of the urban periphery to have more sovereignty over their food supply?
- What ways do we find in the favela to produce, distribute, sell, buy, prepare, process, and consume food? What is our role in this (as residents, researchers, and grassroots social movement activists)?

Our (Difficult) Access to Agroecological Food: On the Connection Between the Countryside and the City

During the Maré Week of Food Sovereignty, Beto said, "When we started to talk about food sovereignty, one of our big challenges was how to organize the entire production and distribution system. Today, in Brazil and worldwide, a few companies control the bulk of food distribution. And in Brazil, there are also only a few that control [it] and [they] are linked to international capital, multinationals.... If you control the distribution, you control the population."[14]

Despite the predominance of a few big players, according to Beto, 70 percent of the food that reaches Brazilians' tables comes from family agriculture and not from agribusiness, which produces mainly commodities for export. Still, he argues, "We have seen that we, the small farmers, do not control the distribution, let alone people organized in the cities. We started to discuss a food sovereignty axis, which is popular supply [that is, supply for the popular classes]. How the countryside and the city are going to build and to organize a production and distribution system."[15]

Brazil is the world's largest user of agrotoxins. In absolute numbers, the country's industrial agriculture uses more agrotoxins than any other country in the world, and many small farmers also frequently use them on their plantations. While in 2000 the total amount of agrotoxins sold in Brazil amounted to "only" 314,000 tons, this number almost tripled by 2013, peaking at 902,000 tons and maintaining this high level in 2014 and 2015, with numbers around the 900,000 tons mark.[16]

In addition to the use of pesticides, the use of genetically modified organisms (GMOs) has also increased significantly in the last two decades. According to data collected by the Campanha Permanente Contra os Agrotóxicos e Pela Vida (Permanent Campaign Against Agrotoxins and for Life), the total land area planted with GMOs added up to just over 7 million acres throughout Brazil in 2003. A mere twelve years later, in 2015, it was over fifteen times that number, reaching 109 million acres.[17] The continuous decrease in crop diversity and the increase in both GMOs and the use of agrotoxins increasingly complicate the access to quality food without traces of toxic substances. In this regard, urban peripheries' residents are disproportionately affected, just as organic food mostly is accessible in middle- and high-income neighborhoods, as we will discuss below.

From the perspective of those who live in the city's peripheries, the question then is where to get poison-free food of organic or agroecological, reliable origin. Our group's researcher Joelma Nobre has been selling vegetables and fruits in a market stall in Vila do João, Maré, for many years. In our meetings, she reported that all her merchandise comes from CEASA and that she can find out little or nothing about its origins. She knows how much she paid for them, how much she needs to charge, and how much she needs to sell to have enough income by the end of the day, but if any consumer asks where her lettuce came from, she can only point to CEASA and the reseller's shed number. After her research experience, she would like to change this picture and sell agroecological products in Maré. Our group intended to support her in putting this idea into practice, yet we were not able to do so during the short course of the project. But the idea remains on the horizon as a post-project task. During the Week of Food Sovereignty Joelma Nobre pondered:

> Yes, I want my favela, my community, to have quality products on the table. But one of the big questions is: who can help me [as a local street market vendor]? Where do I find these

products? Who is going to supply me? I am together with [the agroecology movement] on this journey, and in the struggle. I really want my [market] stand to become an agroecological stand among conventional ones in our conventional fairs. But we don't just work with two or three boxes of lettuce. This is a community where you plant and you harvest, financially speaking. Everything you plant, even if it's a small stand that you set up down your street, will bring a return for you. One of the things is that I need someone to supply me with quality lettuce—but I don't work with one, two, three boxes. I work with twenty boxes; I work with sixty bunches of coriander. I work on Saturdays and Sundays, so I need someone who has this farm, who has this availability ... so that I can provide it to my community at an affordable price. Because it's no use setting up an agroecological stand in the middle of a conventional market and then selling at high prices ... I have to fight the poison with a healthy dish that is also affordable for my clients. I want my stand to be different among the typical ones.[18]

Distributing and selling agroecological products of a known and reliable source is a key issue when discussing the possibilities of improving our food quality here in Maré. There are some consumer networks throughout the metropolitan region and smaller groups of households buy from farmers directly. Juliana Medeiros puts together food baskets that her daughter picks up once a week to deliver to households in the South Zone in Botafogo and surrounding neighborhoods. The most substantial amount of organic and agroecological products that come to the city, though, is sold at organic and agroecological farmers' fairs. And as we will see on the map on the next page, what Joelma Nobre would like to put into practice exists in many places across the city, but so far not in a single favela.

As the map shows, most organic fairs and stores are concentrated in the South Zone of Rio and the southern part of the North Zone—the areas with the most middle- and upper-class neighborhoods. There are much fewer fairs in the North and West Zones. However, the map shows three fairs in the vicinity of Maré's favelas: the Federal University of Rio de Janeiro's Feira Agroecológica (agroecological fair) in Cidade Universitária, located on an island close to Maré;[19] the Josué de Castro

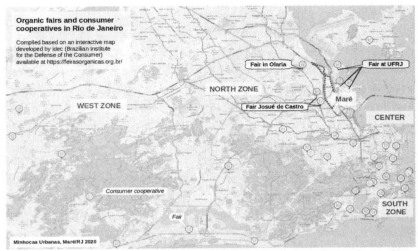

Figure 1. Organic fairs and consumer cooperatives in Rio de Janeiro

Sabores e Saberes agroecological fair, at Fiocruz health research center (Oswaldo Cruz Foundation);[20] and the Circuito de Feiras Orgânicas (Organic Fairs Circuit) in the neighborhood of Olaria. However, as we mentioned above, we estimate that very few Maré residents attend these fairs. Olaria is too far away for daily shopping routines, and the areas where public institutions such as Fiocruz and Cidade Universitária lie are mostly visited by their employees and students. With the pandemic reaching Rio de Janeiro in March 2020, much of the work of public universities and research institutions such as the Federal University of Rio de Janeiro and Fiocruz began to be conducted remotely, so the markets at these sites were suspended due to the lack of potential consumers. Fairs located in city neighborhoods such as the one in Olaria resumed their activities a few weeks after the first lockdown and have been maintained regularly since as essential activity.

The fairs are important initiatives that allow agroecological producers to build regular relationships with conscientious consumers. However, even if these fairs' producers and organizers strive to avoid reproducing the high-price logics of some South Zone fairs, prices are still going to be higher than at regular fairs and in *sacolões*—small stores with vegetables and fruits—in popular areas like Maré. This is also a key point: all favelas of Maré host their weekly fairs, and Nova Holanda's is the largest in the region, historically attracting consumers not only from Maré but also from surrounding neighborhoods. Vila do João also offers a large weekly fair and there are permanent stalls and *sacolões* in several favelas of Maré. Therefore, just as we saw in our interviews, Maré residents routinely purchase vegetables and fruits in local fairs, *sacolões*, and supermarkets. For us to start having access to agroecological products, they need to be available in places where we buy our food.

Another issue, noted by our group's vendor, Joelma Nobre, is that Maré's residents diversify very little when it comes to the food they buy as they always look for the same vegetables and fruits for their daily food routines. When Joelma brings a vegetable or fruit that is not as well known or as common in fairs, and here in the tropics we have a great variety, she notices how little interest many consumers show in them. This can only be changed if alternative agroecological food items are offered here accompanied by information on the benefits of this food and campaigns to promote it.

Considering that food sovereignty is a concept based on agroecological practices and therefore also on urban agriculture, how can favelas organize in the face of this knowledge and these practices?

Our Favela, Our Garden: Urban Agriculture in Favelas

"Because they never have the means to eat well, inside the community. Actually, for the community to eat well, the only way is by growing food."

—Juliana Medeiros, agroecological farmer
and Minhocas Urbanas researcher

According to the *Plano Diretor de Arborização Urbana da Cidade do Rio de Janeiro* (the City of Rio de Janeiro's Master Plan of Urban Afforestation), Maré only has 680 trees of 52 species. According to the goals established by this plan, this would mean a tree deficit of 1,180 units, considering the neighborhood's size. Neighborhoods with the highest municipal property tax revenue, and most residents with high purchasing power, are also those with highest tree density of our city.[21] In recent years, we have seen several large trees being cut down in our Maré neighborhood to make way for small construction works on the sidewalks, while no new trees have been planted. For this reason, the arboreal deficit has most likely even increased since the plan's publication in 2015.

The lack of vegetation and our favela's location turn Maré into a real urban heat island, surrounded by the main access roads to Rio's metropolitan area. Together, these three highways add up to twenty-six lanes with heavy traffic. Respiratory problems are common among residents. Urban agriculture, agroecology, and Maré—do they really have nothing to do with each other, then?

A first step when we start to think of urban agriculture is to break our own perception barrier, which often prevents us from seeing the multiple ways people grow food in the city. Many people are planting in Maré, whether it is on sidewalks, alleys, lanes, terraces, or rooftops. Many of the plants are decorative, while they are also believed to have beneficial properties, such as the espada de São Jorge (snake plant), which supposedly fends off the evil eye, or comigo ninguém pode (dumb cane) and chilli beans that are supposed to protect those who plant and care for them in their house's entrances or halls. But beyond that, we see many green corners as we walk through the streets of Maré—buckets, overturned old refrigerators, concrete beds: people find many ways to gather soil in any kind of receptacle and simply plant. We see flowers and leaves of the most diverse shades of green, herbs, vegetables, and, in the few green areas or where there is at least a little bit of space, we also find animals being bred—from chickens to pigs, from horses to—more rarely—goats.

For a more succinct definition, we understand that urban agriculture is practiced within (intra-urban) cities or at their (peri-urban) margins, and that it aims to cultivate, produce, grow, process, and distribute a variety of food and nonfood products, mostly (re)using locally available material resources. Yet while studies on urban agriculture suppose that worldwide approximately somewhere from 15 to 20 percent of the food consumed comes from agriculture in urban areas, we cannot conclude that in Maré's favelas we are anywhere near this number.[22] Rio as a city hosts two of the largest inner city mountainous forest areas of the world—the Tijuca National Park and the Pedra Branca State Park. In the West Zone of Rio's metropolitan area, we can find intense agricultural activity in gardens, fields, and forest mountain ranges. Yet in areas as densely populated as the Maré neighborhood, free and plantable space is scarce. Despite that, urban gardens have been built with or without city government support; some have perished but others persist, such as the garden in the Mata do Pinheiro, where we developed several activities during our research.

Among the plants we find in Maré's streets and few green areas, several aren't usually considered edible. Still, the movement for agroecology has been making an effort to spread knowledge about these edible weeds or nonconventional food plants (known by the acronym PANC). We do not seek to join the "organic gourmet" trend that has embraced PANCs as something chic to grow and eat, but we wonder whether what we are lacking may already be growing right before our eyes. It seems that our consumption patterns are increasingly confined and standardized so that we eat only what we can buy.

In a visit to the urban garden in Mata do Pinheiro, Geandra Nobre showed us one of these PANCs. "Several PANCs are growing on flowerbeds and street corners with the tiniest bit of soil among this sea of bricks and concrete we live in here in Maré. This one is called João Gomes, and some northeasterners call it língua de vaca. It's an edible plant, but also a weed, that can be a plague. But a good one, you know?"[23]

We need to recover knowledge of these plants and learn how to grow and harvest them even with our limited resources and space—and we do not need to go far for this. Many of the Maré residents who came from states like Minas Gerais or Brazil's northeast are from the countryside and still possess much know-how regarding how to grow, eat, and care for their health with the plants they grow.

In our self-reflection workshop, Amanda Mendonça pondered:

> And there are a few small gardens around the favela. I think it's nice when I pass by Parque União, and there are some doors with basil, like, in a ... little pot. I look and I think, this is basil.... It's cool, right? It's a form of resistance. And there are doors full of ... several plants and flowers and such. They sometimes are not fruits or edible, but then, why is that? Why is that all that's being grown? Is it because our [air] is so polluted? Is it because we don't really know [better]? How can we also invite ... people who understand about this so that they can give workshops? How to do something of a mobilization within the reality people live in, right? Without ignoring this reality?

We visited some of Maré's urban gardens and were convinced that the idea of growing food in the favelas certainly needs to be encouraged. Besides growing healthy food, we improve the air we breathe and create green areas within the city. These gardens allow people to access food grown without pesticides around their homes. Consequently, encouraging local production and consumption reduces costs and environmental impacts related to food transportation. In addition, we have an extraordinary example of critical resistance in Maré—the wisdom of residents like Nova Holanda's Vó Léia. Her empirical knowledge is incredible, and her know-how and practices, although not inserted into theoretically formulated concepts, are part of her being and the space she occupies. When asked if she knew anything about "agroecology," she did not know how to answer. This draws attention to the devaluation of her potential, continuously turned invisible and hampered within our community. Her rooftop garden also works as a tool for sustenance and contact with nature. Amid so much state violence and the deficiencies of so many policies and the lack of rights, it is also possible to note a historical process in our favelas that has links to the social organization of quilombos.[24] Although Maré is a diversified and urbanized space, the roots of our ancestors, be they Indigenous, Blacks, or peasants, are present in our coexistence.

Bruna Pierrout, from the working group on urban agriculture, argues:

> In short, it is hard to say that Maré does not really know about agroecology. Unfortunately, we keep experiencing precarious urbanization under the influence of agro é pop,[25] and the knowledge is being lost with large markets' processes. On the other hand, however, there are still roots. There are still possibilities of urban agriculture through agroecology. We can still provide a better world for our children through freeing environmental education. There is still powerful resistance in an area shaped by the fights of residents that come together for a better community.
>
> Amid so many problems related to the lack of public policies, investments, and fundamental rights [in Maré], we must look at the small solutions that are not seen, nor valued. Against all of the society's unequal conditions, we need to praise the outlook for change of people who critically resist [here] with their traditional knowledge and who, regardless of where it might be, find ways to plant and practice agroecology.

The urban garden at Mata do Pinheiro is a place of urban agriculture, where Seu Bolado takes care of seedbeds where he grows a variety of food. Naldinho Lourenço spoke about the garden in our visit during the Maré Week of Food Sovereignty:

> Parque Ecológico, as a whole, was restructured in 2002. This garden right here is part of [city hall's project] Hortas Cariocas. But in truth the city hall barely collaborates with the space. It sometimes donates fertiliser and a few other things when the [Parque Ecológico] residents' association requests, like fences or irrigation equipment. You can tell things have decayed. And former mayor Eduardo Paes's administration, along with Crivella.... They would send us soil containing crushed glass.... So if we wanted to do something with the children [we would first need to sift that soil].[26]

We did just that for our joint activity on the challenges of maintaining an urban garden in the urban periphery, with the participation of agroecology groups from the Federal University of Rio de Janeiro in November 2018.[27] We sifted the soil to prepare it for the workshops with the children during that day. We also camped out in the garden with a few students from other states who were participating in the III Encontro Regional dos Grupos de Agroecologia do Sudeste (Third Regional Meeting of the Southeast Agroecology Groups), a camp night among trees and near manioc plants in the midst of a favela as densely populated as Maré.[28]

During our research, we connected with a number of movements in the urban agriculture and agroecology field that were also present at the Maré Week of Food Sovereignty. Besides a lot of knowledge exchange, visits to the territory, and moments of hands-on joint effort and intervention, we were able to create links beyond the research project, and the spirit of Urban Earthworms lives on. We hope to continue supporting urban agriculture, agroecology, and food sovereignty to make Maré, along with so many others, a greener and healthier urban periphery to live in.

From this perspective, the idea of popular (self-)education gains importance. For instance, during the research, we connected the activities we carry out with children, who regularly participate in Roça's activities, to the prospects for agroecology.[29] With this in mind,

Alessandra de Lima, in her mid-twenties, spoke of the role that youth and children play, and of our relationship with them:

> I notice that they value material goods more. I have seen people destroying flowerbeds in order to park their motorcycles by their doors, you see? So I think it's pretty challenging to persuade a person who does that, you know? And for a year I've been learning a lot from my friends, especially from Dona Juliana. I see this in older people. When I went to the ENA [June 2018's Encontro Nacional de Agroecologia, or National Agroecology Meeting, in Belo Horizonte]—I had this opportunity. I missed the favela's presence there. There were young people, yes, there were many young people. But most of them were from a rural environment. And then I missed my people. "Gee, where are the favelados? My friends?" And what this research has shown is that it is, in fact, possible, through the children. I like working with them. When we go to the garden, when we take them there, it's so much joy. They participate, they're what motivates us to continue with this work because they make us happy. And when we work there [in the garden] our neighbors also come by, both women and men … and we all exchange knowledge … Most people who come to the favela are migrants. They're northeastern, and they have this thing to share with us, youngsters. But most youngsters aren't paying attention to what they have to teach us. That's a shame.
>
> It's part of our attitude—taking an old refrigerator and laying it down outside and planting in it, on the sidewalks. Even if someone goes there and throws garbage in it—that's our biggest challenge. We made a small garden on a sidewalk where people used to dump their garbage, to put an end to that practice. It, like, didn't do much, but we're still there resisting and trying to keep our garden standing. And the children take care of it.... It is very nice.... I believe in our children's education.[30]

The Distant Reality of Such an Intimate Struggle: For Food Sovereignty in Rural and Urban Peripheries!

Our research process and its dynamism have aggregated perspectives, knowledge, and reflections around the favela's green areas that resist the increasing advances of urban infrastructure. There is also a better understanding of home gardening, both medicinal and decorative.

Talking about food sovereignty in the favela is something new to us. We changed our view of the space we live in and its relationship with the food-sovereignty perspective very much due to meeting agroecological farmers like Juliana Medeiros and the social movements that mobilize around agroecology and urban agriculture.

We learned something every time we walked through the favelas of Maré, our territory, that we looked at it with new eyes—with its cultural abundance and ancestral knowledge, its plants being grown and growing in a space with large clusters of dense housing and an appropriation of most existing space for housing needs. Usually, the favela's most addressed themes are our resistance to the many violations of rights we suffer from regularly, especially from the violent conflicts we face, with the state violently entering the favela in addition to the drug gangs or paramilitaries fighting for territory. We also speak of racism, misogyny, sexism, poverty, and the absence of public and social policies. We speak and fight for everything that affects us directly and indirectly. However, securing healthy food for a population of urban poor that have been historically segregated and impoverished by capitalist society's political-economic organization is another important challenge. Within the context of access to rights, food is something that needs to be discussed beyond access. What sort of food do we have access to and eat every day?

Food is a basic human right regardless of social condition, skin color, ethnicity, place of residence, religious belief, gender, or age. In the current context of capitalism's globalized phase, this human right has been systematically violated as a result of the control that large transnational corporations have over the food market, through which they subordinate this right to their ability to profit and secure accumulation conditions. As a result, people can only have access to food when they have the money and income to buy it.

Faced with the country's current political crisis and an alarming number of agrotoxins in our food, the Permanent Campaign against Agrotoxins and for Life quoted a United Nations rapporteur who said: "Communities are being poisoned in Brazil." The rapporteur denounced the fact that, by the end of 2019, Brazil's government would have allowed the use of over eight hundred toxic substances in agriculture in total, especially pesticides. Some of these pesticides may pose severe risks for producers, consumers, ecosystems, and people in the areas where they are used.[31] In this vast panorama of transformations in food production, we took notice of the barriers to accessing organic products faced by the population of favelas and peripheries. We also paid attention to discussions about healthy foods that were not limited to income alone, but that extended to access to land in order to grow, cultivate, and engage in land and environment sustainability.

When asked about their sources of food, many people we talked to referred to supermarkets, followed by local fairs, and *sacolões* or *hortifrútis*. However, the range of choice is limited for those living in peripheral spaces. Healthy food, especially agroecological food, is hard to find in Maré. However, a considerable part of the interviewees pointed out that they are able to access all the food they need in Maré's fairs. Considering everything we have already discussed regarding products from the conventional food market's circuits, these existing fairs are powerful, dynamic spaces with many people transiting through them as traders and consumers. What these fairs lack is an alternative supply to build a new relationship between agroecological, poison-free products—linked to agroecological and/or family agriculture—and the consumer.

In this context of power over food choices, we discussed throughout our research the importance of food sovereignty, which is based on a broader approach than food security. It is based on the principle that all people have the right to food and that it is the state's duty to provide people with the necessary resources for such access. In this sense João Pedro Stedile and Horácio Martins de Carvalho define food sovereignty as "a set of public and social policies that must be adopted by all nations, in all villages, municipalities, regions, and countries to ensure that the necessary food can be produced for each place's population survival."[32]

From this perspective, it is essential to consider that for a population to be (food) sovereign and master of their own destiny, they must have the necessary conditions, resources, and support to access and/or produce their own food. It is then crucial to think about the processes of sovereignty linked to the culture and ways of life of each territory, region, and population, and then to think about and build strategies for the production and/or access to quality food according to local realities. In order to think about local arrangements, we need to build, together with the population, forms of social interaction and conviviality that diverge from people's current concrete realities, to weave together paths for changing these realities.

Bruna Pierrout's look back at the research's experience captures this spirit: "With each lecture or seminar, I was able to extract valuable knowledge that will contribute greatly to my journey as a young woman and favelada. A woman who seeks to occupy the city's spaces—including a university—exercising her rights as a citizen who seeks change and to break all paradigms imposed by the cruel interest of dominant power in making us more and more invisible."

Sometimes when working at the university-community interface we need to separate our places and the types of involvement we have had in order to evaluate what to change and what to do better the next time we embrace an experience like the NutriCities project in our various roles as university researchers, urban periphery residents, professionals who work in the peripheral territory, and as militants of a grassroots movement. What remains is the certainty that we will continue to work alongside those who struggle for food sovereignty in the favela.

We conclude with Amanda Mendonça's words from our self-reflection workshop: "We can evoke the earthworms' [spirit] at any time. Minhocas [Urbanas] was a reference for everyone here.... It's a work that will add a lot and that can offer a lot to Maré."

NOTES

1   Orlando Fals Borda, *Una Sociología Sentipensante para América Latina* (Bogotá: Siglo del Hombres/CLACSO, 2009). All translations are by the authors, unless otherwise noted.

2   Alexandre Dias, "A Maré no ritmo das ONGs: Uma análise sobre o papel das oficinas musicais de Organizações Não-Governamentais no bairro Maré/Rio de Janeiro" (master's thesis, Federal University of Rio de Janeiro (UFRJ), Music School, 2011), 9.

3   Geandra Nobre quoted during the Maré Week of Food Sovereignty. See a video of this visit at https://soberania-alimentar-mare.home.blog/videos/conhecendo-o-territorio.

4   Naldinho Lourenço quoted during the Maré Week of Food Sovereignty's round-table discussion "Desafios agroecológicos nas periferias urbanas: Práticas e perspectivas." See the video at https://soberania-alimentar-mare.home.blog/videos/mesas-redondas.

5   See a video of the guided visit at https://soberania-alimentar-mare.home.blog/videos/conhecendo-o-territorio.

6   See a video of the roundtable discussion at https://soberania-alimentar-mare.home.blog/videos/mesas-redondas.

7   James C. Scott, *Two Cheers for Anarchism: Six Easy Pieces on Autonomy, Dignity, and Meaningful Work and Play* (Princeton, NJ: Princeton University Press, 2012).

8   See Rachel Pain, "Social Geography: On Action-Oriented Research," *Progress in Human Geography* 27, no. 5 (2003): 649–57; Duncan Fuller and Rob Kitchin, eds., *Radical Theory/Critical Praxis: Making a Difference Beyond the Academy?* (Victoria,

BC: Praxis (e)press, 2004), https://kitchin.org/wp-content/uploads/2020/05/RTCP_Whole.pdf; Kathryn Herr and Gary L. Anderson, *The Action Research Dissertation: A Guide for Students and Faculty* (London: Sage, 2005); Borda, *Una sociología sentipensante para América Latina*; Orlando Fals Borda and Muhammad Anisur Ramnath, eds., *Action and Knowledge: Breaking the Monopoly with Participatory Action-Research* (London: Intermediate Technology Publications, 1991).

9   Timo Bartholl, *Por uma geografia em movimento: A ciência como ferramenta de luta* (Rio de Janeiro: Consequência, 2018).

10   Beto Ribeiro quoted from Maré Week of Food Sovereignty's roundtable "Agroecology: From Production to Distribution." See video at https://soberania-alimentar-mare.home.blog/videos/mesas-redondas.

11   We refer to the Política Nacional de Alimentação e Nutrição (National Food and Nutrition Policy, http://bvsms.saude.gov.br/bvs/publicacoes/politica_nacional_alimentacao_nutricao.pdf.

12   Each state of Brazil's federal union organizes food distribution through a State Supply Center (CEASA).

13   Andrew Jobs and Matt Richtel, "How Big Businesses Got Brazil Hooked on Junk Food," *New York Times*, September 16, 2017, https://www.nytimes.com/interactive/2017/09/16/health/brazil-obesity-nestle.html.

14   Beto quoted from roundtable "Agroecology: From Production to Distribution" during the Maré Week of Food Sovereignty. See video https://soberania-alimentar-mare.home.blog/videos/mesas-redondas.

15   This discussion is detailed on the MPA's website, https://mpabrasil.org.br.

16   "Dados Sobre Agrotóxicos" report by the Campanha Permanente Contra os Agrotóxicos e Pela Vida, see http://contraosagrotoxicos.org/dados-sobre-agrotoxicos.

17   Campanha Permanente Contra os Agrotóxicos e Pela Vida. "Dados Sobre Agrotóxicos."

18   Joelma Nobre quoted during roundtable "Agroecologia: da produção à distribuição," see https://soberania-alimentar-mare.home.blog/videos/mesas-redondas.

19   For more information see https://www.facebook.com/feiraagroecologicaufrj.

20   For information about the fair see http://www.ensp.fiocruz.br/portal-ensp/informe/site/materia/detalhe/46476.

21   Prefeitura da Cidade do Rio de Janeiro, https://www.rio.rj.gov.br/web/fpj/plano-diretor-de-arborizacao-urbana.

22   Lucian Velleda, "Hortas urbanas produzem 20% dos alimentos consumidos no mundo," *Rede Brasil Atual*, March 11, 2017, https://www.redebrasilatual.com.br/ambiente/2017/03/hortas-urbanas-produzem-20-de-todo-o-alimento-produzido-no-mundo. The original study was conducted and published by the Worldwatch Institute in 2011.

23   In English, this plant is called fame flower or jewels of opar. See video of this visit, https://soberania-alimentar-mare.home.blog/videos/conhecendo-o-territorio.

24   Quilombos historically were self-organized communities for the self-defense of former enslaved people who escaped slavery by fleeing to the woods. In recent history many quilombos have revived and reorganized themselves, sometimes using legal means to gain recognition of their groups and territories.

25   Brazil's largest media and TV network, Rede Globo, often runs ads in favor of Brazilian agro-industry, and considers it "Brazil's industry-wealth." The motto

is repeated numerous times on TV and it goes "Agro is tech, agro is pop, agro is everything. It's on Globo."

26   See a video of the visit https://soberania-alimentar-mare.home.blog/videos/conhecendo-o-territorio. Eduardo Paes was Rio de Janeiro's mayor between 2009 and 2016. Before that, he had been secretary for the environment. From 2006 on, this secretariat developed and implemented the Hortas Cariocas program, which enabled the structuring of separate larger-scale urban gardens in some favelas. Marcello Crivella was Rio de Janeiro's mayor from 2017 to 2020. During the last days of his term he was detained for suspicion of corruption and heading a criminal organization.

27   Groups Capim Limão (https://www.facebook.com/projetocapimlimao) and Muda Maré (https://www.facebook.com/mudamare), especially, collaborated with the activities carried out within the research, and provide support and collaborate to this day. We have also maintained a relationship with the Muda Maré group and visited their experimental agroforest in the Living Agroecology and Permaculture Laboratory (LaVaPer) several times, once during the Maré Week of Food Sovereignty. See a video of the visit at https://soberania-alimentar-mare.home.blog/videos/praticas-agroecologicas.

28   For more information see https://ergasudeste.wixsite.com/meusite.

29   The Capim Limão group continues to participate in children's activities alongside the Roça! Collective.

30   Lima quoted during the "Desafios agroecológicos nas periferias urbanas: Práticas e perspectivas," session of the Maré Week on Food Sovereignty. See https://soberania-alimentar-mare.home.blog/videos/mesas-redondas.

31   Campanha Permanente Contra os Agrotóxicos e Pela Vida, "'Comunidades estão sendo envenenadas no Brasil,' denuncia relator da ONU," January 12, 2020, https://contraosagrotoxicos.org/comunidades-estao-sendo-envenenadas-no-brasil-denuncia-relator-da-onu.

32   João Pedro Stedile and Horácio Martins de Carvalho, "Soberania alimentar: Uma necessidade dos povos," March 25, 2011, https://www.ecodebate.com.br/2011/03/25/soberania-alimentar-uma-necessidade-dos-povos-artigo-de-joao-pedro-stedile-e-horacio-martins-de-carvalho.

BIBLIOGRAPHY

Bartholl, Timo. *Por uma Geografia em movimento: A ciência como ferramenta de luta*. Rio de Janeiro: Consequência, 2018.

Bielemann, Renata M., et al. "Consumo de alimentos ultraprocessados e impacto na dieta de adultos jovens." *Revista de Saúde Pública* 49 (2015): 1–10.

Borda, Orlando Fals. *Una sociología sentipensante para América Latina*. Bogotá: Siglo del Hombres/CLACSO, 2009.

Borda, Orlando Fals, and Muhammad Anisur Ramnath, eds. *Action and Knowledge: Breaking the Monopoly with Participatory Action-Research*. London: Intermediate Technology Publications, 1991.

Dias, Alexandre. "A Maré no ritmo das ONGs: Uma análise sobre o papel das oficinas musicais de Organizações Não-Governamentais no bairro Maré/Rio de Janeiro." Master's thesis, Federal University of Rio de Janeiro (UFRJ), Music School, 2011.

Fuller, Duncan and Rob Kitchen, eds. *Radical Theory/Critical Praxis: Making a Difference Beyond the Academy?* Vernon and Victoria, BC: Praxis (e)press, 2004. https://kitchin.org/wp-content/uploads/2020/05/RTCP_Whole.pdf.

Herr, Kathryn, and Gary L. Anderson. *The Action Research Dissertation: A Guide for Students and Faculty*. London: Sage, 2005.

Louzada, Maria Laura da Costa, et al. "Alimentos ultraprocessados e perfil nutricional da dieta no Brasil." *Revista de Saúde Pública* 49 (2015): 1–11.

Pain, Rachel. "Social Geography: On Action-Oriented Research." *Progress in Human Geography* 27, no. 5 (2003): 649–57.

Scott, James C. *Two Cheers for Anarchism: Six Easy Pieces on Autonomy, Dignity, and Meaningful Work and Play*. Princeton, NJ: Princeton University Press, 2012.

Stedile, João Pedro, and Horácio Martins de Carvalho. "Soberania alimentar: Uma necessidade dos povos." *EcoDebate*, March 25, 2011. https://www.ecodebate.com.br/2011/03/25/soberania-alimentar-uma-necessidade-dos-povos-artigo-de-joao-pedro-stedile-e-horacio-martins-de-carval.

CHAPTER THREE

Favela Resistance and the Struggle for Food Sovereignty in Rio de Janeiro

Timo Bartholl

—

Food Sovereignty, Agroecology, and the City

Food sovereignty is concept shaped within rural social movements. In the 1990s, a diverse set of important social movements of small farmers, peasants, and landless workers formed the international Via Campesina network. Linking up their struggles across continents, the movements set out to struggle for land and territory not only in a material sense; they also understood it was necessary to struggle for terms, definitions, and concepts involving food and its production on a more semantic, symbolic, and theoretical level. In this sense, Via Campesina critically reviewed the idea of "food security" then in vogue among international organizations and contrasted it with the idea of "food sovereignty."[1] As the Small Farmers' Movement (Movimento dos Pequenos Agricultores or MPA) explains: "The concept of food sovereignty is born in counterpoint to the concept of food security established by the [Food and Agricultural Organization of the United Nations], because it is understood that a people, in order to be free, needs to be sovereign and this sovereignty depends on food."[2]

Since the establishment of the idea of food sovereignty within and by social movements, three short key documents have been published outlining and defending the basic ideas of food sovereignty from a Via Campesina perspective.[3]

In coming up with what we could consider the semantic and conceptual current of its struggle, Via Campesina published "Food Sovereignty: A World Without Hunger." In the document, signed at the World Food Summit in Rome in 1996, Via Campesina states:

We, the Via Campesina, a growing movement of farm workers, peasant, farm, and Indigenous peoples' organizations from all the regions of the world know that food security cannot be achieved without taking full account of those who produce food. Any discussion that ignores our contribution will fail to eradicate poverty and hunger.

Food is a basic human right. This right can only be realized in a system where food sovereignty is guaranteed. Food sovereignty is the right of each nation to maintain and develop its own capacity to produce its basic foods respecting cultural and productive diversity. We have the right to produce our own food in our own territory. Food sovereignty is a precondition to genuine food security.[4]

The document underlines the central role of those who produce food, especially small farmers and peasants, and contains a general critique of the liberalization of trade specifically considering that food is primarily a source of nutrition and should only secondarily be an item of trade. It defends food as a basic human right; points to the importance of agrarian reform to guarantee food sovereignty (especially in countries of the Global South, we should add); and also points to the importance of the protection of natural resources. It positions itself against the World Trade Organization's International Property Rights Agreement in defense of farmer's rights to free use of genetic resources and seeds needed for food production. The document also underlines the central role of women in food production, expressed by Via Campesina's permanent efforts to strengthen women's key role in the struggle for food sovereignty, as is the case at regularly organized international women's assemblies, such as the fifth one held in Derio in Basque Country in Spain in 2017 during Via Campesina's seventh international conference. The conference produced a final document that emphasized the importance of "building the movement to change the world with feminism and food sovereignty."[5] According to Esther Vivas, Via Campesina increasingly incorporated the feminist perspective over time by struggling for gender equality within the movement and making alliances with feminist groups such as the Global March for Women. Concluding her article, she argues:

The current global food system has failed to ensure the food security of communities. Currently more than a billion people worldwide suffer from hunger. The global food system has had a profoundly negative environmental impact; promoting an intensive agro-industrial model that has contributed to climate change and collapsing agro-biodiversity. This system has been particularly detrimental to women.

Developing alternatives to this agricultural model requires incorporating a gender perspective. The food sovereignty alternative to the dominant agro-industrial model has to have a feminist position to break with patriarchal and capitalist logic.[6]

Back to the 1996 document, this also demanded an end to the globalization of hunger and promoted the democratic control of food production. It set a starting point to what are by now more than two decades of broad debates on how food should be produced and nations should formulate their politics and policies around the food issue overall, and in relation to the question of sovereignty in particular.[7]

The initial idea of food sovereignty took the national level or scale as central and departed from the idea that the national political sphere is where mechanisms of global economics should be challenged and dealt with, mainly those with direct or indirect negative impacts for a nation's vulnerable social classes. As such, the approach is based on the idea that the national level is where social movements that struggle for food justice or for the right to produce can intervene in politics. At the same time, it does not ignore the importance of international networking demonstrated by Via Campesina itself as the international network that it represents.

In 2003, in another important step forging food sovereignty as a concept that guides the mobilization and self-organization of struggle, Via Campesina summed up debates since the birth of the concept eight years before, in a brief document titled "What Is Food Sovereignty?" They state:

Food sovereignty is the peoples', countries' or state unions' right to define their agricultural and food policy, without any dumping vis-à-vis third countries. Food sovereignty includes:

- prioritizing local agricultural production in order to feed the people, access of peasants and landless people to land, water, seeds, and credit. Hence the need for land reforms, for fighting against GMOs (Genetically Modified Organisms), for free access to seeds, and for safeguarding water as a public good to be sustainably distributed.
- the right of farmers and peasants to produce food and the right of consumers to be able to decide what they consume, and how and by whom it is produced.
- the right of Countries to protect themselves from too low priced agricultural and food imports.
- agricultural prices linked to production costs: they can be achieved if the Countries or Unions of States are entitled to impose taxes on excessively cheap imports, if they commit themselves in favor of a sustainable farm production, and if they control production on the inner market so as to avoid structural surpluses.
- the populations taking part in the agricultural policy choices.
- the recognition of women farmers' rights, who play a major role in agricultural production and in food.[8]

In light of these statements, a question we raised during our NutriCities action research process, when reflecting on the relationship between the urban periphery and food security and sovereignty, was what role might the urban poor have in the construction of this concept. And what role does the concept have for the urban poor and their territories? And, as discussed in detail by Richard Lee, food security and food sovereignty certainly do not mean the same thing; rather, they complement one another in a rather conflicted way.[9] So if we understand with Via Campesina, that "genuine food security" can only be reached through "food sovereignty," what relationship is there between the urban periphery and food sovereignty?

At first sight, dwellers of urban peripheries are directly mentioned at two points in Via Campesina's definition of food sovereignty: as "consumers [who should have the] right to be able to decide what they consume," and as "populations [in general] taking part in the agricultural policy choices." Even recognizing the broad character of these assumptions, city dwellers here are forced into a very passive role: either as consumers or as people who may vote for political forces that promise to defend their right to food dignity, or people who may campaign in order to pressure for such policies. But of course, much more can be and has been done, both on behalf of and by those who are in cities all over the globe in order to strive for a higher degree of sovereignty when it comes to how we feed ourselves. There is a diversity of forms of making agriculture happen in the peri-urban and the urban: ways of organizing through agroecological networks and consumer cooperatives, and organizing in the cities to link up with those planting and organizing in the countryside, fighting for transparent food product chains, fair trade, and so forth.

Dialoguing with Via Campesina from a perspective of the urban periphery, a few questions need to be asked in regard to the concept of food sovereignty: When we struggle and organize for food sovereignty in the urban and its peripheries, how do we avoid thinking of the urban periphery as the problem to be solved and understand it instead as a core element of a unified rural, peri-urban, and inner-urban perspective of popular-class struggle? How can we approach the struggle for food sovereignty without reproducing a logic that assigns a passive role to dwellers of urban peripheries? How can they all become protagonists of this struggle?

Food Sovereignty Meets Favela Resistance

When it comes to reflections on food and the city, one of the first things that come to mind is the high dependence of the urban areas on food production in non-urban areas. Whatever the city, people need to eat. But there seems to be limited space and conditions to grow crops and breed livestock that would be enough for a city's whole population. "If the countryside doesn't plant, the city doesn't have dinner" is a common saying among social movements that defend small farmers and land occupiers in Brazil that underlines the importance of mainly peri-urban and rural-based small-scale food production for the maintenance of the metabolism of the urban.[10] For cities to live, their inhabitants must have access to food. They need to eat.[11] We have a general idea of just how important urban agriculture is in some urban contexts. Estimates are that 15 to 20 percent of what we eat comes from urban agriculture.[12] For this reason, it has great importance, not only on a mere symbolic level but also in the very material sense of providing food: urban agriculture must be seen as an intrinsic part of urbanization processes. Still though, if the city in general terms depends on less densely populated agricultural areas in order "to have dinner," what is there to be said about those parts of the cities inhabited by the people most struggling to guarantee their urban subsistence and survival, those who live in high density areas with precarious urban infrastructure, those who are repeatedly neglected by public authorities and subjected to contradictory forms of integration into capitalist market relations, or those who live in the urban peripheries? Could it be anything more than a theoretical provocation or challenge (to ourselves, as well as to others) to think of food security and more importantly, food sovereignty, and how to fight for these from the perspective of those at the urban margins? Can food sovereignty ever be attained at the urban peripheries, and if so, how?

What do we mean by *urban?* We do not only find agricultural activities in the more densely populated urban areas within cities, as is the case in the municipality of Rio de Janeiro with its approximately six million inhabitants, but throughout its metropolitan area as a whole, which consists of seventeen municipalities with a total of approximately twelve million city dwellers. With Paulo Roberto Alentejano we can consider that the process of urbanization includes processes that create new urban and new rural and new in-between forms of socio-spatial organization, that are not simply based on "the pure and simple elimination of the rural and its transmutation into the urban, but a more complex phenomenon, where the new urban and the new rural [or new urbans and new rurals, we might want to add], emerge from the shock of both."[13]

Especially in the West Zone of the Rio municipality we find what we can call, with Silvia Baptista, an "urban peasantry" in the region around the Pedra Branca mountain range, known as Sertão Carioca.[14] At the fringes of the metropolitan area we find what we could call a "peri-urban" peasantry. The Rio de Janeiro metropolitan area produces food and some of it at a large scale, as is the case with bananas or manioc.[15] This broader understanding of the urban, suggests that we should also broaden our notion of our struggle for the right to the city.

"Although the right to the city is generally taken almost exclusively as the struggle for access to urban equipment, it transcends this concept. In *The Right to the City*, Henri Lefebvre … makes it explicit that this is the right to fight against the subordination of lives

58

to the exchange value of capital. This insubordination has the city as a privileged locus, place of meetings, of the centrality of power, which can potentiate social transformations. That is, the right to the city is the right to change humanity and society."[16]In this sense the struggle for a right to the city has to be understood as a struggle for another (so)ci(e)ty. Cities cannot be transformed unless society and peripheries—be they urban, peri-urban, or rural—are organized in a different form. They cannot become more (food) sovereign. After all, full sovereignty at local level is only possible once we overcome the structure of current capitalist society based on exploitative and violent power relations toward a society that knows, as the Zapatistas have said, neither centers, nor peripheries.[17]

In light of the diverse forms of agriculture in the Rio de Janeiro metropolitan area, it is important to note that the territory of our research experience was the densely populated favelas in the North Zone of Rio. The favelas of Maré characterize a region where only a few larger urban gardens have been established over the last decades; some of these were quite productive at some point, but could not all be maintained due to problems including the tension of armed conflicts near one of the main urban gardens on the grounds of a public grade school. In more than three hundred short interviews we conducted in mid-2018, not a single one of our interviewees, living in different parts of Maré, mentioned food consumption derived from homegrown food items. Supermarkets, fruit and vegetable stores, fairs, and street stands are the main sources of food here. The Maré region is traditionally home to an urban fishing community that have their boats at the Canal do Fundão from which they access the Guanabara Bay or even the open sea. Since the bay is highly polluted, even though fishing is still frequent, its importance for Maré's population as a whole (be it as fishers or as consumers) has decreased over the past decades. This might explain why our research group never stopped to consider and analyze the importance of these remaining small-scale craft fishing activities throughout the project's duration. Traditional street fish vendors, with whom we exchanged ideas, usually get their fish from main distribution centers such as Rio's main food supply center CEASA-RJ. In general we must consider that in the favelas of Maré the amount of primary local food production is certainly significantly below potentially possible production levels. At the same time, we must consider that even reaching higher amounts of local primary food production, the area would continue to depend on bringing food from other areas that produce more than is locally needed. We must differentiate Maré as a densely populated inner-city periphery from less densely populated or even peri-urban peripheries of Rio's metropolitan area. It is in this general spirit that we experienced our action research. We asked: How can we learn more about, and eventually produce, more agroecological healthy food and how can we get access to all the food that we cannot potentially produce here? Who to collaborate with, whose struggles to connect to, and how to network from the urban to the peri-urban and rural—and vice versa? We can refer to these questions as the challenge to imagine, think through, and bring forward the building and strengthening of rural-, peri-, and inner-urban networks of territories of resistance in the struggle to increase the (food) sovereignty of the popular (or peripheral) classes.

If we seem at times very distant from being able to increase our degree of sovereignty, especially when it comes to food in favelas such as those of Maré, understanding the favelas and their dynamics as territories of resistance can be crucial to grasp what might be essential in order to make food sovereignty here a less distant idea. In doing so, it is important to take sovereignty as a general concept further and to think of it in a self-emancipatory way. When we talk about food, we talk about food production, food distribution, and food consumption; therefore we also necessarily talk about multiple and entangled economic activities of primary importance for the material reproduction of any social group, be it rural or (peri-)urban. Only by collectivizing our ways of thinking and consequently putting all economic and community activities related to food into building stronger networks among more and less densely populated rural and (peri-)urban peripheries, will food sovereignty become a real possibility.[18]

Another World Is Plantable

When it comes to Brazil's large metropolitan areas, the struggle for food sovereignty involves the implementation of a diverse set of practices of urban agriculture following the idea(l)s of agroecology. If sovereignty is a common objective of struggle of all, whether from rural to inner-urban settings, agroecology provides us with a diverse and locally adaptable set of knowledges and techniques. And urban agriculture is what we can engage with in the cities to broaden our access to quality food and reconcile our relationship to nature beyond the asphalt and concrete of the built urban environment.

In general terms, urban agriculture first gained importance in the Global South as a strategy for the material survival of millions of city dwellers mostly from the lower classes. By the end of the 1990s, it was estimated that around 800 million people worldwide were involved in some activity related to urban agriculture, as stated by Severin Halder. Based on experiences with urban agriculture organizing in the Global South and North, Halder argues: "The urban gardening culture is a germ of hope in times of global urban crisis: 'Another world is plantable!' Urban gardens are carriers of hope for a socio-ecological transformation and are surging around the world: from community gardens in New York ... to *organipónicos* in Havana to the gardens of hope in Cape Town ... favela gardens in Rio de Janeiro ... or intercultural gardens in Göttingen, Germany."[19]

Halder refers to a set of studies to summarize that urban agriculture is a multifunctional phenomenon with potentially positive social, economic, and ecological effects including strengthening struggles for food sovereignty, better provision of health-related services, poverty reduction, and environmental justice. It can help diminish urban waste problems through recycling of organic waste and the use and filtering of wastewater, and can help develop economies based on regional solidarity- and commons-based alternatives.

The presence and types of activities of urban agriculture in the municipality of Rio de Janeiro differ strongly depending on the local conditions that each part of the city has to offer. In the very green and less densely populated West Zone, conditions allow many farmers to practice traditional agriculture, while in more densely populated areas urban gardening dominates instead. The available numbers on urban agriculture's yearly outcomes are impressive. Caren Freitas de Lima refers to the figures published by the public agency EMATER to show that in 2015 alone, as much as 18,350 tons of manioc; 10,077 tons of chuchu; 6,320 tons of coconuts; and 3,888 tons of bananas were harvested and commercialized, among many other products, by at least 1,505 farmers registered with the municipality of Rio.[20] Many of these farmers, despite their small-scale production, do not necessarily adhere to agroecological production and use chemical fertilizers, pesticides, and herbicides, but they are able to supply many of the neighborhood fairs all across Rio with a diversity of products. These numbers put Rio's municipality among the leading production zones for a variety of fruits: it holds first place for acerola production, and third, fourth, and fifth places, respectively, for coconut, mango, and caqui. Considering that the west to east expanse of Rio's municipality is about seventy kilometers, and the fact that the favelas of Maré are located in the very urbanized east edge, it is understandable that here we would not comprehend the magnitude and importance of urban agriculture in our city if it was not through studies and numbers like these.[21] *Agroecology* denotes the study of agriculture from an ecological perspective, yet it can be understood as a scientific discipline, or an agricultural practice or technique, and it can also refer to a social or political movement. As Alexander Wezel et al. succinctly put it, agroecology can be "a science, a movement or a practice," while many times it represents a combination of these.[22] If food sovereignty is what we struggle for, urban agriculture is an important pillar of our struggle and agroecology is the set of knowledges, from traditional and movement-embedded knowledges to scientifically anchored knowledges-with and knowledges-how-to, that guide our agricultural practices in the urban and shows ways out of the agro-industrial catastrophe we are currently trapped in, toward an agroecological future.[23] In this sense of radical change, we can say that "agroecology" reaches further than "organic": while the first is often linked to initiatives that are part of broader political struggles, "organic" can more easily be reduced to a healthier production mode of certified foods for those who can afford them. I will refer to both terms affirmatively, while I remain convinced that the fight for rural-urban food justice is that of "urban agriculture—agroecology—food sovereignty," which is fundamental to the wider struggle of overcoming of capitalism itself. In the words of the Small Farmers' Movement: "[We] advocate a systematic process of transition to peasant agroecology, overcoming the degenerative model imposed by agribusiness and the package of the green revolution, imposed harshly by large companies and the state on families in the countryside, for years this model has already demonstrated its weaknesses and impacts on health and life on the planet, the transition to agroecology is a necessity to regain environmental balance, and actually ensure quality food for the people."

Thus, peasant agroecology for us is a concept that seeks to express the operational demand for the development of successive links to achieve food sovereignty. It is fundamental not to untie agroecology from its subjects, the peasants and native and traditional peoples. When it comes to the diverse universe of social movement practices concerning the struggle for food sovereignty, the idea of politics of scale, a discussion introduced by Neil Smith may assume a key role.[24] Family agriculture, peasant, quilombola, and Indigenous struggles on a local level all are part of a mosaic or network (depending on how advanced movement organizing is in a certain region) in which a wide set of practices and knowledges of traditional and modern agriculture and agroecology converge. In a 2014 open letter, the Rio Urban Agriculture Network (Rede CAU) quotes Cândido Grzybowski, director of the Rio-based civil society organization Ibase: "It is in fact impossible to think of the mosaics and fight for them if they are not seen and integrated as a common good of the territory of which they are part. From a socio-environmental perspective, territories need to be seen, themselves, as a common good, as spaces for human life."[25]

In opposition to this sense of territory as a common, rurally based subalternized classes and their movements in Brazil are constantly under attack by territorially expansive and violent Brazilian agribusiness, to which territory is, before all else, a commodity. Capital deterritorializes any kind of community that could be in the way of its interests in profit-making through the exploitation of natural resources. Wherever the agribusiness frontier advances, violence against peripheral and subaltern groups increases exponentially, as sadly proven by reports published annually by the Comissão Pastoral da Terra (Pastoral Commission on Land), which describes the situation rural subalternized groups encounter in Brazil as a "massacre in the countryside."[26] In terms of a politics of scale, diverse social movements that are strong in Brazil's extensive countryside have developed strategies to work locally and network regionally or even globally as do the big rural social movements that comprise Via Campesina. One strategy of their networking is to reach into metropolitan areas, where they inform the residents about their struggles, which are oftentimes far distant from the cities and rendered invisible by mainstream media; they make alliances with urban social movements, unions, political parties, and academia, and they also connect with urban initiatives of food distribution and production. Therefore, when it comes to the struggle for food sovereignty in a metropolitan area such as Rio de Janeiro, we find a diverse set of initiatives across social classes, in more or less central or peripheral territories, including small collectives, networks, and student and research groups that form what we could broadly refer to as an urban-based agroecological movement. For the Rio de Janeiro case, key initiatives can inspire us to take the idea of food sovereignty further as a unified rural to urban struggle.

Politically, some producers organize within the Rede CAU or the Articulação de Agroecologia (Agroecology Network of Rio de Janeiro or AARJ), where they are supported by civil society organizations and sometimes also unions or political parties. The purpose of the Rede CAU is best described in its own words:

> [We are] convinced that food and nutritional security is a basic social need and that this is part of the social functions of our city and should be an objective of urban and territorial policy. Rio's agriculture for decades has been invisible and along with it, farmers, their histories, their rights, and their means of life.
>
> Rede CAU is a social movement that brings together people and organizations for the defense of agroecology in cities. It works together with urban gardens and plantations, defends ethical and responsible consumption, joins in a range of rural-urban struggles, and challenges the adequacy of public policies. In its collective there are representatives of several popular organizations and research and educational institutions as well as nongovernmental agents. It is linked to the AARJ, the National Collective of Urban Agriculture, and the National Agroecology Network.[27]

The AARJ is a network of agroecologically oriented producers, groups, and movements that is embedded in the National Agroecology Network. In Rio de Janeiro state, the AARJ divides its network into six regional sections, one in the metropolitan region, of which the Rede CAU is part. Once again, nothing is better than AARJ's own words to briefly describe their objectives: "We are a movement of social organizations joined together to strengthen agroecological initiatives in the state of Rio de Janeiro."[28]

It was within the context of these political forces that we connected our efforts as Minhocas Urbanas throughout the NutriCities research process, from regional network meetings to the participation in the National Agroecology Network's National Meeting of Agroecology in June 2018. In the context of these permanent mobilization networks, there are a number of civil society organizations in Rio that have been supporting and contributing to these collective efforts to strengthen urban agriculture and agroecology in Rio's metropolitan area.[29] One of them, Family Agriculture and Agroecology, was responsible for giving birth, in 2013, to the permanent campaign called "Produtos da gente" (Our Products), which lives on within the AARJ, with the aim of promoting and making visible agroecological and organic food production and helping to connect interested consumers and producers.[30] An important joint rural-urban effort of diverse social movements with institutional support from Fiocruz, the Rio-based public health research and study center that is the largest of its kind in Latin America, has been the Permanent Campaign Against the Use of Agrotoxins and for Life, which investigates and publishes information on how agrobusiness and its lobbyists and political representatives work to base industrial agriculture on increasingly devastating poisonous crop growing methods.[31] Public institutions such as Fiocruz, the Rio-based Federal University of the State of Rio de Janeiro, and Rio de Janeiro State University are also strong pillars for the agroecological movement. During NutriCities we connected to a vibrant network of university groups that organize around agroecology and reach out to urban society beyond laboratories and classrooms. Especially in the favelas of Maré, with its proximity to the University City of Rio de Janeiro's Federal University on a nearby island, these groups engage with local organizations or grassroots movements to strengthen agroecological practices and to work with children in environmental education. The Association of Biological Farmers of the State of Rio de Janeiro was formed as early as 1984 in the city of Nova Friburgo in the Serra do Mar mountain range, approximately 140 kilometres from Rio's city center. The main goals of the association have since been to stimulate organic food production based in agroecology and agroforestry, to strengthen family agriculture, and to contribute to the population's nutritional security through the building of food sovereignty. The association seeks to support producers technically and logistically and to connect them with urban consumers.[32]

In the West Zone, an interesting initiative has been that of the Articulação Plano Popular das Vargens (Network for a Popular Plan for the Vargens), which is understood as a "grassroot movement with a local basis. It acts together with regional and national agroecological and right-to-the-city movements. It was formed in the struggle against urbanization that is based on gentrification and displacement."[33] The plan has been worked out with the support of researchers of public universities such as the Institute for Urban and Regional Research and Planning of the Federal Public University of Rio de Janeiro. At the interface of social movements with public bodies—in this case the first represented by the Network for a Popular Plan for the Vargens and the latter by the Urban Council of Architecture and Urbanism—the Live and Plant project has recently been implemented in order to link initiatives of urban agriculture with popular housing movements.[34] Another approach with its focus on the empowerment of women in the communities in Rio's West Zone has seen processes of militant investigation and feminist, antiracist cartographies in the project Militiva.[35] The cartographic journey through Rio's West Zone makes visible agroecological relations with the land and the sea:

> The plantations in gardens, on walls and rooftops, and in the woods and favelas provide healthy food and healing. They also build tradition, memory, and ancestry. Artisan and non-predatory fishing, the collection of shellfish in the mangroves, bays, and seas of the region are also a tradition in the West Zone: "We cultivate the antiracist struggle that recognizes the importance and centrality of farmers, fishers, and gatherers of shellfish within the environmental struggle in the West Zone. That is why we build feminist, urban, and peripheral agroecological relations. Without feminism there is no agroecology."[36]

Another inspiring process of resistance is represented by Quilombo Cafundá Astrogilda,[37] a Black quilombo community within the Parque Estadual Pedra Branca (Pedra Branca State Park), which was recognized as such in 2014 by the Palmares Cultural Foundation after a struggle for recognition in which the past surged to the fore "as a tool of struggle."[38] Through the recognition, families whose deep roots lie within territory that is part of the state park were able to reorganize community life as a quilombo and work within the park, recovering their traditional forms of land use and resuming family agriculture. In 2018, the Quilombo School was founded and agroecology, emancipatory education, and antiracist community organizing have become strong pillars of Cafunda's work since—making the quilombo an important point of convergence on Rio's map of Black, feminist, and agroecological resistances. In different favelas across the metropolitan area, small groups or organizations connect urban agriculture and environmental education to the strengthening of community mobilizations. This is the case with groups like Plant in the Streets, who are based in the favela Morro do Cantagalo in Rio's South Zone and organize community and collective urban gardening activities across the city but also provide paid gardening services in order to financially sustain the group and its members. There are organizations such as the Socio-environmental Greening that are based in the region of the favelas of the Complexo do Alemão in Rio's North Zone, and who conduct environmental education and advocate for agroforestry around the inner-city mountain range Serra da Misericórdia; and there are small local community initiatives for agroecology such as Transformiga in the favela Morro da Formiga, in the region of the Tijuca neighborhood.

In terms of urban gardening, the picture of activities in a metropolitan area with twelve million inhabitants, extending approximately 130 kilometers west to east and another 50 kilometers south to north, is extremely diverse. Especially in favelas, we find numerous small-scale initiatives to plant in buckets and pots, on pavement, in small alleys, and on terraces and rooftops. Some larger community gardens have been implemented within a project of Rio's municipality since 2006, the Hortas Cariocas (Rio Gardens) program. Throughout our research we visited some of the forty gardens that are officially part of the program (seventeen are located in favelas and twenty-three in public schools) and saw that their functioning depended a lot on the initiative of those involved locally. The proposal from the public authority's side is that those who work and plant in the gardens can become small entrepreneurs who should gradually try to live off their produce, so that they no longer need public funding, a clearly neoliberal approach that nevertheless does not seem to have much success: the idea would be that new gardens can join the program when their predecessors become economically independent, but this seems to rather rarely be the case. Much more often the gardens remain a hybrid form owing their maintenance to a mix of self-organized community mobilization that is supported by, but does not fully depend on, the program. An interesting proposal is that part of the production of these gardens should go to nearby public schools to find its way onto students' plates. In 2018, under the coordination of the Hortas Cariocas program, the Centro Municipal de Agroecologia e Produção Orgânica (Municipal Center for Agroecology and Organic Production) was launched in Parque Madureira, a public park in Rio's North Zone. We find an impressively extensive urban garden in Manguinhos, sprawling under energy lines that not only inhibit the building of housing, but also the growth of larger trees, which means that the gardens have high exposure to the sun and working in them is difficult, especially in the hot summer months. Yet a dedicated group of Manguinhos residents keep up the garden and its food production. One proposal of the Horta da Mata garden, where we organized activities in Maré during our research, is still linked to the Hortas Cariocas program officially, yet if it was not for resident Seu Bolado taking care of everything on a daily basis the garden might had ceased to exist by now. Fences have fallen apart, and little to no support comes from the public side to maintain the minimum infrastructure necessary to protect plantations from animals. But the garden (which is also the headquarters for the Associação de Moradores, the Favela Parque Ecológico's Dwellers Association) and the hill with a green park it is part of, are the green lungs of the southern parts of Maré. They have so far been kept safe from the advancing construction of housing and economic infrastructure. But community mobilization will need to continue around the park if its existence is to be guaranteed in the long run.

Connecting the Rural and the Urban: Alternative Distribution Networks of Agroecological and Organic Food

If agriculture in (peri-)urban areas is one strong pillar of the struggle for food sovereignty, another is access to—from a consumer's perspective— quality food of agroecological or organic origin, which correlates with the producer's perspective of how to offer and sell their products to interested consumers. This leads, in turn, to the key question of how to organize alternative networks of distribution of agroecological and organic food. All the main initiatives around agroecology pivot on this question in one way or another. The main distribution mechanisms of organic and agroecological food directly from the producers are specific fairs that can be made up of market stands where the actual producers sell their products or where a reselling cooperative has a joint selling point of its participating farmers. A reseller may represent up to forty small farmers, usually from the coastal mountain range areas around Petrópolis, Teresópolis, and Nova Friburgo, where they pick up the products during the night and bring them to Rio in the early morning hours for consumers to buy them at the morning fairs. But there are just as many individual farmers and family farms that have their stands in these fairs. Fairs being a strong pillar of these networks of alternative distribution derives from a generally strong tradition all across Rio, where rich neighborhoods just as much as favelas, have lively weekly fairs that, together with many permanent street stands, also supply numerous consumers with food.

To connect their affiliated, mostly rural-based farmers to urban consumers, the Association of Biological Farmers (ABIO) has built a network of eleven neighborhood fairs, mostly located in middle- and upper-class neighborhoods in the South Zone, where people can afford the higher prices at which the products are offered. With one market in the North Zone's Olaria neighborhood and a supported market in Meier, also in the North Zone, ABIO is taking its first steps beyond the South Zone.[39] Most fairs outside of this "comfort zone" (with its wealthy consumers and good infrastructure) though are (co-)organized with the Rede CAU. Lima identifies eighteen fairs across Rio's North and West Zone as related to this network and emphasizes the importance of the income these fairs generate for participating farmers, most of whom, unlike the ABIO-market farmers, practice inner- and peri-urban agriculture.[40] According to Lima, half of the farmers secure more than 70 percent of their income through their sales at these fairs. In Rio de Janeiro, supermarkets that offer organic food for relatively high prices are mainly located in middle- and upper-class South Zone neighborhoods, so this source of food is not an option for lower-class households in Rio. Also, and this is important to recognize and appreciate, there is a common sense within the agroecological movement of how problematic commercial relations to supermarket chains can be for small farmers, even if organized in networks—farmers may become dependent on one retailer of their product who may pressure them to accept prices too low to sustain their small farms. Therefore, the focus remains on strengthening and expanding alternative networks of food distribution. Besides the fairs, an important pillar of these networks are food basket home delivery services on the producer side, and food cooperatives on the consumer side.

Apart from the regular fairs, mostly to be found around middle- and upper-class neighborhoods or at public institutions, important social movements such as the Landless Workers' Movement (Movimento dos Trabalhadores Rurais Sem Terra or MST) and the Small Farmers' Movement organize sporadic fairs to give visibility to their struggles and establish contact between farmers, their causes, and the urban population.[41] The main market here is the Market of Agrarian Reform: Its name serves as a reminder of the never realized agrarian and land reform, which could diminish profound inequalities of access to land, resources, and food, and stands as a sign that these movements continue to struggle against the odds to achieve agrarian reform. In different regions across Brazil, the Landless Workers' Movement has been successfully working with permanent Stores of Agrarian Reform in order to distribute their produce directly to supportive consumers in the cities. In regions where the movement is well organized, these shops have been functioning for many years, as is the case in Porto Alegre in Rio Grande do Sul. In 2018, the Countryside Warehouse was finally inaugurated in Lapa, Rio de Janeiro's central and bohemian neighborhood, and has since become a hub for struggles of the agroecological movement in general.[42] Already a few years before the warehouse opened its doors, the Small Farmers' Movement was able to rent a hostel and restaurant facility in the middle-class and tourist neighborhood of Santa Teresa. The space, named Raízes (Roots) functions as a hostel, a restaurant with food from Small Farmers' Movement farmers, and also hosts a small food store. On Saturdays, fresh food items are sold at a market stand and a *café camponês* (peasant breakfast) and lunch are served while cultural events take place on site. The Small Farmers' Movement also runs a network to distribute *cestas camponesas* (peasant baskets) of products from farmers that participate in the movement. These are distributed weekly via home delivery to consumers.[43]

As a self-organized consumer cooperative network, the Rede Ecológica deserves attention for its long experience and perseverance as a consumer cooperative, the number of its customers in different neighborhoods of the city, and the number of producers in the state of Rio it has been able to network. The network buys directly from the producers and organizes the logistics of bringing the products to distribution hubs. Consumers order from a long list of available items and then receive their products at the respective hub for their area, usually on Saturdays. Those who make up the network usually contribute voluntary work to make the whole network function. Attempts to implement distribution hubs in favelas in Rio have not been successful, fair prices of organic food items are quite high if compared to the budget available for most who live here; but at the same time, the ways that people organize and the parts of daily life on which they focus their collective resistance also has an influence here.

Beyond changing food distribution, the Rede Ecológica fosters interaction and mutual learning among producers and consumers. The main areas of action characterize the breadth of the approach: "1) Collective buying, 2) Interaction of producers and consumers, 3) Communication and formation, 4) Integration with social movements."[44] The Rede Ecológica links up with regional initiatives through which producers organize in collaborative ways, such as the Association of Organic Farmers of Vargem Grande in Rio's West Zone, but also with associations located thousands of kilometres from Rio such as the of Extraction Commercialization Central Cooperative for the State of Acre, in Brazil's northern region.[45] Following the example of the Rede Ecológica, yet on a smaller scale, agroecological farmers in Rio's peri-urban areas have organized to deliver food baskets for groups of consumers. Usually on a weekly basis consumers can choose, via social media, from the range of fruits and vegetables and other food items available and receive these baskets at their homes in the city or a collectively combined distribution hub. Juliana Medeiros, from our Minhocas Urbanas research group, and her women's production cooperative Colher de Pau (Wooden Spoon) supply food weekly for about fifteen households in Rio's South Zone through this kind of mechanism.[46] There are other private initiatives of resellers that bring agroecological and organic food to the city and have consumers choose from a list or receive a mix of available products in a basket for a fixed weekly price. Within our small Roça! Collective we also have some experiences with (very) small-scale distribution of agroecological products and have recently begun delivering organic food directly from organic farmers near Rio to households in the favelas of Maré and proximate neighborhoods.[47] The objective is to make this kind of food available in favela territory in the North Zone of Rio in the face of the deepening crisis due to the coronavirus pandemic, which has reinforced the importance of the direct contact between producers and consumers; our objective is to see if we can advance from here toward regular deliveries and a permanent small agroecological store or market stand in Maré throughout, and especially beyond, the period of social distancing. The agroecological movement has made several attempts to broaden its activities and make agroecology and its principals better known while making agroecological food more widely available in the many favelas across Rio's metropolitan area. For a number of different reasons—be they higher prices, buying routines, or lack of access to information, as we discuss more thoroughly in our Minhocas text—these attempts have not been as satisfactory as those in the movement would wish for.

Despite efforts within the agroecological movement, and despite the fact that many urban farmers are themselves inhabitants of what we consider the urban periphery, the spatial distribution of, and access to, the fairs with agroecological and organic produce from Rio's peri-urban and proximate rural areas continue to be very unequal. Connecting favelas and their people across the metropolitan area to the alternative networks of distribution of agroecological food therefore remains a key challenge for the struggle toward food sovereignty at the peripheries.[48] Writing in April 2020, it is too soon to assess the impact that the advancing coronavirus pandemic will have on the dynamic of the agroecological movement. Yet it is very clear that the movement has reacted in some very strong and mature ways, such as expanding delivery services so people can stay in their houses and still receive high-quality food, and by defending the reopening of fairs under strict public health measures in times of restricted movement. It has gained lots of recognition for its work and its importance as a provider of secure food distributed through an alternative, non-supermarket-conforming network, that guarantees stable prices and stable producer-customer relations for *comida de verdade* (true food) as the Rede CAU linked agroecological market in Campo Grande promotes in their recent campaign.[49] As all over the globe, the pandemic poses a challenge to social movements and their networks. Amid many understandable and well-founded worries, the first signs of how movements are reacting and organizing allow for some hope that many strong responses are still to be expected from them.[50]

Class-B(i)ased Organic Realities and the Agroecological Movement

Many involved in urban agriculture don't explicitly understand themselves as being "in struggle," or directly connected to any mobilizations or social movement activities. The "agroecological movement" is part of a much wider field of social relations and practices than it can engage with. Yet its own horizon of struggle tries to also extend to all those who do not engage with it directly; the experiences of small farmers and urban gardeners in general are the background for those who mobilize. Yet this does not mean that conflict is not manifold and intense, even among small farmers, many of whom boldly defend the use of pesticides and herbicides and chemical fertilizers convinced that "there is no alternative." Yet overall, when it comes to food production and food justice, the main antagonism is that between family agriculture on one side, and agrobusiness and the agro-industrial complex on the other: a permanent reminder of the "open vein" of an agrarian reform never realized in Brazil, and that remains a common goal for social movements in the agrarian sector.[51] As mentioned earlier, the urban-based sectors of the movement around environmental and food issues in general are to a certain extent organized in a class-based manner. Access to healthy food is an issue for which those from more privileged neighborhoods mobilize. To consume "organic" is a primary concern for some because it is healthier than conventional food. But for others, it stems from the desire to support agroecology as an approach or a movement to change society more deeply and radically. What is exclusive access to organic food at high prices at rather expensive fairs or in specific supermarkets in selected neighborhoods for some, is a difficulty or lack of access to food alternatives for many others. These differences can and do divide us, and by doing so they follow, reproduce, and reinforce spatial patterns of urban inequality. Yet wherever these divisions are revealed and made transparent, mobilizations gain potential. It is very important, in this sense, to understand environmental and food issues within power structures and to stress the (structural or environmental) racism, machismo, and classism that are the foundation of (urban) environmental-, food-, and health-related injustices.

In light of the class-b(i)ased nature of access to organic food, what is quite specific to the agroecological movement in Rio is that very diverse political approaches and ideologies find their place in it; those who politically engage with the movement seek ways to collaborate with it to the extent that is consistent with their political strategies and tactics. In fact, if the common denominator is to refer to urban agriculture, agroecology, and food sovereignty as three key elements of struggle, this already indicates a common ground for a politicized and critical way to organize around the environmental and food issues, from production to consumption. And hardly anyone would oppose, as an idea at least, the importance of widening access to healthy food to the peripheries as well, since the struggle for food sovereignty is understood by many, if not all, to reasonably be part of the class struggle. The sensitivity against class bias is present, but how to translate this sensitivity into political action is the continuous challenge.

The strong presence of the practical side of urban agriculture and agroecology definitely helps overcome ideological differences during collective workdays, commonly organized fairs, or joint mobilizations and protests.[52] I can buy agroecological food from a farmer and we both relate collaboratively through this act, yet we might not necessarily come to common terms if we were to politically organize together. And, among a diversity of strategies to influence and collaborate with political forces and authorities, we find strong commitments to autonomy and political independence among those that are agroecologically engaged. In general, we can say that the main social movements mobilizing around food sovereignty and agroecology in Brazil are rural-based, organizationally independent, but at the same time more or less closely intertwined with political parties including several smaller ones, such as the Socialism and Liberty Party (Partido Socialismo e Liberdade or PSOL), but predominantly with the Workers' Party (Partido dos Trabalhadores or PT). This means many movements were closely related to Brazil's national government from 2003, with Lula's first mandate as president, up until 2016, when the Workers' Party lost power through a parliamentary coup. Among (self-)critical comrades and scholars who reflect on these relations, it is an accepted interpretation that the movement's ties in this quite long period of time of movement-government collaboration had become too aligned with party politics and disputes for political and state power: many times collaboration has given its place to paternalist forms of co-optation, and relative autonomy has turned into institutional dependency. For this reason, with the parliamentary coup against Workers' Party president Dilma Roussef, these movements have been weakened and, from an emancipatory perspective, have yet to reorganize and reorient their struggles by disentangling themselves again from the old world of party politics, and widen again the horizon of social struggle, which at present seems rather narrow. Yet the larger a social movement, the more diverse the sociopolitical spectrum of those who organize in its multiple bases, therefore the movements have continued to generate direct action and interventions at the local level while continuing to help people organize themselves in their struggles for land, food, and a life with dignity.

As the movements that have their strong bases mainly in the rural are currently under permanent attack by right extremist president Bolsonaro's government, more than ever, the objective of their outreach into the cities is to connect to urban political forces in order to gain visibility for their struggles beginning with finding fairs for their farmer's products. These objectives have brought them to middle- and upper-class neighborhoods in the center or the South Zone of Rio.[53] Nevertheless, they make efforts to try and reach out to the urban peripheries, as is the case of the Small Farmers' Movement, which is trying to figure out ways to decrease production costs and make products more accessible for the urban underclass. If the reality of the bigger movements that reach into the cities is diverse, their shared goal is to struggle for a food sovereign future in the urban as well as the rural: and yet how to understand the urban periphery and from there imagine rural-urban movement organizing and networking might still be one of the key challenges ahead. The political spectrum of mobilizations and/ or struggles is broad. While the political autonomy of the movements and networks is given great importance, the movements try to influence party and government politics, sometimes through lobbying as is the case of some civil society organizations. When legislative issues relating to urban agriculture are voted on in the city council, networks like Rede CAU mobilize to be present as a civil society interest group in Rio's Camara dos Vereadores (city hall). Urban agriculture, as much as small farming in the rural, continue to be marginalized by those who govern mostly in the interest of capital, such as agribusiness, which constantly attacks the territories of peasant, Indigenous, or quilombola groups in the rural; and the real estate sector (who claim there is no room for urban gardens); and the big supermarket chains and multinationals in the food sector (who claim there is no need for food other than that from your local supermarket).

Through the movement's diversity and its practices we can learn that Via Campesina's definition of food sovereignty, which in its key documents refers to city dwellers either as "consumers" or "populations" that should take part in "agricultural policy choices," is too limited to cope with food sovereignty's manifold urban struggles. In the cities we can be and are ourselves protagonists as food cooperative organizers, urban farmers, supporters and members of agroecological movements, and also, as discussed in our Minhocas text, as those who prepare food for ourselves and others in thousands of popular restaurants across Rio's neighborhoods and favelas. Food sovereignty needs to be thought and fought for according to this rural-urban perspective, where many local initiatives within the movement universe intertwine as a powerful network in constant struggle.

From a favela perspective, of course, much still needs to be done to strengthen community initiatives in agroecology, and widen existing networks and movements to strengthen the presence of peripheral subjects, their concerns, their struggles, and their protagonism. The following reflections on favelas, resistance, and the grassroots are intended to contribute to this process of urbanizing-peripheralizing the conception and practice (strategy and tactics) of the struggle for food sovereignty.

Favela Territory, Resistance, and the Grassroots: Favelas and Spatial Expressions of Inequality in Rio de Janeiro

"Certainly, not all [popular] neighborhoods and self-built cities represent the same trajectory and in several cases they seem far from forming forms of popular power or local self-government. But it seems beyond doubt that in these spaces dwell powers of social change that we have not yet been able to discover in all their magnitude."

—Raúl Zibechi

Much has been studied and written on favelas in Rio's metropolitan area, a spatial phenomenon with global visibility. Many of these works are

76

embedded in center-periphery power relations of knowledge production and as such are trapped within, or reproduce a "coloniality of knowledges."[54] In this way, they often further stigmatize favelas and their inhabitants, instead of critically reflecting on such stigmas and helping overcome them by a better comprehension of the complex dynamics of relations of domination and subordination/resistance that constitute these territories. Many of these works focus on favelas' internal socio-territorial relations at the local level, somewhat fascinated, it seems, by the specificities of these territories, which make an interesting research object for middle-class researchers. Yet in order to better comprehend the complex dynamics of favelas, we also need to look at external-internal (global-local) and transterritorial dimensions. We cannot fully understand urban peripheries without recognizing the importance of the politics of scale at play.

In global terms, the UN-Habitat Report *The Challenge of Slums: Global Report on Human Settlements 2003* is a key document that brought to the attention of the so-called international community the magnitude of an urbanization process that has seen urban peripheries grow constantly and globally for over a century now. If Mike Davis took the data of this report to write a dramatic book on a "planet of slums," Rio de Janeiro certainly deserves to be at center stage: it has been one of the urban centers of the Global South whose growth very early on was based on and accompanied by severe urban segregation and the constant growth of favelas.[55] However, in recent years the international agenda has moved its focus to other urgent questions faced by humankind, with climate change in the pole position of current dominant narratives. The current global coronavirus pandemic and subsequent global economic crisis, though, will take the pole position for some time to come. In the meanwhile, urbanization continues to increase on a global scale, and urban peripheries continue to mark the expanding urban landscapes. As the economic crisis we face will hit hardest the approximate 1.6 billion informal workers worldwide, we must consider that living conditions in the urban will worsen dramatically in the near future, and urban peripheries will expand further in cities around the globe, especially those of the Global South.[56] In Rio de Janeiro, the word "periphery" indicates the social, economic, and cultural distance between those who have privileges and those who have few or none, those who benefit from relations of exploitation and those who are mainly exploited. *Periphery,* however, does not necessarily indicate spatial distance, as favelas are spread over the metropolitan area, forming a mosaic-like landscape of popular neighborhoods in the midst of skyscraper middle- and upper-class *bairros* (neighborhoods) and gated communities: an urban set of puzzle pieces that at first sight not only do not fit but do not even appear to be part of the same puzzle. Yet, taking all dimensions and scales of reality and analysis into account, they sure are: they form the jigsaw puzzle that is Rio de Janeiro.

The city of Rio de Janeiro, despite its singularities and particularities, shelters in its midst a pattern of power typical of Brazilian society that can well be characterized by the image, simultaneously sociological and spatial, that was given to us by Gilberto Freyre. After all, our cities may be characterized as enlarged reproductions of the *Casa-Grande e Senzala* (*The big house and the slave quarters*).[57]

The first favelas in Rio de Janeiro date back to the end of the nineteenth century and the first favela is commonly attributed to poor soldiers. The soldiers had returned to Rio from the War of Canudos, in which the Brazilian state had violently oppressed a popular uprising in 1886–87. They found no other way to reintegrate themselves in the colonial city (due to low or neglected state compensations) other than through settling on a hill in the central region of the city, and thereby founding the favela of Providência.[58] Over the course of the twentieth century, the rural exodus, common for many countries in the Global South, was propelled by the industrialization of agriculture according to the principles of the Green Revolution. This brought many people from the interior (Blacks, Indigenous, and peasants, mainly from Brazil's northeast) to Rio's growing metropolitan area, seeking better living conditions and some kind of paid work. Once they arrived, they would only find a place to sleep, and later on to call home, in one of the ever more numerous favelas. These favelas have continued to grow ever since and by the beginning of the twenty-first century were home to about 25 percent of the total population of the Rio municipality.[59]

Serrinha, in the neighborhood of Madureira, the Community of Silva in Sacopã, or Rocinha, or Estácio, and all the favelas that converge with the Tijuca neighborhood are examples of spaces of Black resistance. Racism is an important component of our territorial conformation process. Besides the very Rio-specific distribution of favelas across the city, what these favelas have in common with urban peripheries in other Brazilian cities is that the way they came into being and developed made them spatial expressions of how subalternized groups and their cultures and habits found new, urbanized forms. The main groups that continue to compose the favela population today are Black, Indigenous, and nonwhite, as well as whites with a peasant background: they therefore make favelas spatially and historically complex territories of convergence of quilombola, Indigenous, peasant, and working-class ways of living. In turn, they make Rio's peripheries, territories that we have not yet been able to decipher in their full magnitude in dialogue with Zibechi as cited above.

In social sciences in Brazil and beyond, many approaches to researching and understanding favelas have either been unable or unwilling to overcome the center-periphery divide in how we look at and experience social reality in a postcolonial capitalist class society. Therefore, the causes of the massive peripheralization marking cities such as Rio are hidden behind the discussion of how to deal with its effects. As simple as it may seem, many works seem to miss the key point, namely: The "peripheral" situation of an area is created; it is the result of exploitation by another area, that is, the center. Yet, as argued above, in order to grasp the interspatial relations of urban inequality, we have to include "scale" as a category of our analysis of urban power relations and forms of dominance, as these are expressed in the urban periphery. For several years, the Maré-based NGO Redes da Maré (Networks of Maré),[60] used an aerial photo of Maré as the background of its internet home page. The photo gave an idea of the impressive extension of densely constructed favela housing and was accompanied by a Brechtian phrase: "Nothing should seem impossible to change." This arrangement of photograph and text provoked a question: What needs to actually change, so that things in Maré may change (for the better)? And this question can only be tackled if we take aerial photos from much higher levels and start to include those parts of the city that are net beneficiaries of an unequal distribution of resources and opportunities. *Inequality* only makes sense as an analytical category if we understand it not only as a relation, but instead work critically, analyzing this relation and its origin, nature, and dynamics and—the key point—take both ends of the relation equally into consideration. We can read slum areas, such as Maré, as spatial expressions of urban poverty, for example, but reading them as spatial expressions of urban inequality means we have to identify what Maré is unequal to. We need this second end so that we can actually speak of a relation: favelas in relation to the middle- and upper-class neighborhoods benefiting from unequal inner-urban power relations. The spatial expression of inequality, then, in a city like Rio, is that favelas like those in Acarí, in Maré, or Alemão coexist in the same city with middle- and upper-class neighborhoods such as Flamengo, Leblon, or Barra da Tijuca. Are all those that live in this second group of neighborhoods rich capitalists? Of course not, yet given the shifting balance of public and private investment, urban infrastructure, and workforce flows, we can clearly say that these latter neighborhoods benefit while the favelas suffer from the unequal power relations at play. In this sense, Milton Santos and Maira Laura Silveira propose thinking of spatialized power relations in a way that distinguishes between "spaces that command" and "spaces that obey," in a permanent shock to the dialectic pair of abundance/scarcity. As long as neighborhoods of abundance like Barra da Tijuca "command," can living conditions for the majority of those inhabiting neighborhoods of scarcity, such as Maré, ever be essentially improved? A quite simple logical deduction here says that things in Maré cannot change essentially as long as we keep focusing only on Maré itself: only if the dominant neighborhoods in a power relation stop being dominant can the oppressed liberate themselves from said oppression.

Things are complex, of course. Yet, many times, complex questions are discussed in academic terms making it more, rather than less, difficult to understand where decisive antagonisms are, consequently making it more difficult to take decisions about how to struggle or what to struggle for. Relations of domination-subordination/resistance and their dynamics that are at play here are of multidimensional, multiscalar, and multiterritorial nature. The challenge for us is to untangle their complexity. One way we can do so conceptually is by detecting and analyzing the multiple center-periphery antagonisms that are present in all dimensions, scales, and territories. These establish the constitution of sociabilities and territorialities in the urban. In struggles for emancipation, it is crucial to recognize centers and subcenters of domination and to strengthen those who resist on all levels and scales.

As Ana Fani Alessandri Carlos argues in the case of São Paulo: "the contemporary metropolis, the central/periphery contradiction becomes complex without overcoming itself, updating itself through the contradiction of integration/disintegration of places under globalized capitalism. This contradiction deepens the separation between the place(s) of business and its global architecture—the case of the constitution of a commercial business axis, under the guidance of financial capital, which extends from the center of the metropolis of São Paulo—and the heterogeneous peripheries." "Centrality is the constitutive element of the city, its theoretical and practical foundation, it contemplates the meanings of the city as a civilizing process. In contrast, the periphery is the other side of centrality, it denies it."[61]

If the periphery is the negation of centrality, we can deduce that any emancipatory process of transformation of the urban will depend on struggles that derive from an act of double recognition: the periphery recognizing itself as such, and recognizing its role in territorially based center-periphery relations of class struggle. The overcoming of the centers as such can only be the role of the peripheries. In dialogue with Marxist educator Paulo Freire, who thinks of emancipation as an act of liberation in relation to subjects in struggle, we can spatialize-territorialize his idea and formulate that the overcoming of the center-periphery contradiction brings to the world a new social relationship, where there are no more centers, no more peripheries, but rather peripheries liberating themselves (and [self-] emancipating themselves, ceasing to be peripheries).[62] In dialogue with the Mexican Zapatistas, the simple emancipatory idea that underpins these thoughts is a (so)ci(e)ty that overcomes the center-periphery relations constituting it both internally (inner-urban) and externally (urban-rural), in a transition toward (so)ci(e)ties that know "neither the center, nor the periphery."[63]

On Territory and Power: Urban Peripheries Between Domination and Resistance

Place and space as categories have surged within and nourished struggles and their critical reflection upon the urban Global North. At the same time, the power that the notion of territory has gained through mass resistance and social movement struggle in the Global South, outside the urban, has also strongly influenced how we read dynamics and resistances within urban peripheries. If in the Global North we may speak, in general terms, of a spatial turn on how social scientists have tried to read and understand social reality over the past few decades, we may equally speak of an initially territorial, yet increasingly decolonial-territorial turn in the Latin American context, or, as Maristella Svampa argues, an "ecoterritorial" turn.[64] For over a couple of decades now, Raúl Zibechi has been closely working with social movements in Latin America—or as Chris Dixon expresses it, "writing with movements."[65] Based on these experiences, Zibechi has synthesized some of his reflections on the dynamics at urban peripheries, proposing to read these as "territories in resistance": "I am firmly convinced that those at the bottom (that broad conglomerate that includes everyone, and above all women who suffer oppression, humiliation, exploitation, violence, marginalization …) have strategic projects that they do not formulate explicitly, or at least not in the codes and ways practiced by hegemonic society."[66]

Detecting these projects basically means combining a long-term view with an emphasis on underground processes, on forms of resistance of little visibility but which anticipate the new world that those at the bottom weave into the penumbra of their daily lives. This requires a view that is capable of focusing on small actions with the rigor and interest that the most visible and notable actions demand, those that tend to "make history."[67] Zibechi proposes to overcome the coloniality in knowledge production that is based on subject-object relations.[68] In order to generate emancipatory theory, we need to root our reflections in subject-subject relations: not thinking and writing about struggles, their subjects and territories, but much more from within these dynamics or together and in dialogue with "secondary" subjects in movement. These ideas converse with a broad field of decolonial thought that I also connected to in making a case for "geographies in movement" and the importance of "science [as] tool for struggle."[69] Zibechi brings Frantz Fanon and Ramón Grosfoguel into dialogue and elaborates on how peripheries are usually approached and related to as "zones of non-being" (be it by scientists, public agents, or political forces).[70] Those movements—such as Indigenous people, Afros, peasants, and people living in the urban peripheries of Latin America—carry out politics "from the zone of non-being."[71] In "territories in resistance,"[72] instead of "seeing like a state,"[73] as is the case in many takes on favelas that look at its socio-territorial dynamics from the perspective of a sociopolitical "center" (a university, a government institution, etc.), Zibechi set out to cast a very different (we could even say inverted) gaze at these dynamics "behind the official (hi)story."[74] In dialogue with critical geographers from Brazil, such as Carlos Walter Porto-Gonçalves,[75] Zibechi reflects on power relations, resistance, and the increasing importance of territoriality not only in rural, but also in urban struggles: The novelty that illuminates the social struggles of the last twenty years is that the set of territorialized social relations existing in rural areas (Indigenous but also landless) are beginning to become visible in some cities such as Caracas, Buenos Aires, and Oaxaca, with El Alto in Bolivia being perhaps the most complete expression of this trend. "In Latin America, in the heart of the resistance of those at the bottom, 'other territories' have been forming, different from those of capital and the multinationals, which are born, grow and expand in multiple spaces of our societies."[76]

Linking a diversity of empirical experiences to theoretical analysis, Zibechi challenges our notion and reading of the importance of space in social struggle. Inspired by this challenge, approaching the urban peripheries of Latin America as "territories *of* resistance" has been for me, over the past decade, a simultaneous topic of scientific analysis, proposal of practical involvement in struggles, and a projection of other possible futures. (In order to stress the multiplicity of relations of domination-subordination/resistance that mark the peripheries, I prefer to use "of" instead of "in" to link territory to resistance.) Reading territory through its analytical, practical, and normative dimensions is fundamental if we are to understand the transformations taking place in the peripheries, both rural and urban. It is in this sense that Zibechi argues that urban peripheries "continue to grow and, above all, continue to remain different: spaces where diversity is one of their hallmarks and, above all, where there are forms of non-mercantile life, not colonized by capital. The peripheries of cities are the urban equivalent to Indigenous reservations or peasant territories. They are the hope for radical anti-capitalist change because here, we find social relations that can be the basis for the reconstruction of society."[77]

A key question here is how struggles against domination and the construction of resistance are forged at the interface of social relations and space. A key question is as much how the interaction of social relations and space forge these struggles. Here we can understand, with John Holloway, resistance as permanent movement of negation-and-creation, and with Carlos Walter Porto-Gonçalves as *r-existence*: peripheral classes must resist so they can exist as much as their existence is a form of resistance.[78]

Be it to soften the brutalization represented and conditioned by today's cities or to conquer substantially different and fairer cities, it is necessary to reflect and act taking into account what matters most: the dynamics of social relations, in particular the dynamics of power relations, and the links between them and space, in its twofold quality of product and as a conditioner of social relations. Space is product and conditioner, at the same time constituted by and constitutive of social relations. The spatial dimension is crucial in order to read and comprehend how domination and resistance in the urban relate and forge peripheral territories. Ana Esther Ceceña refers to "spaces of resistance" in order to highlight the importance of space for, in our case, urbanized-territorialized class struggle: "The dominated, the subaltern, survive and resist because they find or build their own spaces and dynamics; because they create their own political forms that Ranajit Guha calls 'the politics of the people.'"[79]

The peripheral classes implicitly and sometimes more explicitly refer to a whole set of "(insurgent) spatial practices" in order to build their "spaces of resistance." Marcelo Lopes de Souza discusses these in dialogue with Henri Lefebvre: "Spatial practices have obviously served both domination, coercion, imposition from above or from outside within the laws and norms that regulate the life of a group or society ... —in a word, heteronomy—as well as emancipation, self-determination, legitimate self-defence, self-government, the free and lucid institution of laws and norms by the very body of citizens, directly—in a word, autonomy."[80]

A very fundamental spatial practice identified by Souza in relation to processes of resistance is the act of "territorialization" itself. Rogério Haesbaert, also in dialogue with Lefebvre, discusses territorialization as a "basic resource" of our being and interacting in society: "Territory, seen by many from a political or even cultural perspective, is focused here on a geographical, intrinsically integrating perspective, which sees territorialization as the process of (political-economic) domination and/or appropriation (symbolic-cultural) of space by human groups. Each of us needs, as a 'basic' resource, to territorialize ourselves."[81]

As power struggles unfold spatially, territories are forged. Haesbaert continues: "Territory can be conceived from the imbrication of multiple power relations, from the most material power of economic-political relations to the most symbolic power of relations of a more strictly cultural order."[82] Considering the complexity and multiplicity of social relations that constitute the urban and determine the urbanization process, we may affirm that the constitution of urban peripheries such as favelas in Rio de Janeiro is a process of a multiplicity of acts of territorialization, or, consequently, a process of "multi-territorialization."[83] "Territorialising oneself in this way means creating spatial mediations that give us effective 'power' over our reproduction as social groups … a power that is always multi-scalar and multidimensional, material, and immaterial, of 'domination' and 'appropriation' at the same time."[84]

In dialogue with these discussions on how society and space relate through power struggles, we can read urban peripheries, such as favelas in Rio de Janeiro, as a multi-territorial expression of the encounter of heteronomous (spatial) practices and autonomous (spatial) practices, neither presenting themselves in their pure form. Souza proposes the concept of "autonomous territoriality," which we may conceive as a territoriality that results from emancipatory spatial practices tending toward autonomy.[85] This idea naturally presupposes that there are also heteronomous territorialities, similarly resulting from heteronomous spatial practices. The multi-territoriality that constitutes urban peripheries is the result, in this sense, of the confrontation of dominant territorialities, which tend to heteronomy, and resisting territorialities, which tend toward autonomy, as much as the result of the interplay between hetero-de-territorialization and self-re-territorialization processes. Since these processes are constituted through, as much as they result in, spatial practices, they can strengthen either the heteronomous dominant or the autonomous resisting side of power struggles. Simplifying considerably, if we understand favelas as the "best possible solution" within the power and class struggles that constitute capitalist urbanization, we may still confirm that, without insurgent spatial practices, favelas as we know them simply would not exist.

Favelas: Territories of Resistance

The relationships of domination–subordination/resistance that constitute favelas do not draw or follow clear lines, nor do they exist as pure antagonisms. There are some diffuse forms of domination, while others are more direct, just as there are more explicit or more implicit forms.

Economic exploitation on the one hand is directed against favela residents as a relationship of interclass capitalist domination, while at the same time it is reproduced and multiplied among favela residents as a relationship of intraclass/territorial exploitation. There are homeowners and tenants, and owners of enterprises, shops, and small businesses that employ workers in highly precarious relations: all live in the same favela. At the same time that capital-labor relations and market logics vigorously penetrate and permeate the peripheral territories imposing values of exchange, they encounter relations based on nonmonetary forms of collaboration that generate use values that are important in the genealogy and reproduction of these territories. This means that urban peripheries are characterized by hybrid forms: residents with diverse forms of intraterritorial relations of domination (economic, social, or cultural, etc.) may suffer together or at least likewise from forms of interterritorial oppressions, such as discrimination against "favela inhabitants" or their position in the face of state violence against these territories.

The state makes use of territory as a category of practice, explicitly repressing and relegating favela residents to the position of second-class citizens. Not a day goes by in which we do not count victims of state violence in a direct or indirect and selective manner in favela territory, violence that clearly differentiates according to color, age, and gender.[86] Racism, which expresses itself here in a lethal way, originates in relations of center-periphery domination, or between the zones of being and zones of not being (interterritory). Yet it is also reproduced in favela territories through transclass dynamics, in an intersubjective and intraclass way. "Racism pervades poverty," says the documentary *(in)cômodos* of Cineclube Atlântico Negro.[87] In the favelas, peripheral classes territorialize through more or less collective struggles against domination of the centers. At the same time, in the territories themselves, they reproduce and re-territorialise center-periphery relations at the intersubjective and intraclass/territorial level. The struggles that forge these territories have transterritorial, intraterritorial, and interterritorial dimensions. The multiterritoriality that characterizes the capitalist production of urban space does not permeate the city as a whole in a homogeneous way. On the contrary, we have territories in which specific forms of domination and others in which specific forms of resistance arise or converge. What characterizes favelas as territories of resistance is that only here do we find a diversity of peripheral resistant practices that constitute and reinvent peripheral territories at every moment. If forms of domination constitute society as a whole and many of its forms originate in the spaces of the oppressors, forms of resistance originate in territories of the oppressed. It is in the spaces that these confluences of resistance occur—and they do so rhizomatically, with greater density, forging territories of resistance.[88]

If the centers "want" the favelas and their inhabitants to remain distant or to disappear completely, for all of it "to explode," as singer and songwriter Max Gonzaga states in his song "Classe média" ("Middle Class" [2013]), they still need the favelas and, in many ways, depend on them entirely. It is the vigor and the magnitude with which the state represses and controls favela territories that indicate that favelas are not as much seen as the expression of a social problem that needs to be addressed as such, but rather, as a territorial expression of resistance that represents a threat for the dominant classes. Katherine McKittrick begins her discussion of a "black sense of place" with a quote by Frank B. Wilderson III: "There is something organic to black positionality that makes it essential to the destruction of civil society. There is nothing wilful or speculative in this statement, for one could just as well state the claim the other way around: there is something organic to civil society that makes it essential to the destruction of the black body."[89]

In dialogue with McKittrick, we can say that favela territoriality opposes capitalist-central territorialities, as much as these dominant territorialities permanently "attack" favela territoriality.[90] How we read and what sensitivity we have, in trying to analyze these antagonisms that constitute the modern-colonial world system and its urbanized forms, clearly depends on the angle and perspective from which we look at them. Considering that how we read favela territory also influences what kind of role we assign them in a broader sense of struggle, I consider it useful to synthesise some of the key characteristics of territories of resistance, from a territorially intrinsic perspective:

- Peripheral social classes territorialize in territories of resistance, and in doing so they try to guarantee minimum living conditions for themselves in the face of the exploitation, oppression, and discrimination they suffer from in capitalist class society.

- Urban territories of resistance are those territories where Indigenous, quilombola, peasant, and other originally nonurban cultures of resistance flow together and constitute new and complex forms of territoriality. In urban territories of resistance, popular nonurban cultures of resistance have found, in a historical and in a geographical sense, an open and ever-changing urban form.
- In territories of resistance, territory is instituted by ambiguous and sometimes antagonistic relations. If, for the peripheral classes, territory is a means to sustain and materialize their struggles and to protect themselves and minimally (self-)organize in relation to the dominant classes, territory is simultaneously a means for the dominant classes to materialize and sustain spatial forms of domination. As such, territory is a means/tool for struggle and resistance while it serves, at the same time, as a means/tool of domination.
- In territories of resistance, peripheral subjects face forms of domination and oppression—if not equally, still to some degree collectively—as inter-class and inter-territory relations of domination. That does not mean that all subjects of a peripheral territory stand united in a joint struggle against these forms of domination. It is a consistent effort of the dominant classes to govern and relate to these territories by fragmenting and dividing potential resistances. The multiscale reproduction of trans-class forms of domination leads to the constitution of multiple subcenters of power within peripheral classes and their territories and as such, to forms of intra-class and intra-territorial forms of domination. Yet this means that peripheral subjects may potentially have common interests to defend together and to organize their resistances as collectives or communities.
- In the face of multiple forms of oppression, we may find in territories of resistance multiple explicit and implicit forms of insubordination and resistance. Implicit forms of resistance may result from forms that at some point were explicit and inscribed themselves into a popular culture of territorialized resistance, or that derive from consciously explicit forms of how subjects react when facing a class- and territory-specific form of domination. Explicit forms of resistance can be individual or collective and

constitute processes where a certain class- or territory-related problem is tackled actively through processes of self-organization and community mobilization. In this context, grassroots movements are part of a broader "society in movement."

- Territories of resistance are not some kind of romantic place or projection, where pure revolutionary subjects are ready to join an externally thought-out grand revolutionary project, nor are they territories in which peripheral classes construct ideal ways of living their lives. They are territories where best available solutions are struggled for within the very unfavorable broader context of globalized capitalism, such as a metropolises of the Global South. Yet, through this process, the peripheral classes potentially point to forms of sociability, conviviality, and territoriality that may go beyond the dominant forms of present-day global capitalist society, and as such, keep alive ideas and imaginations of other societies. In strengthening these aspects of territories of resistance we do not mean to minimize the many problems peripheral subjects face in their daily lives (as if we were to say, "Oh, good, they face many problems, so they can find alternatives for us."), rather, they can help us pay the necessary attention to the ways they deal with these problems.

- In and through territories of resistance, the peripheral classes resist—and it is in territories of resistance that other forms of doing and living appear, that partially and/or potentially, subvert or overflow dominant and oppressive logics of the modern/colonial capitalist world system. In this sense, territories of resistance hold capacities of overcoming the multiple forms of domination and oppression that sustain and help maintain the globalized capitalist world order. If self-emancipation of the peripheral classes may only be achieved by the peripheral classes themselves, in territories of resistance they find ways of strengthening their permanent struggle to reach self-emancipation, by overthrowing present-day capitalist or any other class-based system of domination and oppression.

- As much as the globalized capitalist order has its foundation in relations of domination–subordination/resistance, the constitution of territories of resistance can be considered a global phenomenon, even though with very context-related forms of expression and magnitude. Certainly, in the Latin American context, struggles over territory can be found all across the continent, in both rural and urban contexts. It is not a coincidence that a protofascist, neoliberal government such as the one in command in Brazil since 2019 has been leading a broad attack on Indigenous groups, Black quilombola communities, and small farmer movements in their territories in rural Brazil, while promoting and justifying an increased use of brutal state violence in the urban peripheries.

• Territories of resistance can be read as the most striking spatial expression of the contradictions of globalized capitalism and the class struggle that constitutes it. That is a class struggle that comprises many struggles, and wherever peripheral classes may find in territory an ally, their struggles will be strengthened; while wherever dominant classes find ways to make use of territorial means to oppress and to deterritorialize struggles and their protagonists, these struggles may be weakened. If the dominant classes make use of the territory to hide oppression behind spatialized forms of stigmatization, the peripheral classes find in territory a strong ally to conjugate, articulate, and strengthen their particular struggles as part of broader, multiple, complementary inter-class and inter-territorial struggle. A notion of the (multi)territoriality of struggles leads to a notion of the complementarity of struggles (and vice versa), which also leads us to recognize the importance of networks of territories of resistance that need to be deciphered, understood, strengthened, and amplified as an effort of grassroots work, popular mobilization, and (self)organization.

• As a multiplicity and diversity of implicit and explicit forms of resistance flow together in territories of resistance, grassroots movements and community groups that territorialize themselves in these territories become part of a multiplicity-multiterritoriality of peripheral resistances. The objective of politically communitarian interventions through grassroots work is to detect the most appropriate "societies in movement" that constitute these territories of resistance. The objective is also then to organize around issues and through forms of intervention that break down trans-class, inter-class, and inter-territorial forms of domination and oppression, while strengthening the territory and its people in interclass/territory struggles. The protagonists in this process are those who live in these territories; active intervention in these territories from an emancipatory perspective is based on collaboration, mutual aid, self-management, collectivism with autonomy, and (food) sovereignty as guiding horizons of common struggle. A territory of resistance cannot be strengthened through logics and practices that are implemented in top-down, center-periphery, external-internal directions, so they cannot be strengthened through political vanguardism of any kind: peripheral practical knowledge is born from peripheral practice itself.

If we wanted to sum up this attempt to synthesize what characterizes urban peripheries such as Rio's favelas as specific spatial expressions of urban struggle, we can "simply" state: favelas and urban peripheries in general are territories of popular, Black, feminist, LGBTQIA+, class resistance in the very sense of inner-, trans-, and interterritorial relations of dominance and subordination/resistance. If some of these forms of domination express themselves in certain, and oftentimes very violent forms in urban peripheries (be it machismo, racism, or homophobia) to insist on referring to these spaces as "territories of resistance" does not mean to say that these violent forms are considered to be of minor importance. Rather, it is much more to say that they need to be tackled with all strength and effort, also at the intraclass and territorial levels, without leaving out of our scope the origins these forms of domination or how they are constitutive of the modern colonial world system, from the global to the local scale and as trans- and interclass/territorial forms of domination.

Favela territories are shaped by processes of resistance that combine more explicit elements (as when people organize themselves to face a problem or to challenge a relationship of domination) and more implicit ones (as when people build ways of overcoming problems on an individual and collective level in everyday life). As John Holloway reminds us, "It is the moving that is important, the moving against and beyond, the negating and creating."[91] Many times, we find propositional forms of resistance, that we may read, in dialogue with John Holloway's reflections on "how to change the world without taking power," as a composition of movements of negation-and-creation that produce a relationship of against-and-beyond what is being encountered. But we may also read these in the inverse, beyond-and-against: peripheral sociabilities and territorialities can go beyond capitalist relations and the predominance of exchange values and as such, they "stand against" logics imposed by the centers. Movements "resist and create" at the same time.[92]

In the documentary *Te vejo Maré* (*I See You Maré*) produced for *The Guardian Online* by Ben Holman, one of the founders of the Museum of Maré describes the history of the favelas of Maré: "The history here of this whole region ... is one of resistance indeed, of much insistence."[93] Maré's favelas are the result of their residents' decades of struggle, both in the self-construction of housing (the first years before the embankment of the areas on stilts), and in the self-organization of their daily coexistence, having to deal with numerous restrictions and challenges, from the lack of sanitation to the poor conditions of the education systems and health services, and state, paramilitary, and gang violence.

Favela Is Resistance / Maré Come to the Streets / With Se Benze Que Dá

"Favela is resistance!" is a slogan that has gained visibility in the streets since the Jornadas de Junho, the massive street revolts across Brazil that peaked in June 2013.[94] The resisting in this phrase refers to combined elements of defense and of protagonism, an urban form of popular resistance that guarantees the existence of the urban peripheral classes in their territories. This idea dialogues with reflections on Indigenous and peasant resistances in the rural that Carlos Walter Porto-Gonçalves reflects on frum a decolonial perspective: "To say coloniality is to say, also, that there are other matrices of subalternized rationality resisting, r-existing, since colonial domination was established and that, today, they are gaining visibility. Here more than resistance, which means reacting to a previous action and, thus, always a reflex action, we have r-existence, that is to say, a way of existing, a certain matrix of rationality that acts in circumstances, even reacts, from a *topoi*, in short, from a proper place, both geographic and epistemic. In fact, it acts between two logics."[95]

Raúl Zibechi sees the concept of "social movement" coined in classical social sciences as an obstacle to understanding reality in the urban peripheries, since it emphasizes formal aspects from the classification of forms of organization to cycles of mobilization, from definitions of identities to cultural frameworks: "At this point there are entire libraries on the topic. But there is little, very little, work on the Latin American terrain that stands on a proper and therefore different base. In the arduous task of decolonization of critical thought, the debate on the theories of social movements is of primary importance."[96]

Zibechi questions the application of paradigms in Latin America that were forged in analyzing social movement realities and dynamics in the Global North: "In the urban periphery, poor women often do not organize according to the forms of a social movement according to this theorization, yet they play an important role as a factor of social change. Moreover, the women's movements that we know of in the world have a capillary form, not stable or institutionalized, of action, beyond a small nucleus of women organized in a stable way. But this does not mean that it is not a great movement, one that has changed the world from its root."[97]

The prominent role of women is expressed in territories of resistance in many ways. Family relations are organized around the child-mother-grandmother nexus and many community activities in the favelas are led by women: "The image of poor women in move-ment in their neighborhoods weaving territorial networks that are, as Salazar points out, 'community cells,' is the best image of a non-institutionalized movement and of the creation of non-state powers: that is, not hierarchical, nor separated from the whole. In this way, a new way of doing politics is also born from the hand of new subjects, which do not appear fixed or referenced to state institutions."[98]

Zibechi proposes to go beyond the classical notion of "social move-ment" and dialogues with Luis Tapia, who proposed to move from the idea of "social" to "societal" movement. Zibechi suggests that the socioterritorial dynamics we find in the peripheries—whether rural or urban—constitute what we may refer to as "societies in movement."[99] Putting together the pieces of social and spatial relations, then, we may argue that urban peripheries in Latin America represent specific forms of *sociabilities* (societies in movement) and *territorialities* (territories of resistance)—they are favelas in movement and resistance.

This provides us with an analytical foundation to think of how to connect to the dynamics of urban peripheries from the perspective of grassroots movements. Inspired by grassroots movements such as the

Movement of Popular Communities (Movimento das Comunidades Populares or MCP) and community collectives in different favelas in Rio de Janeiro that I have accompanied in militant investigations, we can state that explicitly formed movements in community contexts in favelas in Rio de Janeiro are usually rather small. In the face of numerous NGOs and philanthropic forms of work in the community that institutionalize struggles and make them hierarchical, grassroots movements that work in a (self-)emancipatory perspective seeking to build nonstate forms of popular power are clearly in the minority. The specific ways they make themselves present, though, through spatial practices such as the maintenance of community spaces and regular activities reinforcing a specific "sense of place" in the favelas, and the fact that their members live in the favelas where they are part of networks of family, friendship, and neighborhood ties give these initiatives considerable reach.[100] They connect to other forms of organizing in their favela and to groups and movements in other favelas and parts of the city.

In an attempt to grasp the diversity of forms of popular self-organizing in the favelas, I identified in a graphic (fig. 1) a few key characteristics that can describe how organizing is taking place. Based on various pairs of characteristics, which relate to one another through a continuum of possible combinations, we may think of numerous forms of how people organize in order to exist in favelas. There is no one certain form or best form to do it, rather struggle is strengthened when the different forms communicate with, respect, and complement one another. This also makes clear that explicitly organizing as a grassroots movement in a favela means to be part of something bigger, where the grassroots movement neither takes the lead nor lags behind in mobilizations: grassroot movements territorialize in territories of resistance by forming "societies in movement" that are seeking to strengthen forms of resistance within, across, and between classes and (their) territories against diverse forms of domination that constitute the capitalist metropolis of the Global South. The way I arranged the inner circle in the illustration indicates what I argue would be the most common form of organizing an emancipatory grassroots movement in favelas.

As a member of the Movement of Popular Communities told me, "The important thing for the people is to realize what popular power

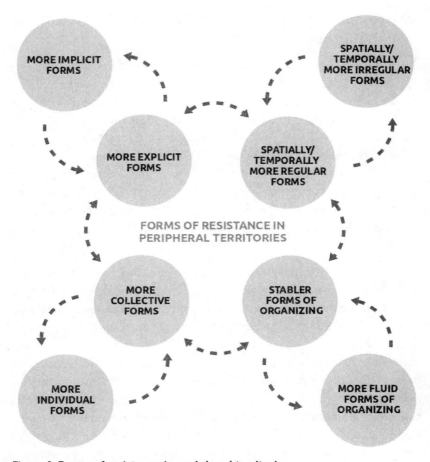

Figure 1: Forms of resistance in peripheral territories

is, so that is our concern. It's popular power in the favelas and in the periphery [that matters], do you understand?"[101] One main objective of territorially based work in the struggles of the peripheral classes is to act on the basis of the needs and problems suffered by the people of these classes together with them, not in their name or representing them in some way. They follow this objective from the perspective of building popular power that is self-institutive power-to that does not negate small advances or reforms that lead to improvements of the people in struggle, but that does not justify means extraneous to the defended ends. The difference between a reform that is won as a result of pressure from self-organized social movements and reformism as a strategy is clearly delineated by the Freunde und

Freundinnen der klassenlosen Gesellschaft (Friends of a Classless Society), who argue:

> But there is a world of difference between the limited struggles for one reform or another to improve one's own life, and even the struggles to prevent it from deteriorating, and reformism. Reformism is a political movement that either aims directly at the preservation of capitalism by mitigating the worst excesses or by institutionalizing the demands that have become inevitable, or it is actually based on the illusion that a long chain of gradual improvements can transform this society into socialism. In either case, however, it is the state that is supposed to accomplish this. Reformism is political representativism; it must keep every grassroots activity on a prescribed course.[102]

At the interface of (self-) emancipatory grassroots movements with societies in movement in territories of resistance, a main objective is to identify the momentum of community mobilizations—be it the more invisible day-to-day forms (networks of neighborhood solidarity) or specific visible moments of convergence of energies (protests against state violence)—and be part of these. Where grassroots approaches most differ from institutionalized approaches is that autonomy and horizontality are key principles of how to organize in order not to reproduce dominant logics, where it is possible and necessary to overcome them in order to strengthen community resistance in a long-term perspective. Larger connections occur through horizontal and federated networks of collaboration and mutual support (reminding us here of classic works of revolutionary thinkers in the Global North, such as Proudhon and Kropotkin) that I have come to identify as "network-territories of resistance."[103]

In the context of the struggle for food sovereignty, which strongly depends on how we organize economically, these networks have great potential for the intensification of rural-urban collaboration, as they are built on nonexploitative forms of economic self-organization, which differ much from neoliberal state- and company-driven, and NGO-supported, ideas of social and community micro-entrepreneurship in vogue in Brazil in recent times. I wish to discuss how far collective economies are of interest in this sense in concluding the second part of this chapter in order to pave the way to the final part.

Collective Economies: Connecting Rural and Urban Resistances

In Brazil, initiatives of "solidarity economy" have a long and diverse tradition and the idea of cooperativism has gained institutional dimensions in different fields such as agriculture, services, and manufacturing. At this point, I will not enter into the discussion of the emancipatory potentials and limits of very diverse and more or less alternative economic approaches, but want to focus instead on some inspiring experiences with collective economies in rural and urban movements.

The Landless Workers' Movement emphasizes the importance of collective struggle: "The struggle for land is a collective struggle, and so are the conquests. After the conquest of the land, the same organization should be maintained so that this land can become productive by providing sustenance for the settled families and contributing to the local economy of the cities.... Agricultural cooperation is part of an intrinsic process of the Landless Workers' Movement. It enables us to overcome the individualism that exists in all of us.[104]

Important rural social movements, such as the Landless Workers' Movement and the Small Farmers' Movement, which have built their movement work around land occupations and self-organization in the agricultural activities of their members, promote cooperative forms of work in the rural settlements as well as collaborative networks of distribution of what they produce. There were more than 6,800 formally registered cooperatives in Brazil in 2019, responsible for 260 billion reals worth of revenues. Writing on experiences of the Landless Workers' Movement, Lu Sudré and Marcos Hermanson confirm "Cooperativism in the countryside generates income for small farmers.... Through the production of healthy food and self-management, small farmers show that the countryside is also fertile ground for cooperativism ... [a] form of organization [that] consolidates itself as a means of subsistence for the peasant population.[105]

The Small Farmers' Movement connects small farmers in different rural regions of Brazil through collaborative networks to foster mutual support among the farmers, and strengthen their position in the market, and organize market access collectively. Reaching out into the cities, as discussed in part one, the Landless Workers' Movement and Small Farmers' Movement work with Agrarian Reform stores, they establish distribution networks and promote the building of consumer cooperatives seeking to boost collectivity and collaboration among those involved. Marcelo Leal of the Landless Workers' Movement explained it this way: "Linked to the 'alternative' universe, cooperatives that consume organic food produced by small farmers politicize the act of consuming and help change the way food is produced. They can be defined as urban nuclei with an economic purpose, because it facilitates sale, and also a political one, since it involves values related to the solidarity economy and agroecology, for example. Because eating is a political act."[106]

Key in the struggle for food sovereignty among rural social movements are alternative, cooperative ways of agricultural production and distribution. One main problem for small farmers in rural areas is their lack of access to the fairs. Since they do not have the logistical means to bring their produce to redistribution centers or directly to fairs or the consumer on their own, they depend on resellers that buy directly from them for very low prices to resell for reasonably higher prices, so that an essential part of the margin is kept as profit by these resellers. The problem here is not only that small farmers work much but stay poor. It is also that they are unable to move from conventional to agroecological production methods, as these would involve slightly, but crucially higher, production costs (especially in the transition phase), which they cannot possibly cover if they do not connect to alternative distribution networks. Therefore, one key challenge for social movements striving toward rural-urban food sovereignty is to self-organize along the full producer-consumer chain in order to distribute food in economically alternative and feasible ways.

For the Small Farmers' Movement, agroecology must be a peasant movement, that is, one affirming the peoples of the countryside and forests as active agents of this process. It must be developed for the masses, in order to be linked substantively to popular supply. There is no possibility of a peasant agriculture project without the perspective of popular supply.[107]

The Small Farmers' Movement poses the challenge of "popular supply" as a key effort to pose the struggle for food sovereignty on an ever broader and ever popular rural-urban basis. In order to strive toward this goal, more collective forms of economic self-organization will be needed.

Some very inspiring experiences of how to collectivize economic relations and activities at the local scale in grassroots work come from the Movement of Popular Communities.[108] The movement has been present in different regions of Brazil for more than four decades now, and has been changing its forms of intervention according to changing sociopolitical conditions over time. Since the 1990s, the movement has been developing a strategy to build popular communities in rural *and* urban peripheries. I stress the *and* here, since the strategy of the popular communities is remarkably adaptable to very diverse local contexts, and is put into practice within the movement in different rural and urban contexts, making this not a rural movement or an urban one, but truly both: a rural-urban movement.

The popular communities are built considering the needs of the people and they correspond to ten sections in which work is developed: economic survival, liberating religion, family, health, housing, school, sports, art, leisure, and infrastructure.

Over time, each popular community seeks to develop work in as many sections as possible, following the guidelines of the Movement of Popular Communities' "Plano Nacional de Lutas e Atividades" (National Plan of Struggle and Activities). This plan was developed through consultations across the base of the movement, through discussion of four basic questions: What are our problems? Why do these problems exist? What have we done to solve them? What are we going to do?

From this consultation the guidelines for each section were formulated. To evaluate the work in the popular community, to find out how it is achieving its goals and to decide on its next steps, members of the community periodically discuss another set of three questions: Which of the guidelines [of the plan] are we putting into practice? What needs improvement? How do we build what we do not yet have in our community?

What makes the Movement of Popular Communities experience so rich is that the strategy finds simple—not simplistic—ways to mobilize the community in very complex peripheral settings, which pose great challenges to the people in general, and to those who organize in particular. In the economic field, all initiatives are based on collective economies, whether they be a self-managed small neighborhood convenience store, a store with construction supplies, community investment groups that work outside the reach of capitalist banks, or community school groups. In Rio de Janeiro, the movement's experiences and initiative were decisive in organizing the Collective Economies Network, which existed from 2013 to 2016, and which our Roça! Collective was also part of. Through several activities that mainly aimed at exchanging experiences of different initiatives in collective economies, and at mutually strengthening our work, we came to a common denominator of how to define collective economies. The 2014 call for the second annual meeting of the network, "Building the Economy That We Want in the Countryside and in the Cities," stated: "We understand collective ways of doing and thinking about the economy in all spheres (production, distribution, consumption, and investment) as a tool of profound social transformation. It is a means (not an end in itself) through which our social movements in the countryside and the cities can organize and strengthen their struggles, without all their agenda focusing on economic issues and without there being a detachment of the question of economy from other social and cultural issues that are the basis of our popular struggle."[109]

Another very inspiring example of strong linkages between rural and urban popular movements and initiatives in the struggle for food sovereignty is the work of the self-managed cooperative called El Almacén Andante (the Walking Warehouse), an experience Emanuel Jurado, geographer and founding member of the cooperative, discussed during the NutriCities Week of Food Sovereignty in Maré in 2018. Based in a common central neighborhood in Mendoza, Argentina, in a collectively organized social movement center called La Casita Colectiva (the Collective House), the Walking Warehouse has more than a decade of experience in the distribution of products from a large variety of cooperative and social movements that come from the greater Mendoza province, or even other parts of Argentina. Weekly home deliveries, market stands, and a fixed store, where they stock the goods, characterize the versatility through which the cooperative has built this strong alternative network of food production.

In a short, unpublished text on their experience, the cooperative Almacén Andante presents itself as part of a larger struggle for food sovereignty in Argentina: "Like other experiences in our country such as Caracoles y Hormigas (Buenos Aires), Puente del Sur (Buenos Aires) and Cooperativa Mercado Solidario (Rosario), we are a solidarity distributor.... We believe that just trade can become a valid alternative to think about and transform commercial conditions in general, through the design and implementation of production-distribution-consumption networks oriented toward solidarity and sustainable development."[110]

Collective economies, such as those developed by rural movements (such as the Small Farmers' Movement and Landless Workers' Movement) that reach out to the cities; and by the rural-urban Movement of Popular Communities, within the urban Network of Collective Economies; or the Almacen Andante, present themselves as an axis around which it appears possible to build strong links between rural and urban struggles toward food sovereignty. To try to make sense of the different parts discussed so far in this chapter we need to take on the challenge of putting together the pieces of experience, concepts, approaches, and ideas so we can see if they do, eventually, form part of the same—far from complete—puzzle.

Putting the Pieces Together: Favela and Food Sovereignty

Food sovereignty is the linking axis of rural and urban resistances. In the first part of this chapter, we saw how the concept of food sovereignty was forged within the context of Via Campesina. We discussed how the basic definitions of the concept delegate to the urban poor the functions of consumers ("decide what they consume") and of voters ("taking part in agricultural policy choice"). But we then saw through the examples of struggle for food sovereignty and how this unfolds in Rio's context, that in practice, the idea of food sovereignty and its protagonists lie on a much broader base. From the practice of movement(s) and common people's actions, we can deduce the manifold possible protagonisms for peripheral subjects in the urban with regard to the struggle for food sovereignty: as urban gardeners and farmers who reuse and compost organic waste, in consumer and food distribution cooperatives, as market vendors, as people who handle and process food (in restaurants and small enterprises/cooperatives of secondary food production), in nutrition and health self-help groups, as conscious consumers, as supporters of campaigns against agro-industry and in support of small farmers, or as environmental and popular educators, to name just a few.

Michel Pimbert closely dialogues with Via Campesina's positions and documents on food sovereignty to defend the need of "reclaiming autonomous food systems" in our struggle "towards food sovereignty."[111]

In an emancipatory take on this struggle, he synthesizes the ideas of food sovereignty in a very fruitful way. According to Pimbert, we are dealing with a struggle on multiple scales: individual, community, people, and national. Pimbert's reflections allow us to think about food sovereignty from a favela perspective, at the interface of individual and community scales, and as a struggle for these rights:

- to define our own agricultural, labor, fishing, food, land, and water management policies, as appropriate to our unique circumstances; and to manage, use and control our life-sustaining natural resources;
- to produce and harvest food in an ecologically sustainable manner and sustain ourselves and our communities with safe and appropriate food; and
- to choose our own level of self-reliance in food.

In the lights of the assumptions, as we also discuss in our Minhocas chapter, we are very far from being sovereign in the favela, food-wise. But should we just accept that in a densely populated urban periphery such as Maré we will always remain highly food dependent? What do our experiences of struggles and of our NutriCities research teach us instead? What kind of perspectives do they bring into the horizon of the possible?

More than a concept, food sovereignty is a principle that guides the peasant struggle. It is an alternative perspective that guides new relations of production and consumption, being one of the bases of the peoples in their struggle against agribusiness and neoliberal policies promoted by financial and transnational institutions.

For the Small Farmers' Movement, food sovereignty is the linking axis between the countryside and the city, it is the material and symbolic element that drives and legitimizes the struggle for agrarian reform and the construction of a new territoriality that has in peasants, and original and traditional peoples, the material and spiritual basis for the construction of a new society.[112]

If food sovereignty is the main link between the countryside and the city, as the Small Farmers' Movement claims, and we are far from reaching it here, then one thing is for sure: we need to connect to the countryside better, more profoundly, and on our own grassroots terms. While we practice as much urban agriculture as possible and promote agroecology in our urban peripheries, we also need to work creatively for new and stronger ways to connect to the countryside and not just any countryside—not to the agro-industrial that transforms the environment into an industrial production site—but to the countryside of the small farmers, peasants, Indigenous, and quilombola. We need to amplify and strengthen the connections between the peripheries of the rural and the urban.

Building Rural-Urban Network-Territories of Resistance and Food Sovereignty

When we consider the possibility of building and strengthening networks of resistance in the rural and in the urban, we must recognize that what we know about each other—our movements, our territories, our resistance—suffers many influences from stigmas (re)produced by corporate media and mainstream news networks: we know little about each other's realities and struggles. If we are to make our struggle for food sovereignty in the rural and the urban an increasingly united one, it is important that get to know each other better. Those of us in the urban must get to know the great creativity the movements in the countryside show when organizing their lives, and how they work and produce in difficult conditions in the rural. Those of us in the rural must recognize that urban peripheries are much more than drug wars, violence, unemployment, or misery. For this common and great task of getting to know each other and recognizing each other's potential to r-exist, we need to strengthen our own channels of communication. We need to visit each other, inviting peasants, quilombolas, and Indigenous to our favelas and visiting their territories to exchange transformative knowledge. These are tasks that agroecological movements and popular education projects in the favelas have had experience with over the past decades.[113]

The continuous challenge to get to know each other's realities and struggles also implies getting to know each other better, and seeing our own reality from different and diverse angles. What potential do favelas present when it comes to the struggle for food sovereignty? Who should we connect to in the rural, in order to become more (food) sovereign in the urban peripheries and in order to strengthen struggles outside cities? As ever, when we get to know different realities, we get to know our own better, as well. In a conceptual theoretical sense, it is this movement of encounters of perspectives that I have tried to lay out here. What happens and what is possible when the struggle for food sovereignty meets and reaches out to favela resistance? Just as important, what happens when favela resistance reaches out to, and becomes part of, struggles for food sovereignty?

Linking back to our reflections on the relation of grassroots movements to favela territorialities (territories of resistance) and sociabilities (societies in movement), a crucial point is how to read the way grassroots movements (inter-)act socio-territorially. My experiences with movements in different favelas in Rio de Janeiro over the past decade and their forms of connecting and networking allow for a few conclusions that build on the territories of resistance approach and try to take it further. The first idea is to look at how they (inter-)act spatially, what their spatial practices are, how they make a sense of place, in order to collaborate with other groups and organizations, with neighbors, friends, networks of sociability, that is, in their nearest proximities, the favela that they are part of and where they have their base. Each small grassroots initiative functions as a core of a network that they continuously build, as much implicitly through preexisting networks of sociability they sprang from and continue to be part of, as explicitly through tactical and strategic decisions on how to network and with whom to network.

One grassroots core can be a single independent collective or part of a wider movement, such as the Movement of Popular Communities, which organizes internally taking centralized decisions democratically and delegating relative autonomy to each base, the popular communities, in the execution of their work. Grassroots cores support other groups that might in turn be currently under formation or already exist in their favela and they get support from related groups in return; usually, the closer the neighborhood relation, the more diverse these relations are politically and ideologically. Yet, the further these cores reach out to other cores, groups, and movements, the more so they share common ideas, ideals, and ways of struggle. They reach out way beyond their own favela, to territories of other favelas as much as to movements and organizations (such as unions and political parties) with bases in formal middle-class neighborhoods or in the city center. As discussed above, favelas spread over the metropolitan area of Rio de Janeiro in a mosaic-like fashion, so the spatial pattern or ground on which these networking activities take place beyond their own favela can be identified as territorially discontinuous.[114]

To help grasp the characteristics of this territorial discontinuity, Rogério Haesbaert discusses the role of territoriality in our contemporary network societies: "The structuring of a network society is not necessarily synonymous with deterritorialization, because in general it means new territories, those in which the fundamental element in the formation of territories is the network, to the point of almost being confused with them ... it is possible to identify a 'territory in the movement' or 'by the movement'.... Today, territorializing oneself also means building and/or controlling flows/networks and creating symbolic references in a space in movement."[115]

Territory therefore is, above all, "action, rhythm, movement that repeats itself,"[116] while at the same time "it is necessary to distinguish, for example, between potential multi-territoriality (the possibility of it being built or triggered) and effective multi-territoriality, realized ... multi-territoriality and network-territories, molded in and by movement, [indicate] the strategic importance of space and territory in the transformative dynamics of society."[117]

And on the relation of network and territory, Haesbaert reflects: "There is no territory without a network structure that connects different points or areas.... Before we lived under the domain of the logics of 'zone-territories,' which hardly admitted overlaps, while today we have the domain of 'network-territories,' spatially discontinuous but intensely connected and articulated with each other."[118]

It is on these grounds that our notion of favelas as territories of resistance, and how to read our interactions as part of these territories, gains conceptual inspiration: First, our ongoing task is to read, analyze, and comprehend the network-territory of favelas in movement that we are intrinsically part of as subjects and activists in peripheral grassroots movements. Second, the idea of favelas as territories of resistance helps us to strategically move forward by choosing our actions in accordance with the specific characteristics of the network-territory of resistance we are part of in terms of how to struggle and how to (inter-)act and connect, so that we can build (on) ever stronger favela-based network-territories of resistance. Haesbaert's reflections on network-territories are inspired by our reading of resistances, just as we are inspired by his insights. Annelise Fernandez and Sílvia

Baptista dialogue with Haesbaert in their discussion of mobilization and networking in the agroecological movement in Rio de Janeiro's West Zone: "Territories are built permanently through meshes, weavings and knots and through borders, limits, belongings. In this way, they are at the same time formed by flows and fixes. The idea, therefore, of network-territories that are constituted from multiple scales and that are connected to different areas, to global flows and political and power structures is a perspective that allows us to understand territories in a more integrative and elaborate way, because it breaks with the dichotomy between territory (as belonging, rooting) and network (as deterritorialization only)."[119]

Starting from this notion of network-territories, the authors trace the history and map agents and their interactions in an integrative struggle toward the recognition of agricultural activities and agroecological distribution networks and fairs as essential economic activities in the urban. They discuss flows of communication that help in setting new common agendas among different agents. In their process, they identify a network-territory of agroecology that connects struggles for food sovereignty in Rio's West Zone to similar struggles in other parts of the metropolitan area (with Rede CAU and Family Agriculture and Agroecology, among others, playing key roles).

This idea of grasping the way the struggle for food sovereignty takes place in Rio de Janeiro as network-territories of agroecology clearly dialogues with experiences and observations as discussed in part 2 of this volume. The way the organizations, groups, and movements mobilize and collaborate points to the existence of a multiscale, multilayer, and multidimensional network-territory of agroecological movement(s) in Rio's urban area. There are more than a few interfaces between this network-territory and the network-territory of favela resistance, yet at the same time, we must recognize that both overlap a lot less than they potentially could and increasingly should.[120] Through NutriCities, we were able to make them overlap a bit further.

When participating as the community research group Minhocas Urbanas in networking activities and events of the agroecological movement at regional and national levels, we saw great openness toward the participation of favela inhabitants. A sincere, shared concern was how to increasingly integrate favela territories into the struggle for food sovereignty. At the same time, at some of these national meetings, we recognized very few favela-specific groups or movements and observed that the urban periphery was clearly underrepresented.

Against this background, one important step in strengthening struggles for food sovereignty in the urban is to recognize the network-territorial nature of struggles, and to create more and stronger common agendas of the network-territories of agroecology and the network-territories of favela resistance in Rio de Janeiro's metropolitan area. In doing so, we can also meet the great challenge we face in strengthening the links among rural and urban peripheries and their movements. Urban network-territories of agroecology already have very strong connections to rural networks of movements, while our network-territories of favela resistance still need to strengthen such ties. We need to reach out more decisively from a favela perspective to rural social movements, while at the same time these movements need to more fully integrate our favela territories in their strategies of reaching out to the urban as a whole. The key to advance, in this sense, can and must be twofold: further integrating network-territories of agroecology and of favela resistance in the urban will also help us strengthen ties to rural network-territories of struggle for food sovereignty as well.

When Zibechi designed his political cartography of urban peripheries in Latin America, he was strongly inspired by the manifold experiences of territorialized struggles across our continent's rural areas. The importance of territory for struggles has its origins outside the urban. Indigenous, Black, and peasant's movements forged (the idea of) territories of resistance decades and centuries before territory was conceived and started being recognized as an important practical category, and subsequently, as an analytical one as well. In this sense, it is beyond banal to state that urban peripheries, such as favelas in Rio de Janeiro, were the way that struggles of Indigenous, peasants, Blacks, and workers territorialized, over the past century, in Brazil's rapidly growing cities.

Bernardo Mançano Fernandes has been closely following Brazil's mass rural social movements since the mid-1990s and has recognized the great importance these struggles had in (re-)molding territories, and the importance territoriality had in (re-)molding the struggles in conflictive processes of de-re-territorialization: "Socioterritorial movements have territory not only as an asset, but it is essential to their existence. The peasant movements, the Indigenous, [but also] the companies, the unions and the states may constitute themselves into socioterritorial and sociospatial movements. Because they create social relationships to directly address their interests and therefore produce their own spaces and their territories."[121]

It was on these grounds that Fernandes recognized movements like the Landless Workers' Movement as socio-territorial movements. These are characterized by their deeply territorializing relation to space and the claim for territory for their material and symbolic reproduction. Silvia Baptista et al. dialogue with these ideas in their reflections on the conflicts around Rio's West Zone inner-urban peasant area called Sertão Carioca: "The conflict is imminent in the construction of a more just society, in which the dispute for territory demonstrates one of the aspects of class struggle.... That is, when social movements incorporate, in their practices, alternatives of production, consumption and coexistence, this dispute becomes socioterritorial."[122]

Bernardo Mançano Fernandes differentiates movements that constitute themselves socio-territorially from socio-spatial movements that represent not their own interests but those of third parties, as is the case with many NGOs. He then goes on to differentiate between socio-territorial movements that are active locally, referring to them as isolated movements, and those who go beyond the local scale.[123] These movements build networks across Brazil's vast territory in order to connect their local resistances. Subsequently we can affirm that resistances in rural Brazil are marked by network-territories in struggles in general and in struggles for food sovereignty in particular. These include symbolic and material networks of political and economic collaboration on multiple levels: territoriality in the rural has been the strong ally of movements while these territorialities have been under constant and increasingly intense attacks, since the neoliberal cycle of the 1990s, and then again during the progressive neodevelopment cycle of the 2000s, up until 2016 and now, during the most recent ultraliberal cycle of Temer's interim and Bolsonáro's government.

Reflections on socio-territorial movements by Fernandes, or on new territorialities of social movements, converge upon the approach of urban peripheries as territories of resistance, inspired by Fernandes's argument that "one social class cannot realize itself in the territory of another social class."[124] Our reflections on the urban peripheries are strongly inspired by our learning from social struggles in the non-urban and peri-urban. Studying closely non-urban experiences of struggle, we have also better been able to dismantle complex power relations in the urban and struggles for the right to (be in) the city.

This sort of "back to the conceptual roots" loop here is meant to help us to fit together the pieces of the puzzle we have in our hands at this point: the comprehension and capacity to read the socio-territorial dynamics that are at play at the multiple peripheries in rural and urban struggles in Brazil; the idea that we are not only part of, but (can) actively build (and increasingly integrate) network-territories of agroecology and favela resistance in the urban; and the recognition of the need and possibility to reach out to, and increasingly integrate these network-territories with the network-territories of rural struggles for food sovereignty: these all open up a horizon of a rural-urban convergence of struggles for popular and food sovereignty in peripheral territories through building and strengthening rural-urban network-territories of resistance and food sovereignty.

This, of course, is as much a projection as an ongoing project for possible futures of our common rural-urban struggle to live in dignity in an ever-less unjust society. While the pieces we have put together so far do not give us the sense of being close to solving the puzzle as a whole, they do open the horizon and suggest that the puzzle we are trying to put together is much bigger than we can account for, at least with the pieces that we have at hand. Yet if the rural social movements reach out to the urban periphery and become increasingly aware of their full potential, and if favela resistance increasingly integrates the perspective of reaching out to the rural, a more food sovereign future seems indeed a possible horizon of our common rural-urban struggles.

Food, Favela, and the Grassroots: Toward a Postpandemic Food Sovereign Future

To pave the conceptual path taken with a concrete practical perspective, I would like to finalize reflecting on a few fields of possible concrete actions in collective cross-movement efforts to further urbanize and peripheralize the struggle for food sovereignty and the idea we have of it as an emancipatory concept or horizon of struggles that encompasses the range from rural to inner urban. The ground of the NutriCities research and the perspectives of our struggles both stem from favela territory, so it is from here that I want to reflect on favela resistance and how it not only meets but can also increasingly become part of a common rural-urban struggle for food sovereignty.

As favela grassroots movements we must understand the importance of urban agriculture and agroecology in the urban, struggle for its recognition, and put it into practice, promote it, and defend it.

As favela grassroots movements together with urban agroecological grassroots movements, we must reach out to rural social movements, get to know their struggles better and find concrete ways to collaborate and mutually support one another. We must connect the rural peripheries with the urban peripheries in manifold ways, learn from each other and overcome the common stigmas that cast a shadow over urban and rural peripheries alike.

As favela grassroots movements we must strengthen and build collective economies and reach out to rural social movements to build rural-urban network-territories for the production, distribution, preparation, and consumption of food; and we must produce in cities what may be needed in the countryside. At every place where we live and work, we produce, we (re)distribute, and we consume what is necessary for the reproduction of the lives of all those who form part of our growing network-territory. We must defend collective economies against many false doubles, such as "micro-entrepreneurship in favelas" and the like.

Based on our comprehension of favelas as territories of resistance, we can affirm the great potential the urban peripheries present for the struggle for food sovereignty. If rural social movements in the city most easily connect to the middle class and its territories, as people there have the means to afford higher-priced food and to support the social movements, favela territories present a full range of possible interactions with the rural: their vivid fairs can host agroecological stands, their inhabitants can work in secondary food processing, the territories can have stockage and hub functions, favela communities can organize themselves as consumer cooperatives or organize distribution hubs of the rural-urban networks for the flow of agroecological products.

Any person involved at any point in the food chain has to have the power of decision over their labor activity; and be collectively organized, be it as a family or as a group, in the work process; and collectively own the land to grow and breed; and own the means of production to harvest, transport, distribute, process, and prepare food. The chain of capitalist middlemen and resellers (which is one of the main reasons for the low price the small farmer receives and the relatively high price the consumer pays in the city) has to be replaced by cooperatives that organize the logistics of our rural-urban and urban-rural food and goods exchange network.

One key issue of overcoming the conventional capitalist food production chain logic is to break with its mostly linear structure. Trucks come from monocultural agro-industries to bring commodity crops to the main distribution hubs in the big cities and ports (when for exportation), oftentimes traveling empty on their way back. An alternative food production and distribution network needs to be based on circular logics that substitute these linear understandings of resource-destructive capitalism.

We can only achieve large-scale "popular supply" in strong alliances with social movements from the countryside. At the same time, urban agricultural activities have great importance for our striving for food sovereignty at the urban peripheries. Wherever possible, we must plant: the greener our favelas, the less we are affected by extreme heat and air pollution. We cannot only plant complementary food items, we must also plant for phytotherapeutic purposes to decrease our dependence on the pharmaceutical industry when it comes to solving our health problems.[125] In urban peripheries that dispose of larger areas of unconstructed lands, we can plant and harvest on a larger scale.

We must constantly learn and build transformative knowledge exchange networks between the rural and the (peri-)urban. We can only strive for food sovereignty at the urban peripheries if we have a deep understanding of how we (self-)organize in these territories of resistance and how common capitalist market food distribution and supply work. Only based on this knowledge, can we (self-)organize in order to think-create alternative ways of producing, distributing, preparing, and consuming food that provides us with good energy in a healthy way for us, for the environment, and for those who work at any point of the food-production chain.

As favela grassroots movements, we must read carefully the present moment of the severe global pandemic crisis of COVID-19. We are presently only starting to learn what it means when a sick system (global capitalism) is infected by a deadly virus (the coronavirus pandemic). It is necessary to engage with the fortunately numerous solidarity campaigns and help distribute food among those who most suffer from economic deceleration. But we must be aware that the food we have access to and can distribute is bad quality food.[126] A sick system in a deadly crisis can only respond to an emergency by utilizing what it has on hand.[127] Emergency mobilizations must not be channeled into and reduced to spontaneous philanthropic aid, they must become acts of true solidarity and be strengthened as grounds for the widening of struggles. In rich countries such as the US, millions of tons of food are destroyed due to damaged production and distribution chains, while many of the poor in the country lack the means to get decent food on their plates. The coronavirus pandemic is most likely to lead to a hunger pandemic—and it is the poorest in the poorest countries who will suffer most. The Global North will do little to invert this situation; global capitalism will not have much to offer to invert it either, it is part of the problem, not the solution.

Social movements are in action facing the pandemic. In a remarkably broad mobilization, on April 8, 2020, the National Agroecology Network presented a proposal to the federal government signed by 774 social movements and civil society organizations, to increase the financial volume of the Program for the Acquisition of Food from Family Agriculture from less than 200 million to 1 billion reals for the present year.[128] Knowing the government we are speaking of, hopes are few that considerable action will be taken by Brazil's current disastrously governing political leaders. To survive, alternative distribution networks will depend on their capacity to self-organize and build strong rural-urban bridges for producers and consumers. In a statement on April 7, 2020, the International Panel on Food Sovereignty points to the repression that small-scale producers and their fairs are facing due to pandemic-related state interventions, but declares: "Small-scale food producers stand in solidarity and will fight to bring healthy food to all!"[129]

If we were to summarize all this in one phrase: favela grassroots movements must take food seriously, now and in the future. And we have many examples to inspire us: the historical example of how the Black Panthers strengthened communities and their own resistance work through the practice of community meals in many Black US neighborhoods, as discussed by Raj Patel;[130] the community restaurants in urban peripheries across Argentina, that lived on way beyond the 2001 economic crisis that had riddled the country's economic and political landscape; the impressive network of solidarity community restaurants of the poor for the poor in the urban periphery of Bañados, Asunción, fiercely facing the pandemic's effects on the poor households;[131] the inspiring experiences of the Movement of Popular Communities' monthly, collectively prepared community lunch in the movement's popular communities across Brazil, their collective food shopping, or community agriculture; and the many experiences and initiatives of the agroecological movement near and around us and the work and networks of rural social movements in the cities, such as the distribution of agroecological food by social movements such as the Workers' Party and the Small Farmers' Movement in solidarity campaigns in some of Rio's favelas during the pandemic.

We must take food seriously.

We must work to further converge our network-territories of favela resistance and the network-territories of urban agroecology to reach out to the rural network-territories of struggle for sovereignty and to inspire those who build and maintain them reach out to us in the favelas. Only together can we further build and strengthen these rural-urban network-territories of resistance and food sovereignty. Pandemic-ridden crisis capitalism will riddle the world for years or decades to come, our answer can only be to keep striving beyond what there was and is, toward a food sovereign egalitarian postpandemic and postcapitalist future.

Striving for food sovereignty as part of striving for better living conditions at the peripheries is no more and no less than striving for a radical change in how the whole thing we call society works. True food sovereignty in a nation-state capitalist society is not only a no-go for the dominant political and economic classes: it is a logical contradiction. Food sovereignty as a pillar of an egalitarian society can only be reached by overcoming the exploitative food systems that structure present-day global food distribution systems.

An increasing movement for food sovereignty at the peripheries will necessarily shake the foundations of capitalist fairs, the more so the stronger the struggle. And in face of the current pandemic, the opposite becomes as evident as it will ever get: the more the foundations of global capitalism are shaken, the more urgent it will be that we advance with our struggles for (food) sovereignty. Be it in favelas, urban occupations, rural settlements, Indigenous territories, quilombos: all (in struggle) for food (sovereignty) and food (sovereignty) for all!

NOTES

1   Richard Lee, 2007. "Food Security and Food Sovereignty" (Centre for Rural Economy Discussion Paper Series No. 11, 2007), 3.

2   MPA website, subsection "Soberania Alimentar" (Food Sovereignty), https://mpabrasil.org.br/soberania-alimentar. All translations are by the author unless otherwise indicated.

3   Via Campesina, "Food Sovereignty: A Future Without Hunger," November 11–17, 1996, https://viacampesina.org/en/wp-content/uploads/sites/2/2021/11/1996-Rom-en.pdf; Via Campesina, "The Doha Round Is Dead: Time for Food Sovereignty," July 29, 2006, https://viacampesina.org/en/the-doha-round-is-dead-time-for-food-sovereignty; Via Campesina "What Is Food Sovereignty?" January 15, 2003, https://viacampesina.org/en/food-sovereignty.

4   Via Campesina, "The Doha Round Is Dead."

5   Via Campesina, "VII International Conference: Women's Assembly Declaration," Committee for the Abolition of Illegitimate Debt, August 14, 2017, https://www.cadtm.org/VII-International-Conference-Women.

6   Esther Vivas, "La Via Campesina: Food Sovereignty and the Global Feminist Struggle," December 18, 2012, https://archive.foodfirst.org/la-via-campesina-food-sovereignty-and-the-global-feminist-struggle.

7   Vivas, "La Via Campesina."

8   Via Campesina, "What Is Food Sovereignty?"

9   Lee, "Food Security and Food Sovereignty."

10   The quote is from a talk by Beto Ribeiro of the Small Farmers Movement at the Week of Food Sovereignty held in Maré on behalf of the NutriCities project in December 2018. It is estimated that 70 percent of food consumed in Brazil originates in small-scale *agricultura familiar* (family agriculture).

11   Despite the economic predominance of, and importance given to, Brazil's agro-industrial complex, which mainly produces commodities for exportation, it is estimated that 65 to 75 percent of the food on Brazilian tables comes from smaller-scale, family-based agriculture. See MST, "70% dos alimentos do mundo vêm da agricultura familiar, afirma economista," May 29, 2014, https://mst.org.br/2014/05/29/70-dos-alimentos-do-mundo-vem-da-agricultura-familiar-afirma-economista.

12   According to a study by the Worldwatch Institute published in 2011. See https://cityfarmer.info/farming-the-cities-feeding-an-urban-future-worldwatch-institute.

13   Paulo Roberto Alentejano, "As relações campo-cidade no Brasil no século XXI," *Terra Livre* 21 (2003): 25–39.

14   A few weeks before I concluded this text, Geandra Nobre and I discussed our experiences with the Roça! Collective and samba block Se Benze Que Dá at a workshop on urban struggles at the School of Architecture and Design of the Federal University at Minas Gerais in Belo Horizonte (August 3–November 3, 2020). There, we had the fortunate opportunity to share our session with Sílvia Baptista and Caren Freitas de Lima. They are active in the Popular Collective of Women in the West Zone (https://www.facebook.com/COLETIVAPOPULARDEMULHERESZO), and participated in the elaboration

of a participative and popular plan for land use in Rio's West Zone ("Articulaçã Plano Popular das Vargens," http://sertaocarioca.org.br), and have also engaged with militant and feminist investigation (Militiva, https://www.militiva.org.br).

15   The 2006 agricultural census counted 1,055 agricultural establishments within the municipality of Rio de Janeiro, of which 790 were based on family agriculture. And even though in administrative terms none of the municipality's territory is considered "non-urban," some areas have many similarities with rural areas. Meanwhile, of course, the pressures of urban expansion are higher here. Morgana Mara Vaz da Silva Maselli, "Conflitos e resistências na agricultura familiar da cidade do Rio de Janeiro," *Revista Agriculturas* 12, no. 2, (June 2015): 27–32.

16   Caren Freitas de Lima, Silvia Baptista, Susana Arruda, and Cristhiane, "A rede carioca de agricultura urbana e o direito à cidade," *Campo-território: Revista de Geografia Agrária* 14, no. 34, (December 2019): 313–37.

17   Subcomandante Insurgente Marcos, *Nem o centro e nem a periferia—sobre cores, calendários e geografias* (Porto Alegre: Deriva, 2008).

18   The main ideas that I bring into dialogue with our experiences during the NutriCities research have been more broadly discussed in previous works that are part of ongoing research efforts titled "Peripheries in Movement" (Periferias em movimento) and "Knowledges, territories, movements" (Saberes, territórios, movimentos). I share some of the main results on my blog, "Territórios de Resistência," https://www.territoriosresistencia.wordpress.com, mostly in Portuguese. Wherever no other reference is mentioned, the (articulation of) ideas derive from two works that I cite here to avoid repetition: Timo Bartholl, "Movimentos sociais de base e territórios de resistência: Uma investigação militante em favelas cariocas" (PhD diss., Geography Department of Fluminense Federal University, 2015), https://territoriosresistencia.files.wordpress.com/ 2016/03/tese-territorios-de-resistencia-tbartholl-6mb.pdf; and Timo Bartholl, *La ciencia como herramienta de lucha: Por una Geografía en movimiento* (Bogotá: Desde Abajo, 2024); for the original Portuguese version see Bartholl, *Por uma Geografia em movimento.*

19   Severin Halder, *Gemeinsam die Hände dreckig machen* (Bielefeld: Transcript, 2018), 122–23.

20   EMATER is the Portuguese abbreviation of Company for Technical Assistance and Rural Outreach. These are public agencies, organized at the state government level, which are responsible for technical support of agricultural activities. See http://www.emater.rj.gov.br.

21   Caren Freitas de Lima, "Agricultura na e da cidade do Rio de Janeiro: Dicotomias e as especificidades da agricultura urbana" (master's thesis, Federal Rural University of Rio de Janeiro, 2019).

22   A. Wezel, S. Bellon, T. Doré, C. Francis, D. Vallod, and C. David, "Agroecology as a Science, a Movement and a Practice: A Review," *Agronomy for Sustainable Development* no. 29 (2019): 503–15.

23   This term is a hybrid, inspired as much by John Holloway's distinction between dominant "power-over" and emancipatory "power-to" as by Carlos Walter Portio-Gonçalves's differentiation between colonial "knowledge over" from decolonial "knowledge with," the latter an idea that I connect to making a case "for a geography in movement(s)" (Bartholl, *Por uma Geografia em movimento*).

24   Neil Smith, "Geography, Difference and the Politics of Scale," in *Postmodernism and the Social Sciences*, ed. Joe Doherty, Elspeth Graham, and Mo Malek (London: Palgrave Macmillan, 1992), 57–79.

25 Rede CAU, "Carta Aberta da Rede Carioca de Agricultura Urbana," December 14, 2014, https://aarj.wordpress.com/2014/12/14/carta-aberta-da-rede-carioca-de-agricultura-urbana.

26 All annual reports can be accessed at https://www.cptnacional.org.br/index.php/publicacoes-2/conflitos-no-campo-brasil.

27 Rede CAU, "Carta Aberta."

28 See Articulação de Agroecologia do Rio de Janeiro, https://aarj.wordpress.com.

29 Among those doing important work are: Verdejar Socioambiental, https://www.verdejar.org; Agricultura Familiar e Agroecologia, https://aspta.org.br; Alternative Politics for the Global South, http://pacs.org.br; Centro de Ação Comunitária, https://www.facebook.com/centrodeacaocomunitaria/; Federação de Órgãos para Assistência Social e Educacional, https://fase.org.br; Centro de Integração na Serra da Misericórdia, https://www.facebook.com/CEMIntegracaoNaSerra; and Cooperação e Apoio a Projetos de Inspiração Alternativa, https://www.capina.org.br. More complete lists of relevant links see "Networks," Militiva, https://www.militiva.org.br/links; or our Minhocas Urbanas website "Soberania Alimentar Maré," https://soberania-alimentar-mare.home.blog/links.

30 For information about Our Products see https://www.facebook.com/produtosdagente.

31 For more information see Campanha Permanente Contra os Agrotóxicos e Pela Vida, https://contraosagrotoxicos.org.

32 For more information see Associação de Agricultores Biológicos do Estado do RJ, https://abiorj.org.

33 See Rede Ecológica, http://redeecologicario.org.

34 For more information see "Fernanda dos Santos: agricultura urbana como ferramenta de transformação social," https://www.caurj.gov.br/fernanda-dos-santos-agricultura-urbana-como-ferramenta-de-transformacao-social.

35 See Militiva, https://www.militiva.org.br.

36 Militiva, "Relações agroecológicas do mar e da terra," accessed April 1, 2024, https://www.militiva.org.br/relac-oes-agroecologicas-no-mar-e-n.

37 See "Quilombo Cafundá Astrogilda," https://pt-br.facebook.com/quilombocafundaastrogilda. See an interesting presentation of the Museum Cafundá Astrogilda, http://www.museuafrorio.uerj.br/?work=museu-astrogilda-cafunda-quilombo-de-vargem-granderj.

38 The Palmares Cultural Foundation is a public institution that works for the promotion and preservation of Afro-Brazilian culture. Luz Stella Rodriguez Cáceres, *Pelos caminhos do Cafundá* (Rio de Janeiro: FAPERJ/Papéis Selvagens, 2019).

39 For more information see Agenda Feiras Orgânicas ABIO, "Circuito carioca de feiras orgânicas," https://abiorj.org/agenda-feiras-organicas-abio.

40 Lima, Caren Freitas de, "Agricultura na e da cidade do Rio de Janeiro: Dicotomias e as especificidades da agricultura urbana" (master's thesis, Federal Rural University of Rio de Janeiro, 2019).

41 For more information see Movimento dos Trabalhadores Rurais Sem Terra, https://mst.org.br.

42 For an interesting article on Countryside Warehouse see "Inauguração do Armazém do Campo reúne centenas de pessoas no Rio de Janeiro," *Brasil de Fato*, September 15, 2018, https://www.brasildefatorj.com.br/2018/09/15/inauguracao-do-armazem-do-campo-reune-centenas-de-pessoas-no-rio-de-janeiro. See also "Armazém do Campo–RJ," https://www.facebook.com/armazemcamporj.

43   See Cesta Camponesa de Alimentos Saudáveis, http://www.cestacamponesa.com.
      br.
44   Rede Ecológica, http://redeecologicario.org.
45   For specific information about all producers that offer their products through
      Rede Ecológica see "Introdução à relação Acompanhantes e produtoras/es,"
      http://redeecologicario.org/areas-de-atuacao/interacao-entre-produtores-e-
      consumidores/produtores.
46   See Cozinha Colher de Pau, https://www.facebook.com/Cozinha-Colher-
      de-Pau-1395175540735871.
47   Roça! Collective, https://roca-rio.com.
48   See AARJ's extensive list of where consumers can find access to agroecologi-
      cal products, including not only fairs but also directly from some small farms.
      See "Onde Adquirir Produtos Agroecológicos," https://aarj.wordpress.com/
      onde-adquirir-produtos-agroecologicos.
49   See Feira Agroecológica de Campo Grande–RJ, https://www.facebook.com/
      feiraagroecologicacgrj.
50   For an early assessment of social movements' response to the pandemic
      across Latin America see Raúl Zibechi, "Los movimientos en la pandemia,"
      Desinformémonos, Periodismo de abajo, April 2, 2020, https://desinformemonos.org/
      los-movimientos-en-la-pandemia.
51   Dialoguing here with Eduardo Galeano's *Open Veins of Latin America*.
52   An already traditional encounter within Rede CAU is the annual Mutirão "Tira
      caquí" (Collective workday "Harvest caqui fruits"), organized in the West Zone.
      As much as a workday, it is also a get-together and moment of mutual strength-
      ening and support.
53   Other ways for big rural social movements to reach out to the city have been
      either to fund and build new urban movements or to support existing ones in
      their urban struggles.
54   Edgardo Lander, ed., *A colonialidade do saber* (Buenos Aires: CLACSO, 2005).
55   Mike Davis, *Planet of Slums* (New York: Verso, 2006).
56   International Labour Organisation, "LO: As job losses escalate, nearly half of
      global workforce at risk of losing livelihoods," April 29, 2020, https://www.ilo.org/
      global/about-the-ilo/newsroom/news/WCMS_743036/lang--en/index.htm.
57   Carlos Walter Porto-Gonçalves and Rodrigo Torquato da Silva, "Da lógica do
      favor à lógica do pavor: um ensaio sobre a Geografia da violência na cidade do
      Rio de Janeiro," *Polis* 28 (2011): 3. The authors refer to Gilberto Freyres's contro-
      versial work *Casa-Grande e Senzala*, published for the first time in 1933. Many
      criticize his analysis off how violent and racist Brazilian colonialism and society
      have been. See, for example, "Relações raciais em Casa Grande e Senzala ainda
      geram polêmica," *Pernambuco*, http://g1.globo.com/pernambuco/noticia/2013/12/
      relacoes-raciais-em-casa-grande-e-senzala-ainda-geram-polemica.html.
58   Their return coincided with the formal prohibition of slavery in Brazil in 1888.
59   Fernando Cavallieri and Adriana Vial, *Favelas na Cidade do Rio de Janeiro: o
      quadro populacional com base no Censo* (Rio de Janeiro: Prefeitura da Cidade do
      Rio de Janeiro–Instituto Pereira Passos, 2012), 5.
60   Most recently, the NGO's home page has started using a photo taken from the
      top of Morro do Timbau and zooming in on parts of favela Nova Holanda, not
      accompanied by any text. Politically, the NGO materializes countless projects
      locally and tries to influence public policy-making extra-locally in a clearly

reformative perspective, yet not without taking into consideration the multiple scales at play. See Redes da Maré http://www.redesdamare.org.br.

61 Ana Fani Alessandri Carlos, "A prática espacial urbana como segregação e o 'direito à cidade' como horizonte utópico," in *A cidade contemporânea: Segregação especial*, ed. Pedro de Almeida Vasconcelos, Silvana Maria Pintaudi, and Roberto Lobato Corrêa (São Paulo: Contexto, 2013), 95–126.

62 Paulo Freire, *Pedagogia do oprimido* (Rio de Janeiro: Paz e Terra, 2014).

63 Marcos, *Nem o centro e nem a periferia.*

64 Svampa, *As fronteiras do neoextrativismo na América Latina: Conflitos socioambientais, giro ecoterritorial e novas dependências,* (São Paulo: Elefante, 2019).

65 Raúl Zibechi, *Movimientos sociales en América Latina: El "Mundo Otro" en Movimiento* (Mexico City: Bajo Tierra/El Rebozo, 2017). Chris Dixon, *Another Politics: Talking Across Today's Transformative Movements* (Oakland: University of California Press, 2014). "Writing with movements" is the way Chris Dixon refers to his work of critically accompanying and reflecting on transformative movements across North America. See "Writing with Movements," http://writingwithmovements.com.

66 Raúl Zibechi, *Territorios en resistencia: Cartografía política de las periferias urbanas latinoamericanas* (Buenos Aires: Lavaca, 2009), 6.

67 Zibechi, *Territorios en resistencia,* 6.

68 Raúl Zibechi, *Descoloniza: El pensamiento crítico y las prácticas emancipatorias* (Bogotá: Ediciones Desde Abajo, 2014). Raúl Zibechi, *Movimientos sociales en América Latina: El "Mundo Otro" en Movimiento* (Mexico City: Bajo Tierra/El Rebozo, 2017).

69 Bartholl, *Por uma Geografia em movimento.*

70 Zibechi, *Descolonizar,* 28. See Frantz Fanon, *Black Skin, White Masks* (London: Pluto Press, 2008); Ramón Grosfoguel, "El concepto de racismo en Michel Foucault y Frantz Fanon: teorizar desde la zona del ser o desde la zona del no-ser?" *Tabula Rasa,* no. 16 (2012): 79–102.

71 Zibechi, *Descolonizar,* 28.

72 Zibechi, *Territorios en resistencia.* Since I have been working with the Spanish version of "Territories in resistance" I have translated quotations from it. English readers may prefer the translation: *Territories in Resistance: A Cartography of Latin American Social Movements* (Oakland: AK Press, 2012).

73 Zibechi, *Territories in Resistance.* James C. Scott, *Seeing Like a State* (London: Yale University Press, 1998).

74 James C. Scott, *Los dominados y el arte de Resistencia: Discursos ocultos* (Mexico City: Era, 2004), 24.

75 Carlos Walter Porto-Gonçalves, *Geo-grafías: Movimiento sociales, nuevas territorialidades y sustentabilidad* (Mexico City: Siglo XXI, 2001); Carlos Walter Porto-Gonçalves, "A Reinvenção dos Territórios: a experiência latino-americana e caribenha," in *Los desafíos de las emancipaciones en un contexto militarizado,* ed. Ana Esther Ceceña (Buenos Aires: CLACSO, 2006), 151–97.

76 Zibechi, *Territorios en resistencia,* 5.

77 Zibechi, *Territorios en resistencia,* 149.

78 John Holloway, *Change the World Without Taking Power: The Meaning of Revolution Today* (Ann Arbor: Pluto Press, 2005); Porto-Gonçalves, "A Reinvenção dos Territórios."

79 Ana Esther Ceceña, 2008. "De saberes y de emancipaciones," in *De los saberes de la dominación y de la emancipación,* ed. Ana Esther Ceceña (Buenos Aires: Consejo, 2008), 21.

80 Marcelo Lopes de Souza, "Com o estado, apesar do estado, contra o estado: os movimentos sociais urbanos e suas práticas espaciais entre a luta institucional e a ação politica," *Revista Cidades* 7, no. 11 (2010): 23..

81 Rogério Haesbaert, *O mito da desterritorialização: do 'fim dos territórios' à multi-territorialidade* (Rio de Janeiro: Bertrand, 2011), 16.

82 Haesbaert, *O mito da desterritorialização*, 79.

83 Haesbaert, *O mito da desterritorialização*, 79.

84 Haesbaert, *O mito da desterritorialização*, 97.

85 Marcelo Lopes de Souza, "O território: sobre espaço e poder, autonomia e desen-volvimento," in *Geografia: Conceitos e temas*, ed. Ina Elias de Castro, Paulo Cesar da Costa Gomes, and Roberto Lobato Corrêa (Rio de Janeiro: Bertrand Brasil, 1995), 77–116.

86 Anistia Internacional, *Você matou o meu filho! Homicídios cometidos pela Polícia Militar na cidade do Rio de Janeiro* (Rio de Janeiro: Anistia Internacional, 2015).

87 Cineclube Atlântico Negro, *(in)cômodos*, https://vimeo.com/111809569. The film was exhibited during the First Week of Audiovisual Sovereignty in a session at the Roça! Community Space in Maré on November 20, 2015.

88 Gilles Deleuze and Félix Guattari, *Rhizom* (Berlin: Merve, 1977).

89 Frank B. Wilderson III, "The Prison Slave as Hegemony's (Silent) Scandal," in *Warfare in the American Homeland: Policing and Prison in a Penal Democracy*, ed. Joy James (Durham, NC: Duke University Press, 2007), 23.

90 Katherine McKittrick, "On Plantations, Prisons, and a Black Sense of Place," *Social & Cultural Geography* 12 no. 8 (2011): 947–63.

91 Holloway, *Change the World Without Taking Power*, 19.

92 Zibechi, *Movimientos sociales en América Latina*, 49.

93 See trailer with links to all episodes of *Te Vejo Maré (I see You Maré)*, https://vimeo.com/10814898.

94 The heading is a translation of the Portuguese lyrics "Favela é resistência / Maré vem pra rua / Com o Se Benze Que Dá" by the Maré based samba block Se Benze Que Dá.

95 Porto-Gonçalves, "A Reinvenção dos Territórios," 165.

96 Zibechi, *Autonomía y emancipaciones*, 197.

97 Zibechi, *Autonomía y emancipaciones*, 197.

98 Zibechi, *Territorios en resistencia*, 39.

99 Zibechi, *Territorios en resistencia*; Luis Tapia, *Movimientos sociales, movimiento societal y los no lugares de la política: Democratizaciones plebeyas* (La Paz: Muela del Diablo, 2002).

100 Doreen Massey, "A Global Sense of Place." *Marxism Today* (June 1991): 24–29; McKittrick, "On Plantations"

101 The statement was recorded at a militant investigation workshop at the MPC's Popular Community Chico Mendes in Rio's North Zone in the region of Pavuna, May 22, 2015.

102 Freunde und Freundinnen der klassenlosen Gesellschaft. 2007. "28 Thesen zur Klassengesellschaft." *Kosmoprolet*, June 1, 2007, https://www.kosmoprolet.org/de/28-thesen-zur-klassengesellschaft.

103 Bartholl, "Movimentos sociais de base e territórios de resistência."

104 Movimento dos Trabalhadores Rurais Sem Terra, "O cooperativismo como bandeira na luta pela Reforma Agrária Popular," July 5, 2019, https://mst.org.br/2019/07/05/a-luta-pela-terra-e-uma-luta-coletiva-e-diante-disso-as-conquistas-tambem-sao.

105 Lu Sudré and Marcos Hermanson, "Cooperativismo no campo gera renda para pequenos agricultores," July 16, 2019, https://mst.org.br/2019/07/16/cooperativismo-no-campo-gera-renda-para-pequenos-agricultores.

106 Gisele Brito, "Understand What a Food Consumer Cooperative Is (and How It Works), MPA, July 27, 2016, https://mpabrasil.org.br/noticias/entenda-o-que-e-e-como-funciona-uma-cooperativa-de-consumo-de-alimentos.

107 See MPA's website subsection "Soberania Alimentar" (Food Sovereignty), https://mpabrasil.org.br/soberania-alimentar. Beto Ribeiro, an MPA militant, based in the Rio area, confirmed the importance of the "popular supply" approach for the movement in his participation in NutriCities' Week of Food Sovereignty in December 2018.

108 A self-reflection on the MPC's work is part of Bartholl, "Movimentos sociais," and is available separately, https://territoriosresistencia.files.wordpress.com/2016/03/326-341_cap4-2_chico-mendes_tese-territorios-de-resistencia-tbartholl.pdf. On the history of the MPC see Marianna Penna, "À procura da comunidade perdida: História e memórias do Movimento das Comunidades Populares" (PhD diss., Fluminense Federal University, Niterói, 2016).

109 This is translated from the invitation to the second annual meeting of the network in 2013.

110 Almacén Andante, "El Almacen Andante, justo entre la producción y el consume," unpublished manuscript. I thank Emanuel Jurado for sharing it.

111 Michel Pimbert, *Towards Food Sovereignty: Reclaiming Autonomous Food Systems* (London: IIED, 2008).

112 MPA, "Soberania Alimentar."

113 In the many community preparation classes for university access tests in Rio's favelas, issues such as the struggle for agrarian reform, unequal land distribution, and the protagonism of rural social movements usually get reasonable attention. But the question of how to actively connect to these struggles from the urban periphery is not sharply in focus.

114 For graphical representations of how grassroots movements in favelas act as cores of network-territories of resistance see Bartholl, "Movimentos sociais," 404.

115 Haesbaert, *O mito da desterritorialização*, 279–80.

116 Haesbaert, *O mito da desterritorialização*, 281.

117 Rogério Haesbaert, "Território e multiterritorialidade: Um debate," *GEOgraphia* 9, no. 17 (2007): 41–42.

118 Haesbaert, *O mito da desterritorialização*, 79.

119 Annelise Caetano Fernandez Fraga and Silvia Regina Nunes Baptista, "Territórios-rede de agroecologia: ciência(s) e saberes locais na ambientalização de lutas na zona oeste e região metropolitana do Rio de Janeiro." Paper presented at the 38th annual meeting of ANPOCS (Brazil's National Association of Post-Graduate Studies in Social Sciences) in Caxambu (Minas Gerais) in 2014, 4.

120 Verdejar Socioambiental (Alemão), Centro de Integração na Serra da Misericórdia (CEM, Penha), and Muda Maré work with agroecology and environmental education and are inspiring examples of encounters of favela resistance and the agroecological movement. At the same time, during NutriCities we had the interesting experience of seeing outreach groups from the Federal University, such as Muda Maré and Capim Limão, amplify their political notion of what different approaches are present in favelas. While they typically had experience with more institutionalized forms of community work, NutriCities got them in touch with a less institutional, grassroots perspective. It is this perspective that

most needs strengthening in our efforts to converge our territory networks of favela resistances and agroecology in the urban.

121   Bernardo Mançano Fernandes, "Movimentos socioterritoriais e movimentos socioespaciais: contribuição teórica para uma leitura geográfica dos movimentos sociais," *Revista Nera* 8, no. 6 (January/June 2005): 31.

122   Silvia Regina Nunes Baptista, Carlos Osvaldo Motta Formoso, and Ivani Rosa da Silva, "Sertão carioca: A construção social de um território agroecológico," in *Paisagens do sertão carioca: Floresta e cidade*, ed. Rogério Oliveira and Annelise Fernandez (Rio de Janeiro: PUC-Rio, 2020), 140

123   Fernandes, "Movimentos socioterritoriais e movimentos socioespaciais," 14–34.

124   Fernandes quoted in Zibechi, *Territorios en resistencia*, 148.

125   Rede Fitovida, a network of traditional medicinal and phytotherapeutic knowledges and practices, is an amazing example. See Rede Fitovida, https://www.facebook.com/FitovidaRede.

126   Silvio Porto is correct in stating that the population will only have access to terrible food during the pandemic. See Lu Sudré, "População só terá acesso a alimentos de péssima qualidade durante pandemia," *Brasil de Fato*, April 27, 2020, https://www.brasildefato.com.br/2020/04/27/populacao-so-tera-acesso-a-alimentos-de-pessima-qualidade-durante-pandemia.

127   The lack of support for family agriculture by recent governments makes responses to the pandemic harder, while small farmers are at risk of losing the food they produce due to failure of the distribution networks. See Lu Sudré, "Sem apoio, agricultores perdem produtos enquanto populações vulneráveis passam fome," *Brasil de Fato*, April 28, 2020, https://www.brasildefato.com.br/2020/04/28/sem-apoio-agricultores-perdem-produtos-enquanto-populacoes-vulneraveis-passam-fome.

128   See Articulação Nacional de Agroecologia, "Movimentos sociais apresentam solução emergencial de 1 bi para alimentar população vulnerável," April 8, 2020, https://agroecologia.org.br/2020/04/08/paa-programa-de-aquisicao-de-alimentos-da-agricultura-familiar-comida-saudavel-para-o-povo.

129   See International Planning Committee for Food Sovereignty, "COVID-19—Small-Scale Food Producers Stand in Solidarity and Will Fight to Bring Healthy Food to All," April 7, 2020, https://www.foodsovereignty.org/covid-19.

130   Raj Patel, "Survival Pending Revolution: What the Black Panthers Can Teach the US Food Movement," in *Food Movements Unite: Strategies to Transform Our Food Systems*, ed. Eric Holt-Giménez (Oakland: Food First Books, 2010), 115–35.

131   As described by Raúl Zibechi, "Bañados de Asunción: dignidad y autonomía," *Desinformémonos*, April 13, 2020, https://desinformemonos.org/banados-de-asuncion-dignidad-y-autonomia.

BIBLIOGRAPHY

Alentejano, Paulo Roberto. "As relações campo-cidade no Brasil no século XXI." *Terra Livre* 21 (2003): 25–39.

Anistia Internacional. *Você matou o meu filho: Homicídios cometidos pela Polícia Militar na cidade do Rio de Janeiro.* Rio de Janeiro: Anistia Internacional, 2015.

Baptista, Silvia Regina Nunes, Carlos Osvaldo Motto Formoso, and Ivani Rosa da Silva. "Sertão carioca: a construção social de um território agroecológico." In *Paisagens do sertão carioca: Floresta e cidade,* edited by Rogério Oliveira and Annelise Fernandez, 119–44. Rio de Janeiro: PUC-Rio, 2020.

Bartholl, Timo. "Movimentos sociais de base e territórios de resistência: uma investigação militante em favelas cariocas." PhD diss., Geography Department of Fluminense Federal University, Niterói, Brazil, 2015. https://territoriosresistencia.files.wordpress.com/2016/03/tese-territorios-de-resistencia-tbartholl-6mb.pdf.

———. *Por uma Geografia em movimento: a ciência como ferramenta de luta.* Rio de Janeiro: Consequência, 2018.

Borda, Orlando Fals. *Conocimiento y poder popular: Lecciones con campesinos de Nicaragua, México e Colombia.* Bogotá: Siglo XXI, 1986.

Cáceres, Luz Stella Rodriguez. *Pelos caminhos do Cafundá.* Rio de Janeiro: FAPERJ/Papéis Selvagens, 2019.

Campos, Andrelino. *Do Quilombo à favela: A produção do 'Espaço Criminalizado' no Rio de Janeiro.* Rio de Janeiro: Bertrand Brasil, 2007.

Carlos, Ana Fani Alessandri. "A prática espacial urbana como segregação e o 'direito à cidade' como horizonte utópico." In *A cidade contemporânea: Segregação especial,* edited by Pedro de Almeida Vasconcelos, Silvana Maria Pintaudi, and Roberto Lobato Corrêa, 95–126. São Paulo: Contexto, 2013.

Castells, Manuel. *The City and the Grassroots: A Cross-Cultural Theory of Urban Social Movements.* London: Edward Arnold, 1983.

Castoriadis, Cornelius. *Figuras do pensável: As encruzilhadas do labiritino,* vol. 6. Rio de Janeiro: Civilização Brasileira, 2004.

Cavallieri, Fernando, and Adriana Vial. *Favelas na Cidade do Rio de Janeiro: O quadro populacional com base no Censo 2010.* Coleção Estudos Cariocas do Instituto Municipal de Urbanismo Pereira Passos. Rio de Janeiro: Prefeitura da Cidade do Rio de Janeiro, 2012.

Ceceña, Ana Esther. "De saberes y de emancipaciones." In *De los saberes de la dominación y de la emancipación,* edited by Ana Esther Ceceña, 15–35. Buenos Aires: Consejo, 2008.

Davis, Mike. *Planet of Slums.* New York: Verso, 2006.

Deleuze, Gilles, and Félix Guattari. *Rhizom.* Berlin: Merve, 1977.

Dixon, Chris. *Another Politics: Talking Across Today's Transformative Movements.* Oakland: University of California Press, 2014.

Duarte, Fábio. *Space, Place and Territory. A Critical Review on Spatialities.* London: Routledge, 2017.

Editorial El Colectivo, comps. *Reflexiones sobre poder popular.* Buenos Aires: El Colectivo, 2007.

Escobar, Arturo. *Sentipensar con la tierra: Nuevas lecturas sobre desarollo, territorio e diferencia.* Medellin: UNAULA, 2014.

Fanon, Frantz. *Black Skin, White Masks.* London: Pluto Press, 2008.

Fernandes, Bernardo Mançano. "Movimentos socioterritoriais e movimentos socioespaciais: Contribuição teórica para uma leitura geográfica dos movimentos sociais." *Revista Nera* 8, no. 6, (January/June 2005): 14–34.

Fernandez, Annelise Caetano Fraga, and Silvia Regina Nunes. "Territórios-rede de agroecologia: Ciência(s) e saberes locais na ambientalização de lutas na zona oeste e região metropolitana do Rio de Janeiro." Paper presented at the 38th annual meeting of the Brazilian Association of Postgraduate Programs and Research in Social Sciences (ANPOCS), 2014.

Freire, Paulo. *Pedagogia do oprimido*. Rio de Janeiro: Paz e Terra, 2014.

Freunde und Freundinnen der klassenlosen Gesellschaft. "28 Thesen zur Klassengesellschaft." *Kosmoprolet* 1 (2007): 10–51.

Grosfoguel, Ramón. "El concepto de racismo en Michel Foucault y Frantz Fanon: Teorizar desde la zona del ser o desde la zona del no-ser?" *Tabula Rasa*, no. 16 (2012): 79–102.

Haesbaert, Rogério da Costa. *O mito da desterritorialização: do 'fim dos territórios' à multiterritorialidade*. Rio de Janeiro: Bertrand, 2011.

———. *Território e descolonialidade: Sobre o giro (multi)territorial/de(s)colonial na "América Latina."* Buenos Aires: CLACSO, 2021.

———. "Território e multiterritorialidade: um debate." *GEOgraphia* 9, no. 17 (2007): 19–45.

———. *Territórios alternativos*. São Paulo: Contexto, 2002.

———. *Viver no limite: território e multi/transterritorialidade em tempos de in-segurança e contenção*. Rio de Janeiro: Bertrand Brasil, 2014.

Halder, Severin. *Gemeinsam die Hände dreckig machen*. Bielefeld: Transcript, 2018.

Harvey, David. *Spaces of Capital: Towards a Critical Geography*. New York: Routledge, 2001.

———. *Spaces of Global Capitalism: A Theory of Uneven Geographical Development*. New York: Verso, 2006.

———. *Spaces of Hope*. Edinburgh: Edinburgh University Press, 2000.

Holloway, John. *Change the World Without Taking Power. The Meaning of Revolution Today*. London: Pluto Press, 2005.

Kropotkin, Pëtr. *Mutual Aid: A Factor of Evolution*. London: Freedom Press, 1987.

Lander, Edgardo, ed. *A colonialidade do saber*. Buenos Aires: CLACSO, 2005.

Lee, Richard. "Food Security and Food Sovereignty." Centre for Rural Economy Discussion Paper Series No. 11 (2007).

Lefebvre, Henri. *A produção do espaço*. Belo Horizonte: UFMG, 2006.

Lima, Caren Freitas de. "Agricultura na e da cidade do Rio de Janeiro: Dicotomias e as especificidades da agricultura urbana." Master's thesis, Federal Rural University of Rio de Janeiro, 2019.

Lima, Caren Freitas de, et al. "A rede carioca de agricultura urbana e o direito à cidade." *Campo-Território: Revista de Geografia Agrária* 14, no. 34, (December 2019): 313–37.

Machado, Décio, and Raúl Zibechi. *Os Limites do progressismo. Sobre a impossibilidade de mudar o mundo de cima para baixo*. Rio de Janeiro: Consequência, 2017.

Marcos, Subcomandante Insurgente. *Nem o centro e nem a periferia—sobre cores, calendários e geografias*. Porto Alegre: Deriva, 2008.

Maselli, Morgana Mara Vaz da Silva. "Conflitos e resistências na agricultura familiar da cidade do Rio de Janeiro." *Revista Agriculturas* 12, no. 2 (June 2015): 27–32.

Massey, Doreen. *For Space*. London: Sage, 2005.

———. "A Global Sense of Place." *Marxism Today* (June 1991): 24–29.

———. *Space, Place and Gender*. Cambridge: Polity Press, 1994.

McKittrick, Katherine. "On Plantations, Prisons, and a Black Sense of Place." *Social & Cultural Geography* 12 no. 8 (2011): 947–63.

Patel, Raj. "Survival Pending Revolution: What the Black Panthers Can Teach the US Food Movement." In *Food Movements Unite: Strategies to Transform Our Food Systems*, edited by Eric Holt-Giménez, 115–35. Oakland: Food First Books, 2010.

Penna, Marianna. "À procura da comunidade perdida: História e memórias do Movimento das Comunidades Populares." PhD diss., Fluminense Federal University, Niterói, 2016.

Pile, Steve, and Michael Keith, eds. *Geographies of Resistance*. London: Routledge, 1997.

Pimbert, Michel. *Towards Food Sovereignty. Reclaiming Autonomous Food Systems*. London: IIED, 2008.

———. *Transforming Knowledge and Ways of Knowing for Food Sovereignty*. London: IIED, 2006.

Porto-Gonçalves, Carlos Walter. "A Reinvenção dos Territórios: A experiência latino-americana e caribenha." In *Los desafíos de las emancipaciones en un contexto militarizado*, edited by Ana Esther Ceceña, 151–97. Buenos Aires: CLACSO, 2006.

———. "De saberes e de territórios: Diversidade e emancipação a partir da experiência latino-americana." In *De los saberes de la dominación y de la emancipación* edited by Ana Esther Ceceña, 37–52. Buenos Aires: Consejo, 2008.

———. *Geo-grafías. Movimiento sociales, nuevas territorialidades y sustentabilidad*. Mexico City: Siglo XXI, 2001.

Porto-Gonçalves, Carlos Walter, and Rodrigo Torquato da Silva. "Da lógica do favor à lógica do pavor: um ensaio sobre a Geografia da violência na cidade do Rio de Janeiro." *Polis* 28 (2011): 1–28.

Proudhon, Pierre-Joseph. *Do princípio federativo*. São Paulo: Imaginário, 2011.

Santos, Milton, and Maria Laura Silveira. *O Brasil: Território e sociedade no início do século XXI*. São Paulo: Record, 2001.

Saquet, Marcos Aurélio. *Abordagens e concepções de território*. São Paulo: Expressão Popular, 2010.

———. *Saber popular, práxis territorial e contra-hegemonia*. Rio de Janeiro: Consequência, 2019.

Scott, James C. *Seeing Like a State*. New Haven: Yale University Press, 1998.

———. *Los dominados y el arte de resistencia: Discursos ocultos*. Mexico City: Era, 2004.

Silva, Carlos Alberto Franco da. *A modernização distópica do território brasileiro*. Rio de Janeiro: Consequência, 2019.

Smith, Neill. "Geography, Difference and the Politics of Scale." In *Postmodernism and the Social Sciences*, edited by Joe Doherty, Elspeth Graham, and Mo Malek, 57–79. London: Palgrave Macmillan, 1992.

Souza, Marcelo Lopes de. *A prisão e a ágora: Reflexões em torno da democratização do planejamento e da gestão das cidades*. Rio de Janeiro: Bertrand Brasil, 2006.

———. "Autogestão, 'autoplanejamento', autonomia: Atualidade e dificuldades das práticas espaciais libertárias dos movimentos urbanos." *Revista Cidades* 9, no. 15 (2012): 59–93.

———. "Com o estado, apesar do estado, contra o estado: Os movimentos sociais urbanos e sua práticas espaciais entre a luta institucional e a ação política." *Revista Cidades* 7, no. 11 (2010): 13–47.

———. *Dos espaços de controle aos territórios dissidentes: Escritos de divulgação científica e análise política*. Rio de Janeiro: Consequência, 2015.

———. "O território: sobre espaço e poder, autonomia e desenvolvimento." In *Geografia: Conceitos e temas*, edited by Iná Elias de Castro, Paulo Cesar da Costa Gomes, and Roberto Lobato Correa, 77–116. Rio de Janeiro: Bertrand Brasil, 1995.

————. *Os conceitos fundamentais da pesquisa sócio-espacial*. Rio de Janeiro: Bertrand Brasil, 2013.

Sudré, Lu, and Marcos Hermanson. "Cooperativismo no campo gera renda para pequenos agricultores." July 16, 2019, https://mst.org.br/2019/07/16/cooperativismo-no-campo-gera-renda-para-pequenos-agricultores.

Svampa, Maristella. *As fronteiras do neoextrativismo na América Latina: Conflitos socio-ambientais, giro ecoterritorial e novas dependências*. São Paulo: Elefante, 2019.

Tapia, Luis. *Movimientos sociales, movimiento societal y los no lugares de la política: Democratizaciones plebeyas*. La Paz: Muela del Diablo, 2002.

UN-Habitat. *The Challenge of Slums: Global Report on Human Settlements*. London: Earthscan, 2003.

Via Campesina. "The Doha Round is Dead: Time for Food Sovereignty." July 29, 2005. https://viacampesina.org/en/the-doha-round-is-dead-time-for-food-sovereignty.

————. "Food Sovereignty: A Future Without Hunger." 1996. https://viacampesina.org/en/wp-content/uploads/sites/2/2021/11/1996-Rom-en.pdf.

————. "What Is Food Sovereignty?" January 15, 2003. https://viacampesina.org/en/food-sovereignty.

Vivas, Esther. "La Via Campesina: Food Sovereignty and the Global Feminist Struggle." December 18, 2012. https://archive.foodfirst.org/la-via-campesina-food-sovereignty-and-the-global-feminist-struggle.

Wezel, Alexander, S. Bellon, T. Doré, C. Francis, D. Vallod, and C. David. 2009. "Agroecology as a Science, a Movement and a Practice: A Review." *Agronomy for Sustainable Development* 29 (2009): 503–15.

Worldwatch Institute. "Farming the Cities, Feeding an Urban Future." Press release, June 16, 2011. https://cityfarmer.info/farming-the-cities-feeding-an-urban-future-worldwatch-institute.

Zibechi, Raúl. *Autonomía y emancipaciones: América Latina en movimiento*. Lima: UNMSM/Programa Democracia y Transformación Global, 2007.

————. *Brasil potência: Entre a integração regional e um novo imperialismo*. Rio de Janeiro: Consequência, 2014.

————. *Descolonizar: El pensamiento crítico y las prácticas emancipatorias*. Bogotá: Ediciones Desde Abajo, 2014.

————. *Movimientos sociales en América Latina: El "mundo otro" en movimiento*. Mexico City: Bajo Tierra/El Rebozo, 2017.

————. *Territories in Resistance: A Cartography of Latina American Social Movements*. Oakland: AK Press, 2012.

————. *Territorios en resistencia: Cartografía política de las periferias urbanas latino-americanas*. Buenos Aires: Lavaca, 2009.

CHAPTER FOUR

Pacifying Hunger: Lessons from/for Rio's Urban Periphery

Christos Filippidis

—

This essay is the result of two different research paths. It reflects two research projects: NutriCities, which was based at Loughborough University, and Urban Fragility as Military Object, based at Durham University. The two projects attempted, each in its own way, to shed light on the informal space-times of the Rio de Janeiro urban periphery. Favelas comprise a unique environment that has long been a favorite research subject among geographers and, more broadly, among those who investigate urban phenomena. In this sense, this essay is by no means original and admittedly has its limitations (the most fundamental of which is linguistic) as I hesitantly enter the vast field formed by the continuing production of knowledge and discourse on favelas. The initial impetus behind the present essay was the issue of food (in)security in Maré, a cluster of seventeen favela communities in the North Zone of Rio. The starting point was therefore thematically and spatially predetermined. Along the way, however, and as the two research paths intersected at multiple points, it became necessary to reformulate this particular question in terms that had not been visible at the outset. The intention to explore the issue of food (in)security and its link to informal urbanization—a relationship that has become increasingly relevant, as a large part of the so-called Global South continues to be rapidly urbanized—added new dimensions to the initial question when examined in light of urban informality in Rio. It soon became clear that food (in)security is but one of many articulations of the security concept as encountered in the discourse around the favelas. Yet this concept is not only expressed in the form of "human security," a term which has been highlighting, in the language of the international community, the multifaceted vulnerability of populations of the urban periphery since the end of the Cold War, but also in the form of "public security," that is, as a matter of public order.

Tracing the dominant discourse on life in the favelas today, one realizes that the food question is central to a broader debate on poverty, "underdevelopment," and the challenges these raise at the public security level. As currently manifested in the urban periphery of Rio, the food question raises a host of other issues that have long been a concern for governance cadres. First and foremost among them is the question of whether access to food is an indicator, or even a prerequisite, of social peace. In the face of this realization, I have therefore decided to examine the food question in the favelas from what is perhaps a paradoxical perspective. Instead of investigating food (in)security per se, I chose to examine food *in* security, to examine how the food question is being problematized as a matter of public security, and how it is introduced into the planning of related professionals. In order to do so, it is necessary to delve deeper into the security landscape as this has been shaped over the past decade in the urban periphery of Rio. This was the core mission of the second research project. Investigating food in security therefore resides precisely at the intersection of the two aforementioned research paths.

In order to understand Rio's security landscape, we had to examine in detail the policing policies that have been in effect in the favelas in recent years. More specifically, we had to focus on the so-called pacification program, which had already been in place in the municipality of Rio de Janeiro for about ten years at the time when our research began. I therefore decided to shed light on the details of the program, even though it was conducted at a time when the program appeared to be slowly coming to an end. The program may still be formally in force at the time these lines are being written (mid-2019). However, both the election of Jair Bolsonaro as head of the country and Wilson Witzel at the helm of the state of Rio marked, in a sense, a paradigm shift in public security policies and a clear departure from the pacification model, which had been mistakenly seen by many as a "soft power" exercise. By focusing on the pacification operations, I therefore decided to set the day that Bolsonaro and Witzel assumed power, that is, January 1, 2019, as a time limit for the collection of the research material. In short, this essay could not encompass the rapid changes that have taken place and continue to take place in Rio since the election of the two ultraconservative politicians.

The pacification operations were initially advertised as an innovative community policing program that would not only focus on maintaining and restoring order, but would also seek to provide social services to the communities under its supervision by implementing social policy programs. In the context of this ambition, the food question would acquire a very special, though not immediately obvious, position. Looking at the structure and the individual characteristics of the pacification operations, one can see that their originators had indeed attempted to integrate elements of social policy into a policing program. This finding would soon highlight the two key pillars in the design of these operations: security and development, with the latter assuming the form of either economic development or community development within the pacification discourse. This same finding would also force the present research, after thoroughly examining the functionality of this duality within the particular program, on one hand, to look back at the history and, more specifically, at the poisonous legacy left behind by the Cold War period, and on the other, to broaden its geographical scope in order to highlight the central role played by the development-security nexus in the design and implementation of a number of other pacification/counterinsurgency operations (notions that are identical in the vocabulary of police-military science) around the world. It is therefore appropriate to read the operations that are still being carried out in Rio's favelas through the theories and practices of pacification that have been, and are still being, tested in various police and military laboratories around the world today. And that, not simply with a view to making sense of the genealogies of pacification that still cast shadows on life in the favelas today, but also with the aim of understanding the central place occupied by the concept of food in the pacification/counterinsurgency agenda.

It is therefore precisely the understanding of pacification in terms of development and security that has served to highlight the central role played by food in the history of counterinsurgency. Food plays a key role in the latter's repertoire, as counterinsurgency is nothing but a specific political police-military methodology of population management. As the bloody history of counterinsurgency teaches us, the food question is structurally involved in individual police-military planning at both the strategic and tactical levels. I emphasize this involvement, focusing on the ways food is employed both in terms of military operations and development, just as the pacification agenda itself dictates. Moving across the repulsive landscapes of counterinsurgency operations, I seek to understand how food enters into the wider field of strategic and geopolitical planning that has shaped the postcolonial world. At the heart of this planning was also the so-called Green Revolution, a rural modernization program aimed at resolving the global food question that frightened postwar Western cadres at a time when starvation was being examined as a major cause of social unrest, political destabilization, and, ultimately, alignment with the Communist bloc. For this reason, I briefly focus on the particular features of the Green Revolution, aiming to demonstrate how a rural modernization program became, within the American Cold War agenda, a prominent geopolitical tool for countering the question of "Third World insurgency." Brazil has played a key role in the design of this agenda in the broader context of US foreign policy in Latin America. My aim is therefore to reveal how the Green Revolution was implemented in Brazil, how the country's rural landscape was reshaped by its geopolitical goals, and how this reshaping was ultimately decisive in the colossal spatial and demographic changes that have left so many scars on the country since the mid-twentieth century. Following those indelible scars, I found that what is now called Rio's urban informality is largely the result of these changes. In other words, a program of rural modernization implemented within the context of global pacification—the pacification, in effect, of the surplus populations of the capitalist periphery and their food needs—has led to the mass displacement of rural populations and to a new accumulation of surplus life thronging into the urban periphery, which in turn now finds itself to be the object of yet another pacification process.

The remaining concern of this essay is therefore to focus precisely on how the food question developed alongside the ongoing pacification program over the last decade in Rio's favelas. Following up on certain urban agriculture initiatives promoted through the sustainable development agenda—which was largely drawn up by the city of Rio—and supported in one way or another by the pacification program, I attempt to reveal how the issue of food turns into an object of securitization and therefore, an issue of public security policy. The

practical relationships of these initiatives with the pacification operations in certain favelas is explored; critical points and individual goals
within the theoretical framework that supported the promotion of
these initiatives are highlighted, and their involvement in the wider
mission of the pacification program—which is nothing other than the
management of urban informality as such—is examined. By examining
the specificities of this peculiar sustainable development-pacification
nexus through the promotion of urban agriculture, I attempt to reveal
how the interplay of (green) community development and (community) policing sought to formalize the spatial and social relationships
that make up the informal space-times of the urban periphery. The
transition from the grand narratives of modernization and the Green
Revolution to the "humble" declarations of sustainability and green
development thus reveals continuities and discontinuities within the
context of pacification/counterinsurgency. We are able to track these
by following the thread that unravels the issue of food during the peculiar transition from Green Revolution to green governmentality. As we
know, of course, food lies at the core of our biological necessity. The
intention of the present research is to show that it also lies at the core
of police-military planning, thereby blurring the boundaries between
biopolitics and thanatopolitics in the course of history.

Food *in* Security

"What is going to diminish the violence is good policing, more
intelligence work, a police force that is more community-
oriented, a police force that is closer to the population, with
another professional preparation, another civil mentality. All
this is correct. You can do all this. However, if you don't have
food in people's mouths, if you don't have jobs, if you don't
have education and good schools, there will be the possibility
of people falling into criminal behavior."
—Luiz Inácio Lula da Silva

Brazilian president Luiz Inácio Lula da Silva's telling paraphrase of
a classic sociological position, the renowned concept of the "social
question," casts light on the ways this manifests itself in modern Brazil,
and on how it relates to the notion of public security in particular.[1] His
position is certainly not surprising. It follows a long sociological and

criminological tradition of connecting "delinquent" behavior to human material needs. His reference, however, to the issue of food (scarcity)— that is to say, the phenomena of hunger, malnutrition, and food (in) security in general may sound somewhat paradoxical and incomprehensible insofar as it concerns Brazil, one of the largest producers and exporters of agricultural and livestock products in the world. It is especially so when coming out of the mouth of a man who had long declared war on those very phenomena. Yet the case of Brazil, long known for its extreme social contrasts, is a privileged field of reflection over the food question and its troubles, not only because it concerns a key regulator of food production processes around the world, nor because the international community has considered the case of Brazil as a blueprint in tackling the food question through relevant social programs and provisions, but also because it highlights the critical economic and (geo)political implications of food—its production and circulation—and the close, but often invisible, relationships that connect the food question with the theories, technologies, and applications of the security apparatus, as, for example, described by Lula.

The issue of food (in)security is of great concern to the international community today. This is clearly seen, first of all, at the level of governmental rhetoric and discourse. For example, the food question has now been positioned at the top of the global governmental agenda. This is easily understood by looking at the structure of the sustainable development agenda, as this was established following the UN Sustainable Development Summit in September 2015 in New York. The second of the seventeen Sustainable Development Goals adopted, and whose aim is to tackle the global food problem, was titled "Zero Hunger," evidently named after the namesake program (the Zero Hunger Program) implemented in Brazil and engineered by Lula himself. But the critical importance of the food question is first manifested through the endless material outbreaks of hunger and malnutrition, as they continue to take place primarily in the deprived topographies of the capitalist periphery. According to the *Global Report on Food Crises 2018*, for example, "In 2017, almost 124 million people across 51 countries and territories faced *Crisis* levels of acute food insecurity or worse."[2] This is a significant increase when compared with the previous year: "In 2016 the population in need of urgent action was estimated at 108 million across 48 countries."[3] The main reasons however remain the same: protracted conflict and climate shocks—drought in particular.

Yet hunger and malnutrition are by no means natural phenomena, however dependent they may be on the dramatic changes taking place in the natural world today, or on global demographic transformations. As Gustavo Oliveira rightly points out, "We must be careful ... with this discourse that naturalizes scarcity as a given condition of our times. Scarcity cannot be merely viewed as a 'natural' phenomenon; it is embedded in social relations with particular historical geographies. Above all, the current 'scarcity' results from particularly inefficient forms of resource use." He goes on to add: "We must analyze this 'scarcity' in terms of anthropogenic, political and economic struggles taking place simultaneously as conflicts between states, competition between companies and struggles between classes all around the world."[4] The food question has therefore been dependent on specific mechanisms of food production and circulation management for a long time, and is first and foremost subject to market mechanisms, as well as a series of stringent regulations, the most basic of which is obviously its exchange value. The issue of food and its accessibility cannot simply be translated into a simple proportion of the total amount of food produced to the total world population, as it would be in a Malthusian reading. Rather it must be understood in terms of the regulation of production and circulation, and as one of the main objects of economic and political governance today.

To understand the importance of the food question as a governmental—and by extension, a biopolitical—issue we must in a way "naturalize" the debate: we must first consider food in the context of an inescapable biological need/necessity. It is a well-known fact that within the cycle of biological processes, food and water are the most important prerequisites for the biological preservation and reproduction of human life. As such, food occupies the most eminent position in the set of functions that support our biological and existential survival. By virtue of its eminence, it also raises certain demands regarding the circumstances and conditions that must be met in order to satisfy these functions securely. Food quality must be continuously monitored, its quantity constantly assured, and its circulation persistently regulated; all these nutritional parameters must be constantly secured. This is why nutritional phenomena are consistently described in terms of security.

This is also how the notion of food (in)security acquires its meaning, referring as it does to "the lack of secure access to sufficient amounts of safe and nutritious food for normal growth and development and an active and healthy life."[5]

Yet reading the food question as an issue of security does not mean merely assessing its effect on human biological functions, as an issue, that is, of safe consumption at the individual organic level. Rather, it means to perceive it in terms of a population phenomenon established on the basis of certain normalities; as a cohesive element of any human grouping and thus as a structural element of its regular social reproduction. Problematizing food as an issue of security means controlling and regulating dietary quantities, qualities, and flows and understanding them through their interaction with wider population indicators and phenomena. Within this discourse of security, food is perceived not only as a prerequisite for biological preservation at the individual level but also as a precondition for the existence and reproduction of an entire population. And by extension—and one has to be emphatic here—it is perceived as a constitutive element of human communities, that is, of their proper functioning and social peace, and, therefore, as a wider public security issue—just as Lula framed it. Food is an archetypal expression of human existence. And as it resides at the core of our biological necessity, it also constitutes an inescapable biological prerequisite that under certain and extraordinary conditions—that is, conditions of scarcity—may come into tension with the idea of boundaries and restrictions. Not just physical boundaries but also those boundaries outlining the very idea of human grouping. That is to say, pending food needs that remain unfulfilled may manifest themselves as an unavoidable conflict not only with the subject's own bodiness but also with its moral principles, its conscience, its sociability, and ultimately with its sense of community. Furthermore, as we shall see below, the subject may find itself in a fundamental clash with the law that bounds a particular community and regulates the relationships that comprise it. This obviously raises questions concerning the functioning of human groupings and instantly turns the food question into a social one: a question of population problematization and management—and therefore, a broader security issue.

As a universal common biological truth, food necessity therefore imposes certain objective and nonnegotiable limits on the subject.

Breaking these results in the release of a deregulating, undermining, and destructive energy. An energy that is sometimes inward—in the form of biological deterioration or suspension that remains within the confines of an individual, interior physical decline—and sometimes outward, in the form of rebellious action that demands from its immediate environment the means to meet and satisfy any need. According to the teachings of political philosophy, and more specifically, those of the founding philosophers of the state, this outward movement is capable of causing rifts in common human space, disrupting its regular function and consequently threatening social peace and social cohesion.[6] This outward movement and the fear it generates constitute, in the narratives of the theorists of governance, a founding element for the very legitimacy of a higher authority that regulates and circumscribes human needs and relationships. More specifically, they are the basis upon which the notion of the state is founded with all its attendant protective, controlling, repressive, and regulatory frameworks. This is why the food question and its threatening potential have long become an area of governmental control and management. It is for this reason that we must look more closely at the relationship between food and the notion of (public) security. We must examine, in other words, food *in* security. Therefore, if food (in)security refers mostly to the internalized and subcutaneous outbursts of necessity, food *in* security brings its exteriority to light. By revisiting and rephrasing this notion, which has become so popular as of late, we will strive to position food, this primary necessity, in the discourses and practices of public security.

To look at the food question from the perspective of security does not simply mean to understand its governmental dimensions as mere expressions of a preventive and protective mechanism that aims to safeguard the normalities and prevent the deregulation of population phenomena: to safeguard, in other words, the smoothness of social reproduction. It also entails exploring how food is deliberately transformed into a tool of population control, social engineering, and the exercise of power. This is because its eminent biological importance, in all its irreversible and addictive dimensions, can turn food into a tool for a totalitarian management of human existence. Our close and constant dependence on food and water transforms both these (re) sources and their circulation into a biopolitical field for the exercise of power and population control. In short, within the context of the nonnegotiable and inescapable processes of survival, the food question serves to highlight something that, besides being a primal human dependency, is also a privileged field for managing life itself. Because by controlling the production and circulation of food one can easily control the preservation and reproduction of an entire population and therefore determine the probabilities and conditions of its very survival. In this way, this biopolitical field is in certain cases transformed into a laboratory of applied thanatopolitics. It is therefore important to problematize food on the one hand as a field of governmental regulation and intervention and, on the other, as a domain for the exercise of power. It is important for us to understand, that is, not just how power is exercised through food but also how food affects the exercise of power, the design of political agendas, the implementation of governmental practices and even the conduct of war itself. To explore how food is involved in the regulation of biological needs and population phenomena as well as in the production of subjects and the regulation of social relations as a whole.

Whether as an issue of safe individual consumption, of population preservation and social reproduction, or of exercising power, the food question takes on its vital importance precisely because it is (im) posed in terms of primary necessity. It therefore acquires a certain significance as the notion of necessity haunts all of human history and underlines the strong dependence of much of our social, political, and cultural reality on the inescapability of our bodily needs. From the very beginning, (bodily) necessity lies not only at the heart of any social constitution and political institution but also at the core of philosophy itself: loaded, to a great extent, with a certain structural negativity/externality. It is a notion that has repeatedly caused philosophy embarrassment and repulsion alike. Unattractive to thinkers, it has been variously labeled "antijuridical"[7] or "antipolitical."[8] If we were to look at the history of Western philosophy overall, and that of political philosophy in particular, we would see that human thought has most persistently been plagued by notions understood through their relationship to necessity, and to its bodily expressions in particular. Think of binaries such as *oikos/polis*, private/public, *zoe/ bios*, and notions such as freedom, security, happiness, violence, work, toil, or pain: together, they comprise a conceptual sum that originated from the dialogue with the inescapable reality imposed by our bodily necessity.[9] For Epicurus, for example, true pleasure arises when "the stomach is soon full, the body satisfied"; it is "the calm that takes hold in the soul once the tensions of the body disappear."[10] For Aristotle, humanity's bond to its bodily needs constitute the boundary between mere natural life and political life; between ζωή/zoe and βίος/bios.[11] And for Socrates "the genuine philosopher disdains food ... because his 'concern is not for the body' but for 'the soul,'" as Maria Christou points out. Socrates "does not only seem to oppose body to soul and food to philosophy ...but also food to 'proper' humanness."[12] More generally, as Hannah Arendt reminds us, the distinction "between activities related to a common world and those related to the maintenance of life" was considered self-evident and axiomatic for ancient political thought as a whole: "To be free meant ... not to be subject to the necessity of life."[13]

In addition, as Giorgio Agamben shows, necessity must be understood as the origin of the law: "Necessity constitutes, so to speak, the ultimate ground and very source of the law."[14] Dwelling briefly upon the relationship between necessity and law, we would notice this lies at the core of both modern political philosophy and the philosophy of law: after all, the very notion of the state is founded upon the tension generated by their encounter. According to Santi Romano, "It is to necessity that the origin and legitimation of the legal institution par excellence, namely, the state, and its constitutional order in general, must be traced back."[15] Similarly, Mark Neocleous writes, in his study of the basic principles of liberalism and John Locke's thought in particular: "The underlying basis of the exercise of power is necessity."[16] As a consequence, we need to trace the beginnings of the law itself as made by the state in necessity. But the relationship between necessity and law is proving to be more complicated: necessity does not simply constitute the zero point of the law—it is also its conditional end. More specifically, necessity may legitimately lead to the suspension of the law—in the sense that this possibility is provided by law itself—when circumstances dictate so. The renowned concept of the state of exception or state of emergency indicates precisely the compelling presence of necessity, either as constitutive force or as a radical caesura in the very body of law.[17]

Necessity therefore maintains a close relationship with the state and its law—whether as the actual basis of the law or as its conditional suspension. However, necessity—and here lies the crux of this entire debate—also maintains a close relationship with violence. Not only with the lawmaking and law-preserving violence of the state, as Walter Benjamin would put it, but also with the violence that comes "from the outside" in order to abolish it; that is, revolutionary social violence.[18] Arendt reaches the same conclusion when she locates the necessity that lies at the core of human biological preservation and reproduction at the root of revolutions, with "violence and necessity being in motion and dragging everything and everybody into their streaming movements."[19] Critically drawing on the lessons of the French Revolution, Arendt shows us how "the irresistibility of violence" was linked "with the necessity which we ascribe to natural processes, not because natural science used to describe the processes in terms of necessary laws, but because we experience necessity to the extent that we find ourselves, as organic bodies, subject to necessary and irresistible processes."[20] Managing this elemental necessity—which in times of revolution/insurgency and crisis is often expressed as elemental violence and demands immediate release from the burdens of life—therefore becomes the primary task of the state and the focus of its security apparatus.[21] The figure of the hungry crowd makes regular appearances over the course of human history. Food has historically been the driving force behind plebeian uprisings, social unrest, political claims, and revolutions. And this is well-known to the cadres of governance, especially when it concerns the production of urban space. As Michel Foucault reminds us during his study of a particular historical period in which the very food question was shaping a new governmental paradigm: "The immediate and most perceptible consequences of scarcity appear first of all, of course, in the urban milieu, since it is always relatively less difficult to withstand food shortage—relatively—in a rural milieu. Anyway, it appears in the urban milieu and, with great probability, almost immediately leads to revolt. Now after the experiences of the seventeenth century, urban revolt is, for sure, the major thing for government to avoid."[22]

This insurrectional potential inherent in food necessity is clearly no mere object of historical contemplation. Quite to the contrary, in this time of global food crises and high food inflation, it still haunts the planning of governance cadres.[23] Returning to Lula's position for a moment, we would note that this hungry collective subject that he refers to is nothing but a modern manifestation of the hungry mob—those who are subject to the most powerful necessity that imbues our bodies, which Arendt positioned at the center of the modern perception of history and its own "necessities."[24] It is the actor par excellence of the renowned "social question" that was formulated later, in the nineteenth century, as a distinct sociological problem and which has been keeping governance cadres busy ever since. However, as Patricia Owens reminds us, "the Social Question was not about human suffering per se. The problem was not primarily with the existence of mass poverty itself, but with its consequences on 'social' cohesion and political order."[25] Lula, therefore, does not seem to engage in a compassionate contemplation of the outcasts of this world. Instead, he focuses on the revolutionary, insurrectional, and ultimately dangerous potentialities that this mass of hungry people carries with it. He knows full well that there can be no social peace without food in people's mouths. What lies at the heart of Lula's claim is obvious: public order cadres have to bend over the material needs of the poor and marginalized in order to pacify them and hold at bay their revolutionary instincts; or in the case of Rio, to keep them away from the unmapped landscapes of illicit or shadow economies and the violence these are identified with.

Security as Pacification

Lula's claim was made in July 2008, during an interview on Rio's public security policies.[26] An extremely ambitious police program was to be launched in the municipality of Rio de Janeiro a few months later: the so-called pacification program was specifically designed to address public security issues in the favelas. In the wake of announcements that Brazil would be hosting two consecutive sporting mega-events, the 2014 FIFA World Cup and the 2016 Rio Olympic Games, public security policies were redesigned largely with the favelas in mind; mainly the favelas that bordered sports venues hosting the games, main thoroughfares, or tourist areas in the city's Southern Zone. Public security was a key prerequisite for the emergence of Rio and, by extension, of Brazil as a place ripe for investment, mass tourism, and capitalist development. This is also evidenced by the fact that in 2008, just a few months before the notorious Pacifying Police Units (Unidade de Polícia Pacificadora [UPP]) inaugurated the pacification program by making their appearance in the Santa Marta favela, Lula ordered the

Ministry of Defense to publish the first "National Defense Strategy" in the history of the country. A highly symbolic move that sought to demonstrate to the international community that Brazil would be a safe host for the two upcoming sporting events in the country.[27]

Pacification was not merely a response to the public security issues urgently raised by the two mega-events, however. It was also an addition—in theory at least—to a series of interventions and reforms in the field of public security that sought to gradually democratize security forces and rid them of the authoritarian logic inherited by the military government (1964–85). The 1988 constitution would essentially mark the transition to a new era that sought to get rid of the authoritarian legacy of past decades, instead emphasizing the protection of human rights. The democratization of the country's political life and its security forces alike was both a challenge and a promise, especially for Lula's left-wing government. This would, in a sense, attempt to redirect the country back onto the left-wing path set by João Goulart before his violent overthrow by the 1964 coup d'etat. Pacification is meant to follow the spirit of this "democratic" shift and is based on a "holistic" conception of public security: instead of focusing on the management of violence as a social symptom alone, it also aims to tackle its root causes. In practice, this is done through community/proximity policing and, secondarily, through an intervention policy aimed at community development, with particular focus on infrastructure and social provisions. Pacification sought—in theory at least—to distance itself from a notion of public security that was based on restoring public order alone. Instead, it highlighted the importance of social inequalities in the production of crime and violence and took certain initiatives to improve day-to-day life. In the words of José Mariano Beltrame, minister of public order of the state of Rio for the period 2007–16: "The UPPs have come to stay. It is not just a security project; it is a state policy of life improvement and hope development for the people of Rio de Janeiro."[28]

Pacification operations, as a specific conceptualization of public security, have already been in effect for a decade—even though they seem to be officially coming to an end. Many have been referring to them as a program that failed to achieve the goals it set for itself, despite its having been presented as an innovative public security program. After all, pacification has only concerned a small proportion of Rio's population to date: 38 Pacifying Police Units were deployed in total, which served 264 out of the nearly 1,000 favelas spread across the city.[29] This is also confirmed by the program's original scope "to 'pacify' around 30 favelas each year up to 2016."[30] Even though Michel Temer signed a presidential decree on February 16, 2018, mandating the armed forces to maintain law and order on the streets of Rio, this did not signal the end of the pacification program. It did, however, certainly outline its finite potential as well as the federal government's intention to bypass the state of Rio and the local security authorities alike in the short term.[31] Nevertheless, an investigation into the characteristics and implications of the pacification plan is still of interest. This is not only because pacification units remain active in some areas, even if their numbers have been shrinking, but mainly because the program, as argued by Beltrame above, is "not just a security project": rather, it constitutes a paradigm of the problematization of public security and a privileged field of study for understanding the issues and links between public security and modern urban phenomena, in light of a wider urban agenda that does not focus exclusively on Rio. Pacification operations in particular allow us the opportunity to shed some light upon the present dominant framework, as constituted by the development-security nexus. This is important because, by understanding the crucial role of development within the public security agenda, we can in turn come to understand the food question itself as an object of securitization.

While the contact point between the food question and pacification operations may not be visible at first glance, there is a certain thread that connects them. Pacification operations do not simply constitute a public security policy but, as Beltrame has already pointed out and as we shall see later on, it is also a broader problematization and management of the "social question" as this has been manifesting itself for decades in the Brazilian landscapes of urban informality.[32] Inevitably, food needs comprise one of the objects of this management process—being as they are a fundamental element of the "social question." To better understand their place in the pacification context, we must consider them, as already mentioned, as an object of public security. We must evaluate them, that is, in light of specific policies of favela intervention and of broader public order policy reform. We must also underline the specificity of the operations in Rio in light of the knowledge and information we have at our disposal today concerning other pacification operations around the world, from the end of World War II onward, and the emphasis of the latter on the development-security nexus. In so doing we will be able to understand both the idioms of pacification as a special category of military-police operations and the role of food in its related theories and practices. Finally, we must read the modern food question through the changes that occurred in the second half of the twentieth century in the field of agricultural production in the country. As we shall see, these changes are linked both to a wider pacification operation that had been in full swing globally at the time, but also with the production of urban space overall, and urban informality in the city of Rio in particular.

"Pacification" is no random or unfortunate choice for a term. Quite to the contrary, one would be hard-pressed to believe that the heavy semantic load it carries escaped the designers of the operation. As Neocleous shows us, pacification as a concept first appeared in 1599, when Captain Bernardo de Vargas Machuca wrote *Milicia Indiana*, "the world's first manual of counter-revolutionary warfare."[33] However, it gradually established itself as a specific military-police methodology between the late nineteenth century and the Second World War as part of the colonial operations of France, Britain, and the United States.[34] Its fundamental theoretical corpus and practice ultimately become entrenched within military science, almost like an epistemological paradigm, during the decolonization era. The aim here was to suppress the popular uprisings and guerrilla movements that were breaking out in various parts of the capitalist periphery. Pacification is essentially a synonym for counterinsurgency (COIN). Therefore, the operations that take place in Rio cannot be considered a Brazilian exception, either in terms of terminology or operationally. Rather, they must be understood as yet another part of, and as a modern expression of, this particular military-police tradition. They should be interpreted through the tools and methodologies of counterinsurgency. As to whether or not this interpretation is valid, let us first turn to the experts. According to US diplomats in Brazil: "The Favela Pacification Program shares some characteristics with US counter-insurgency doctrine and strategy in Afghanistan and Iraq. Like counter-insurgency, the population is the true center of gravity, and the program's success will ultimately depend not only on effective and sustained coordination between police and state/municipal governments but also on favela residents' perception of the legitimacy of the state."[35]

David Kilcullen, perhaps the most important counterinsurgency theorist today, seems to be thinking along the same lines. Describing pacification operations in the Rocinha favela, he writes: "Patrols roam the narrow streets on foot and by motorcycle, working the areas between outposts and checkpoints, in an operational pattern that looks a lot like a police-led version of urban counterinsurgency, Baghdad style."[36] Robert Muggah and Albert Souza Mulli also concede that "there are uncanny similarities between Rio's pacification strategy and ongoing counterinsurgency operations in Afghanistan and elsewhere."[37]

Yet in addition to the assessments provided by the experts above, it is also important to consider this question within the context of the contemporary counterinsurgency doctrine. First of all, it is obvious that, in the case of Rio, we are not dealing with any organized insurgency of the kind that surfaced during the Cold War or during the campaigns in Iraq and Afghanistan. However, as far as police-military experts are concerned, this does not mean that the security environment in Rio and the ongoing pacification operations there cannot be interpreted using the counterinsurgency vocabulary. When one examines the relevant military discourse and terminology, what becomes immediately noticeable is that the terms by which the phenomenon of insurgency is being problematized change over time. On the notional level, insurgency does not appear to constitute an atemporal, ahistorical notion for military cadres. To the contrary, it is a notion characterized by a distinct plasticity—taking on, as it does, different meanings as the global geopolitical landscapes, the actors involved, and the nature of the challenges raised at both the national and public security levels change over time. And as the counterinsurgency discourse shows, it is a concept nowadays identified with a wide range of phenomena, challenges, and security risks in which traditional "insurgency," in the way we had perceived it until recently, is but one phenomenon among others.

According to the current US Army counterinsurgency manual, "An insurgency is the organized use of subversion and violence to seize, nullify, or challenge political control of a region" (meaning to wrest political control of a region from the state). Counterinsurgency respectively constitutes those "comprehensive civilian and military efforts designed to simultaneously defeat and contain insurgency and address its root causes."[38] Based on these definitions one would be right to conclude that a specific kind of insurgency has been taking place in Rio since the mid-1980s and that the pacification operations could indeed be viewed as counterinsurgency operations. The common admission by security experts that the state is not merely absent in the favelas but also essentially unable to be present there, further testifies to the fact that political control of the region is being challenged. It is precisely on the basis of this impossible state presence that the favelas are described as ungoverned spaces and occupied territories[39] and the broader city of Rio as a fragile city—a "paradigmatic fragile city" according to Muggah— or even a feral city.[40] What links up all these definitions is precisely the phenomenon of ungovernability—that is, the absence of the state and of state control—that characterizes certain regions.

But what exactly challenges state control in these regions? How does this insurgency in the informal neighborhoods of Rio manifest itself? It does so in the form of armed nonstate actors, as they are called, mainly drug gangs, which operate and control specific areas in the favelas. Counterinsurgency therefore takes the form of a war on gangs. The pacification program focuses precisely on reestablishing state control in these areas and consolidating its presence in every possible way. Problematizing these phenomena of ungovernability—and gang violence in particular—through the counterinsurgency vocabulary has long been a common place in public security debates and is by no means restricted to Rio. As Kristian Williams points out, "A growing body of literature now specifically argues that gang violence should be treated as a type of insurgency."[41] This is clearly shown, for example, in the current US counterinsurgency doctrine, and in the so-called "theory of competitive control" proposed by Kilcullen.[42] It is also evident in the multitude of literature sources currently focusing on issues of gang violence, illicit economies, and organized crime, which present their interpretations and methodologies through the prism of counterinsurgency.[43]

According to Kilcullen's theory of competitive control, for example, "In irregular conflicts (that is, in conflicts where at least one combatant is a nonstate armed group), the local armed actor that a given population perceives as best able to establish a predictable, consistent, wide-spectrum normative system of control is most likely to dominate that population and its residential area." These local actors may be "urban street gangs, communitarian or sectarian militias, insurgents, bandits, pirates, armed smugglers or drug traffickers, violent organized criminal networks, vigilantes and armed public defender groups, terrorist organizations, warlord armies, and certain paramilitary forces."[44] What is striking in the above statement is not the plethora of actors who challenge state control in some parts of this world today, but the crucial role taken on by the notion of population in relation to the power and ultimately the very existence of those actors. As a notion, population is essentially the center of gravity of counterinsurgency theory. And we can start from here in identifying some initial links to the previous part's observations.

Looking back on the classical theorists of counterinsurgency, one would note that pacification does not constitute a representative category of military or police operations. It is not a typical "adversary-centric" or "enemy-centric," "red versus blue" kind of approach,[45] but is rather constituted on the basis of "population-centric" terms.[46] For example, the counterinsurgency expert John Nagl writes in his foreword to David Galula's foundational work, *Counterinsurgency Warfare*, that, for an insurgent, "the civilian population is its main target and also the battlefield on which the war is fought. Key terrain in an insurgency is not the physical space, but the political loyalty of the people who inhabit that space."[47] So at the heart of counterinsurgency theory is the position that the strongest weapon at the insurgents' disposal is nothing else but their relationship with local populations and communities. The advantage of an irregular enemy is a social and political, not a military, one. It is for this reason that military machines have been focusing on this very relation between insurgents and the materialities, phenomena, and social networks that make up the population—and it is here that the staggering importance of pacification/counterinsurgency lies today.

Civilians have therefore moved from being a protected entity, as they were, for example, according to the law of war and the normative narratives of international law for Europe and the so-called civilized world. They have now ended up becoming the actual field of military operations themselves. They have become the "social milieu" with its particular class, racial, and gender characteristics, within which the enemy resides and which must be transformed in such a way that will allow the enemy to be displaced physically as well as politically.[48] The well-known Maoist dictum according to which the population is to the guerrilla as water is to fish has become the main motto of counterinsurgency think tanks. Military operations would therefore soon spread beyond the physical terrain and into the so-called human terrain[49]—that "flesh-and-blood terrain"[50]—and would be planned on the basis of a strong population/territory dependence. The relationship between insurgents/guerrillas and wider population groups made the counterinsurgency forces focus directly on this relationship, which consequently became a new field of intervention. Pacification, therefore, becomes established when population phenomena and needs begin to be problematized as a specific object of military management and as a field of operations per se. Which, as Patricia Owens shows us, is a phenomenon of decolonization, at least as far as European military machines are concerned.[51] This element carries an originating gravity, in the sense that, if we understand the biopolitical significance of the notion and the phenomena of population for military practices, we can then provide an interpretative framework for a number of contemporary phenomena and thus perceive their lineage. One of them is the pacification program that has been in effect in Rio for over a decade.

The purpose of these operations in Rio is therefore to regain state control over specific territories and their populations. The field in which these operations are conducted is therefore first and foremost the human environment itself. What the relevant theory and its individual applications then show is that the war on gangs does not aim exclusively at combating these, as would be the case with typical "enemy-centric' approaches. Rather, it raises issues of political/social legitimacy and control over individual areas and populations Designing the public security agenda therefore rests on understanding broader socio-spatial phenomena. And by extension, the aim of pacification is to manage these phenomena in particular, not just any armed or criminal activity. This is precisely what Lula demonstrates when addressing the public security challenges posed by the spatial accumulation of poverty and the material needs of the populations in the urban periphery. This is because crime and the surplus populations that are squeezed in the chaotic landscapes of urban informality constitute, in a sense, communicating vessels. In the dominant view of criminologists, security experts, development theorists, and police-military cadres, any sections of the population that cannot meet their basic needs within the formal economy may resort to informal activities, criminal activities, or violence, and may possibly be recruited by existing gangs in order to make a living.[52] Pacification, therefore, focuses on those potentialities and not simply on gangs that control particular areas, ultimately understanding "surplus life as a threat to order."[53] As Neocleous puts it, "The war [on drugs] has paved the way for the pacification of groups perceived as the least useful and most dangerous parts of the population, of regions regarded as 'ungovernable' and borders regarded as 'insecure.'"[54]

The question of regaining control of an "ungoverned/ungovernable" territory proves to be a multidimensional one in practice. According to Saskia Sassen, "The emerging roles of major gangs in cities such as São Paulo contribute to produce and/or strengthen types of territorial fractures that the project of building a nation-state sought to eliminate or dilute."[55] Based on this particular reading, these gangs do not merely engage in "criminal" activities within the discontinuous geographies formed by these fractures but substitute for the state itself: they undertake, that is, a number of state functions and provide social benefits, covering the basic needs of populations in the areas they control. And, "they ... obtain freedom of action and, crucially, legitimacy and support from the local population," utilizing what Vanda Felbab-Brown calls the political capital of illicit economies.[56] Pacification operations therefore aim at intervening directly in the field shaped by social relations themselves—relationships between gangs and local populations, relationships based on material needs and interests, and relationships based on silence and enforced by the fear of reprisals. These operations seek to (re)legitimize the state and delegitimize gangs in the eyes of the population, and to maintain the constant presence of security forces in the areas where these gangs are active. In other words, we are faced with a proper battle to win hearts and minds.[57]

The notion of the population therefore plays a leading role in the context of pacification; in a sense, it constitutes both the field itself and the object of these operations. This is why population phenomena (and the food question among them) are of central importance. In Rio's case, the pacification program clearly follows the typical "population-centric" logic of counterinsurgency. As explained, the object of pacification includes entire regions and their populations, not just armed gangs operating in those areas; it presupposes recovering control over both the physical and the human terrain.[58] But this recovery is not attempted exclusively by force; on the contrary, it follows the familiar carrot and stick method. Pacification in Rio, as in other bloody police and military laboratories around this planet, is not limited to law enforcement and the restoration of order alone. Instead, it is a typical example of the interlocking of security and development, as dictated by the fundamental principles of counterinsurgency theory. As the current US counterinsurgency field manual points out, "All population groups are controlled by some combination of consent and coercion."[59] The notion of development in this debate therefore emerges to provide the first part of this combination because force alone does not suffice in order to achieve the legitimacy of the state, nor to secure popular support for it. As Patrick Donley puts it, "Economic development is the provision of sufficient basic services, infrastructure, and economic essentials to garner popular support and engender government legitimacy."[60] This is the fundamental reasoning behind the development-security nexus, where development is problematized as security technology, given that "development reduces poverty and hence the risk of future instability."[61] Development should therefore be viewed as a (sometimes preventive) counterinsurgency technology, a method of remodeling the social milieu at hand, and as a social engineering tool, as we shall see. Development should be understood as a means of containing the challenges and threats posed by the accumulation of poverty in the favelas, "managing and containing the effects of underdevelopment."[62]

The presence of development within the public security agenda—especially when articulated in terms of community development—should not be surprising, particularly when it comes to pacification/counterinsurgency. As Austin Long points out in reference to the formation of postwar counterinsurgency theory, "The initial focus of COIN research was on the problems of modernization and economic development."[63] As for the term "pacification" itself, he stresses that "it will be used to mean the combination of security and development in a given unit of political administration (e.g., village, neighborhood, province)."[64] The two are intimately related, as development without security is hostage to insurgents and security without development provides little (though some) incentive to support the government. The presence of development within the pacification/

counterinsurgency agenda is therefore by no means accidental. And not simply because, as Mark Duffield notes, the long lineage of the relationship between security and development goes back to the beginnings of liberal ideology.[65] But also because during the postwar period, when the main corpus of counterinsurgency theory was being formed, the notion of international development also emerged as a venture "focused primarily on building nation-states from the former colonies through modernization and economic transformation."[66] As Duffield points out, "It was not until the early part of the twentieth century and, especially, following decolonization, that development took on its present geopolitical and human focus."[67] Development, therefore, has been playing a leading role in counterinsurgency policies implemented since the end of World War II and across various regions of strategic importance. The current US counterinsurgency doctrine also highlights this fact: "internal defense and development," we read, "is the full range of measures taken by a nation to promote its growth and protect itself from subversion, lawlessness, insurgency, terrorism, and other threats to its security."[68] These are the two complementary categories of political-military actions that, according to French general Jacques Allard, constitute the mission of pacification: destruction and construction.[69]

However, the bloody history of counterinsurgency clearly teaches us that if there is something that characterizes it, something that overcame the resistance of populations—wherever this happened—this was neither "construction" nor development: it was organized violence, population displacement and containment, and planned destruction. In addition, in the case of Rio, we know that pacification operations are based primarily on security—and its most militarized manifestations in particular—and less so on development.[70] However, we also know that the city has long been a field of continuous militarization of public security, the exercise of state violence and human rights violations—and it is even officially a military testing laboratory today. In the words of army general Walter Souza Braga Netto, the commanding officer responsible for the implementation of the presidential decree that called for the aforementioned federal intervention: "Rio de Janeiro is a laboratory for Brazil."[71] Judging from the outcomes so far, the city has turned into a laboratory of applied necropolitics. "Violence has increased since the federal intervention in Rio de Janeiro began in

February 2018," write Juliana Cesario Alvim Gomes and Andrés del Río. "According to the Intervention Observatory report, the facts are alarming: from February 16 to April 15, 1502 shootings were reported, which resulted in 284 deaths and 193 people injured.... Crossfires also produced 12 massacres and 52 casualties."[72] According to the same data, "The number of people killed in the two months of the federal intervention more than doubled compared to the same period in 2017."[73] The final report for 2018 is indicative: "Rio's security forces had their deadliest year on record in 2018, with 1,444 police killings" writes Anna Jean Kaiser, while Júlia Dias Carneiro reports 1,532 murders by the police—an increase which according to the coordinator of the Violence Analysis Laboratory, Ignacio Cano, was clearly dictated by federal intervention directives.[74] This toll would not surprise the inhabitants of the favelas, as "the Military Police of Rio de Janeiro is considered the most lethal one in Brazil, having killed over eight thousand people in the last decade": the exact same decade in which the pacification program has been in effect.[75]

While these numbers reveal a series of unpleasant truths for the program's supporters, they also highlight the essence of the debate. They make us aware of the fact that pacification is nothing but an actual military operation aimed at the "fabrication of a social order," and as such it sows death and destruction.[76] It is an operation which reminds us that behind the references to "peace" and "pacification" lies war or, as Foucault would put it, "Beneath the omissions, the illusions, and the lies of those who would have us believe in the necessities of nature or the functional requirements of order, we have to rediscover war: war is the cipher of peace."[77] These numbers reveal that, just like the other bloody examples that preceded it, this operation is based primarily on destruction: destruction as method. They reveal that development not only constitutes a necessary supplement to security but also presupposes it. And this is empirically proven by looking, for example, at the framework in which these operations were planned.

The framework in question is based on the four successive stages: tactical intervention, stabilization, unit establishment, and evaluation and monitoring. This operational framework constitutes an additional reminder of the effect that the US counterinsurgency dogma has had on the operations conducted in Rio, as it has similarities with corresponding American frameworks. In broader terms, we would say that it follows the "clear-hold-build" logic that contemporary counterinsurgency operations are based on.[78] In strictly operational terms, during the first stage of the plan the more militarized troops of the Brazilian police, the Special Police Operations Battalion (Batalhão de Operações Policiais Especiais [BOPE]) and the Riot Police Battalion (Batalhão de Polícia de Choque [BPChoque]), invade specific favelas. This invasion takes place, where necessary, "with the support of substantial, battalion-sized and heavily equipped units of the Brazilian Army or Marines."[79] The aim of these forces is to "clear" local gangs from these areas, before handing control over to the Pacifying Police Units (UPPs), which will then position themselves there for as long as necessary. The operation thus moves into its second phase, which involves direct contact with the community as dictated by the aforementioned operational framework. This contact manifests itself in two ways: One is through community or proximity policing practices—or through the permanent and stable presence of Pacifying Police Units in these areas (the "hold" stage). The other is through the implementation of community development programs and the construction of infrastructures that aim to improve the quality of life in these areas (the "build" stage). Here security precedes development—just like in the classic examples of postconflict stabilization and reconstruction.[80] By drawing on the theory of nation-building, and projecting its core principles upon the urban scale, we discover exactly the same logic at work: "Security is an essential precondition for productive investment."[81]

Much could be said for this direct contact with the community. I would like to highlight just one of these points, temporarily diverging from my main argument. This point concerns the widespread claim that community/proximity policing is the opposite of militarization, as an expression of soft power over hard power. The question here is not whether these operations are governed by the spirit of community or proximity policing. It is rather to show that, first, the logic of community policing lies at the core of counterinsurgency theory and practice, and second, not only does it not conflict with the logic of militarization but on the contrary, community policing complements this logic.[82] These operations are in their essence typical examples of applied counterinsurgency. As Williams rightly observes, this is nothing but a combination of militarization and community policing.[83] In Rio, as elsewhere, militarization is a vital supplement and a prerequisite for community policing. In this sense, there is no conflict between the two as public security methods.[84] This is evidenced as much by the direct involvement of the armed forces and the most militarized police forces in the operations in question, and by the fact that the armed forces have been repeatedly and independently called upon to restore order in the ten years that the pacification program has been in effect.

However, this involvement of the armed forces is not an incongruity, nor does it in any way undermine the "population-centric" spirit of pacification and community policing. This is because pacification/counterinsurgency, as a particular operational modality, demands from the outset the collaboration of police and military forces—that is, the military is expected to undertake a series of police activities that essentially constitute population mapping and management, and which are ultimately aimed at enforcing and maintaining social peace. But it is also because the Brazilian army specifically has a long experience in pacification and stabilization operations, and therefore its presence on the streets of Rio could in no way prove incompatible with the overall spirit of the pacification program. As Maíra Siman and Victória Santos point out, the Brazilian military's leading of the United Nations Stabilization Mission in Haiti (2004–17) shows vast similarities to the pacification operations in Rio—both at the level of applied methods and at the level of understanding the operational environment.[85] In any case, pacification allows us the opportunity to look beyond normative dichotomies such as war/peace or army/police, and to realize that, within the context of capitalist accumulation and the security state it requires, "war and police are always already together"; that is, "war and police as processes working in conjunction as state power."[86]

Admittedly the literature on the militarization of public security in Rio is already fairly extensive today and we will not dwell further on this. Let us end this brief diversion by examining, on the contrary, the other means of daily contact with the community, that is, the "build" stage. By investigating the role of "construction" in this program, and highlighting the role of this ostensible (community) development, we will be better able to understand the importance of development and, by extension, the position of the food question in the context of pacification and the wider development-security nexus. As illustrated earlier, in the postwar era pacification was linked to the modernization of the capitalist periphery.[87] The end of World War II marks the transition to a time when the notion of development would assume the decisive role fairly evidently assigned to it by security cadres: as a measure of counterinsurgency, whether preventive or not, and as a measure of pacification of populations and their needs. The notion of development was thus at the heart of this political-military debate and, as will be shown later, largely related to the (global) food question. Development surfaced in the modernization theories of the time as a factor in stabilizing the capitalist periphery and its surplus populations. Within the Cold War context, "hunger and poverty were no longer seen as the universal human condition but as a danger to international stability."[88] Poverty and underdevelopment were in this way problematized as security threats because they were the cause of social unrest, radical demands, and potential reasons for aligning with the communist bloc at the time.

This rationale required, along with the deployment of military force, the introduction of measures aimed at improving the living conditions of these populations. This move was clearly based on self-interest on the part of Western powers, which perceived social instability in the periphery as a threat to their own national security and national interests, thus making "modernization an instrument of Cold War strategy."[89] Development packages delivered at that time, mainly in the context of US foreign policy and largely as part of a nation-building policy, were therefore strategies to contain this threat and policies seeking to manage and contain the effects of underdevelopment. The same preventive rationale guides policies regarding the so-called fragile states today, where we observe "the reinvention of development as a civilian form of counter-insurgency" in the name of a self-proclaimed "responsibility to reconstruct."[90] This rationale is also at the heart of Lula's original position, now applied at the urban level of this "paradigmatic fragile city," and which essentially drives the pacification operations on its streets. As Siman and Santos make clear, the implementation of pacification's social agenda effectively means "the deployment of 'social projects' only to the degree necessary to control the risk posed by vulnerable populations."[91]

This preventive role was initially taken up at the pilot stage, two years after the pacification program was officially launched, by a specialized body called UPP Social. According to a World Bank report, "The 'post-occupation' phase of the UPP model comes with the entrance of UPP Social, the social development arm of the program that aims to coordinate social services in these areas and thereby integrate the favelas into the rest of the city."[92] The arrival of UPP Social marks, in theory, the transition to the so-called social occupation phase, where this specialized body undertakes the implementation of specific social programs in the context of a particular kind of armed social work whose aim was crime prevention and the "providing of sustainability to the pacification" in certain communities.[93] The UPP Social program was piloted in 2010 and officially launched a year later, under the auspices of the municipal government of Rio, specifically the Pereira Passos Institute (Instituto Pereira Passos [IPP]), a research center responsible for municipal urban planning, and UN-Habitat. In 2014 the program was renamed Rio+Social. According to La Rocque and Shelton-Zumpano, by the end of the same year, 770,000 people lived in communities supported by the program: that is, over half the inhabitants of all favelas of the municipality of Rio de Janeiro.[94]

Whether or not this figure describes the reality shaped by the pacification program, we must highlight the rationale behind this particular social policy. As Patricia Owens stresses, in a particularly enlightening way, the notion of social policy has historically emerged as a technology for managing the radical demands of the early industrial proletariat: as a method of pacifying workers.[95] And it is precisely in this targeting that counterinsurgency comes into contact with a large part of social theory that emerged at the time and therefore with social policy itself. So if we were to look at the social pillar of the Rio pacification program, we would see precisely this preventive function and counterinsurgency targeting lying at its core. It attempts to pacify the surplus populations of the urban periphery by helping improve their daily lives, in the hope that this improvement would keep them away from informal—and particularly criminal—means of making a living. Yet in the case of Rio, the limits of this narrative soon proved that the aim of this so-called development was not to actually improve the living conditions of the favela inhabitants, but primarily to enforce its own spectacle, barely making an effort to whitewash the bloody outcomes of security.

It soon became apparent that the much-advertised community development and related initiatives would suffer the familiar symptoms of a short-circuited bureaucracy. But most importantly they were limited from the outset to a handful of token gestures and to the maintenance of an urban profile that served as a powerful propaganda tool. As Sebastian Saborio notes, the pacification program essentially sought "to achieve a beautification strategy of the favelas visible from the mega events sceneries but not to bring about meaningful improvements in social welfare."[96] To put it another way, pacification predictably focused on security and set community development aside. It opted to invest not so much in the creation of services and infrastructures of general interest, but in the production of development-as-spectacle. Even security experts attest to the fact that "the UPP project ... remained mostly a security operation, with the holding and building phases being overlooked."[97] Similarly, Maíra Siman and Victória Santos note that this program was criticized "due to its failure to promote effective community participation in decision-making and to generate significant results, as well as for making investment in public services in favelas conditional on the presence of UPPs."[98] They conclude that, as with other pacification and stabilization operations, this, too, was marked by "a prioritization of order over the always postponed progress." The inhabitants of those areas were the first to come to that conclusion. In the words of a social activist from Complexo do Alemão, "The security that we always needed was investment in health and education. If the state had invested more in the human being and less in this war on drugs, we would all have had a positive return."[99] Similarly, after speaking with residents of Rocinha, another favela integrated in the pacification program, Erika Robb Larkins points out that no substantial improvements have been made to the three main issues of their daily lives—namely healthcare, education, and basic sanitation. "What they get from the state are substandard services, accompanied by a punitive politics of policing.... The focus is always on security to the exclusion of other core issues"[100]

The UPP Social program has therefore largely proved to be a showcase of development that has taken care to conceal existing social problems behind the pretense of beautification and strategic symbolism. But there is hardly anything new about this. The role of UPP Social / Rio+Social essentially highlighted familiar issues in the ongoing debate about the implementation of development programs in the favelas overall: how the areas due for development are selected, what the objectives are behind the respective programs, and how investment flows are directed. For example, Larkins similarly describes the traces left in Rocinha by the infamous Growth Acceleration Program (Programa de Aceleração do Crescimento [PAC]). PAC was implemented into two stages—PAC I and PAC II—and was the Lula administration's main investment program since 2007. As she claims, "PAC is a project of winning favela hearts and minds but is also, crucially, a political performance for outside audiences, tied to party politics and election cycles."[101] PAC was implemented in a small number of favelas,[102] as a program that would work in tandem with the National Program for Public Security with Citizenship (Programa Nacional de Segurança Pública com Cidadania [PRONASCI]): a public security program promoting the idea of community policing, "tying public security to the enhancement of citizenship."[103] It was implemented as the purely developmental part of a typical development-security framework.

It is true that a number of critical projects and infrastructures implemented in some of these favelas have improved the daily lives of the residents.[104] But as in the case of UPP Social, PAC was similarly plagued by funding constraints, significant delays, and highly symbolic actions in specific favelas, such as Complexo do Alemão, Manguinhos, and Rocinha. In some cases, flagship infrastructures such as the Oscar Niemeyer–designed bridge at the entrance to Rocinha, the elevator entrance and housing units in Cantagalo/Pavão-Pavãozinho, or the Complexo do Alemão cable car, were effectively employed as political and propaganda showcases for the program. Even within these specific favelas, the program's impact has been relatively small. Since its inception, it has faced serious delays "with much less money being spent than originally intended."[105] However, for the Lula administration, PAC played an additional role: the role of consolidating the electorate for the upcoming 2010 election.

PAC was replaced by the Crescer program during the Temer government and is now monitored for project overpricing and waste of federal funds, thereby displaying all the familiar symptoms of corruption that characterize the wider political life of the country. Yet just like UPP Social or Rio+Social, its legacy has been considerable—and it has been more political than infrastructural at that. PAC demonstrated that the notion of development is in the first instance implemented in the context of a strategy of urban spectacle and promoted as a security technology. But it also revealed something else: the implementation of this particular kind of development aims at the destruction of specific informal forms of life and of a particular conception of urbanity, destruction then becomes not just a method but a goal in itself. PAC revealed that, in the context of pacification/counterinsurgency, "construction" largely manifests itself as an inverted destruction. This reversal is one of the key targets, not only of the pacification program but also of other development initiatives that have been attempting to "urbanize" the favelas for years. For example, development as inverted (and imminent) destruction became evident to several Rocinha residents when they resisted the construction of yet another giant cable car that would be funded by the PAC program, "pointing to the cable car as a high-cost marketing project, the high number of evictions and the potential of the project to produce gentrification."[106] Pacification therefore proves that the return of the state to these areas does not take place in a socially minded fashion, nor is it simply aimed at tackling gangs or safeguarding the prosperity of local communities. Rather, it attempts to open up a new field of economic exploitation in the form of a peculiar land grabbing. And it tries to (re)inscribe, within the strict confines of state control, a spatial environment and a human terrain that lay outside the formal economy's flows. This (re)inscribing will either take the form of tax audits and forced contributions to state revenue or a source of profit for private capital—as proven, for example, by the expansion of electricity, cable, and internet companies, and the replacement of illegal connections with legal ones.[107]

From the pacification point of view, urban informality as a whole is problematized as the field and object of operations. The type of development that takes place in the pacification context attacks the core elements of urban informality and its day-to-day life, attempting to (re)integrate into the flows of formal economy whatever is (re)produced and consumed in informal terms. As Larkins puts it, "Pacification and its economic side effects are reincorporating favela residents into the formal market economy."[108] As a result, pacification actually performs an utterly antisocial role alongside its supposedly social function. Much of the daily life of the inhabitants, which acquires its meaning in the context of informal economy and informal social reproduction, is deliberately destroyed as pacification constructs the conditions allowing formal economy to function and imposes the presence of the state on their daily space-times. But this destruction does not matter to those who shape public opinion. For them, it is important that any development results statistically reflect the public security landscape, that is, in terms of crime prevention. And at the same time, it is vital to incorporate as many physical and social territories as possible into profit's frantic flows. This incorporation was ironically described as a reintegration of communities into democratic society in the decree outlining the structure and functioning of the UPPs: in Sergio Cabral's words, at the moment when special pacification units are permanently installed in the community, they prepare it "for the arrival of other public and private services that allow it to be reintegrated into democratic society."[109] This is the ground zero of state presence/return in the areas in question. This (re)foundational moment is accompanied by what, in the language of the World Bank and former Rio mayor Eduardo Paes, is called the "shock of order." As we read in a related World Bank report, the installation of UPPs in these areas is "often accompanied by a 'choque de ordem' (shock of order) against various forms of informality, from precarious housing to street vending."[110]

The similarities between this example and others drawn from the destructive panorama of pacification/counterinsurgency are obvious. In describing similar operations in Afghanistan, Patricia Owens, for example, focuses on the critical importance of producing a specially formulated "social realm as a form of pacification" that allows intervention and adjustment. A key prerequisite for the production of such a realm is the "modernization"/privatization of the economy and the "neoliberal restructuring (or rather invention) of the Afghan 'political economy,'" which creates "a greater need for public (and private) regulation and control of economic activity."[111] Regulating the social and economic sphere therefore becomes a priority, even if it means destroying existing socio-economic structures and social reproduction practices that have long contributed to the well-being of local communities.[112] Because, as Duffield aptly puts it, "The reimagining of underdevelopment as dangerous in, for example, the literature on war economies ... or descriptions of international criminal networks ... points to another more challenging and edgy form of self-reliance. This is adaptive self-reliance as radical autonomy. It signals the discovery of effective means of existence beyond states and free of aid agencies."[113] This "radical self-reproduction equates with threatening forms of innovation and circulation, including the ability to survive beyond states and sap the walls they erect."[114] And speaking specifically of

Afghanistan, which is described as "an important zone of fragile state experimentation," he points out: "Self-reliance has a dangerous ambiguity in relation to attempts to strengthen state authority. When successfully and innovatively pursued, rather than being a process of governmentalization, self-reliance supports resistance and imparts independence. The 'actually existing development' of informal trade, illegal commodity procurement, transborder smuggling networks and diaspora enterprise can encourage centrifugal forces of autonomy and alternative claims to legitimacy and rights to life."[115]

The tension generated between this "actually existing development" and development as perceived by governance cadres therefore lies at the heart of pacification operations. The creative destruction exerted by this "aggressive economic formalization"[116] proves that its priority is not the well-being of communities but rather the imposition of a specific notion of development and the fabrication of a certain social order and a "durably pacified social space."[117] After all, this priority is expressly stated in the theory of postconflict stabilization, reconstruction, and nation-building, which can be applied to the urban scale of "feral" or "fragile" cities: "The prime objective of any nation-building operation is to make violent societies peaceful, not to make poor ones prosperous, or authoritarian ones democratic. Economic development and political reform are important instruments for effecting this transformation, but will not themselves ensure it. Rather, such efforts need to be pursued within a broader framework, the aim of which is to redirect the competition for wealth and power, which takes place within any society, from violent into peaceful channels."[118] This redirection of economic and social competition from "violent" to "peaceful" channels, or more precisely, from "violent" channels to channels of legitimate violence, does not come about with wishful thinking: to the contrary, it requires brute force, arms, and coercion. It requires, as we saw, destruction-as-method.

Contrary to what the pacification/counterinsurgency cadres claim, this is most probably where we can identify the true meaning of the "armed social work" notion. This strange and almost contradictory notion is key to the counterinsurgency agenda and encapsulates how the mission of pacification/counterinsurgency is described by those directly involved in it. As stated in the US counterinsurgency manual, "COIN operations can be characterized as armed social work. It includes attempts to redress basic social and political problems while being shot at."[119] A few years later, in response to criticism from anthropologists and other social scientists against the use of the term, Kilcullen would emphasize that "armed social work" is "community organizing, welfare, mediation, domestic assistance, economic support—under conditions of extreme threat requiring armed support."[120] Such representations of this particular kind of social work aim to distract the public from the spectacle of police-military violence. The main goal, according to these narratives, is the provision of social services and community development: the presence of guns is merely a necessary evil. Guns are indispensable as a means of self-protection for the completion of an otherwise peaceful social program.

Descriptions of this kind consciously bypass the intentions and strategic goals behind the planning of these operations, thereby normalizing the presence of armed forces among populations and limiting the discussion on issues of social work methodology.[121] Nevertheless, direct experience in the field demonstrates that the term "armed" carries more weight than "social work"; that security is a priority over "community development." This means either that there are more armed officers present in the field than "social workers," or that the "social workers" are there as agents of a preventive counterinsurgency policy meant to pacify needs and community grievances before they are expressed in the form of unlawful or criminal activity. As Siman and Santos point out, in the discourse linking poverty to crime, security takes precedence over development while development is limited to "practices of 'armed social work,' as seen in relief assistance and to projects aiming to support community resilience and small-scale reconstruction."[122] That is, to the minimum level of development required to prevent the explosive mixture comprising the communities of the urban periphery from going off. Any social work is therefore provided as a method of crime prevention.

How an agent of armed violence is "naturally" transformed into an agent of armed social work is vividly described by Galula:

> At some point in the counterinsurgency process, the static units that took part initially in large-scale military operations in their area will find themselves confronted with a huge variety of nonmilitary tasks which have to be performed in order to get

the support of the population, and which can be performed only by military personnel, because of the shortage of reliable civilian political and administrative personnel. Making a thorough census, enforcing new regulations on movements of persons and goods, informing the population, conducting person-to-person propaganda, gathering intelligence on the insurgent's political agents, implementing the various economic and social reforms, etc.—all these will become their primary activity. They have to be organized, equipped, and supported accordingly. Thus, a mimeograph machine may turn out to be more useful than a machine gun, a soldier trained as a pediatrician more important than a mortar expert, cement more wanted than barbed wire, clerks more in demand than riflemen.[123]

While impudently concealing the colonial dimension of the French presence in Algeria, Galula hereby describes a particular kind of military mission that is consistent with social work. As is well known, the French military had been present in Algeria for over a century through a colonial campaign that, just like other colonial operations, was characterized by violence, imprisonment, mass murder, and torture. But it was, first and foremost, a population management project and as such it focused on the needs, daily lives, social networking, and movements of the people. It is precisely within this aspect of the operation that both the population-centric interpretation of counterinsurgency and the fanciful neologism of armed social work become meaningful. As in the example of French colonial presence in Algeria, which was nothing but a military operation aimed at exploiting natural resources, land, and human labor, so in the case of Rio the object of operations is the population itself. It is the imposition—whether armed or not—of a certain social order that requires the formalization of the social and economic relations that comprise the human geographies of the urban periphery.

Judging by the goals of the Rio pacification program and noting that (creative) destruction is a preeminent feature among them, we may conclude that weapons are not simply present in the field to protect "social workers." They are there to impose a certain social order and ultimately to accomplish what Clausewitz described as the purpose of war. War, wrote the Prussian general, "is thus an act of force to compel our enemy to do our will."[124] Or in the case of Rio, to compel the populations crammed into the uncharted landscapes of urban informality to conform to the flows, requirements, and normalities of the formal economy—regardless of whether that means population displacement, or integration into a formal and identifiable transaction framework with the state and private companies. It is precisely this goal that therefore requires any kind of "social work" within these communities to be "armed." Because weapons do not just indicate the need for (self-)protection of those who implement social programs in the field, they are also the means by which the social and economic relations that make up the informal space-times of the urban periphery will forcibly be reshaped and formalized. We are therefore not dealing with "armed social work," but rather, with armed social engineering; with a violent process that attempts to reshape the field of social relations by shaping new types of subjectivity. This violent process, thereby confirms an established tenet in the field of civil-military operations today: "A military force introduced during times of crisis becomes a tool of social engineering."[125] This is not simply because, as military historian Andrew Birtle writes, the "army's expertise in human leadership and management made it an ideal instrument for social engineering."[126] It is mainly because security forces have the power to apply and enforce this kind of engineering. And obviously, it is because the notion and the phenomena of population have long been turned into objects of military management.

Owens shows us how "armed social work"—whose roots she traces, in a sense, to the French school of counterinsurgency—is linked to social engineering. To do so, she draws from the history of counterinsurgency and from the involvement of soci(ologic)al theories in the planning and conducting of operations:

> French practitioners were much more likely to deploy new sociological language to understand and rationalise their activities. Strategists wrote pioneering articles on the "social role" of the colonial soldier and how to fight war in "the social milieu." Commentators spoke of the need to "socialise" the local population, social re-engineering, the functional interrelations between parts of the "social body" and the deeper sociological causes and remedies of anti-colonial resistance. These are the French origins of claims about the power of armed social work. The

inner core of local resistance to pacification would be undone through the destruction and reconstitution of the native "social" base: exemplary massacres, forced removals and re-concentration, selective distribution of basic supplies, the co-optation of local enforcers and opening new markets.[127]

Armed social work is therefore guided by the spirit of creative destruction mentioned above. It is a process that is carried out deep within the human terrain, constructing through destruction and destroying through construction. But this particular kind of "social-ization" of war is not exclusively French. It appears repeatedly as an operational motif in counterinsurgency campaigns all around the world. "In the Philippines, variations on these activities were called 'policies of attraction'; in French Morocco, the 'policy of the smile'; in Britain's late-colonial wars, 'hearts and minds' and 'rehabilitation'; in America's war on Vietnam they were the 'Other War,' or the policy of 'fuck 'em and feed 'em'; in Afghanistan and Iraq they were 'population-centric.'"[128] All these operations were designed on the basis of what is called social engineering, that is through programs "designed to reshape the subject society": exactly what has been taking place in the favelas of Rio throughout the past decade.[129]

The insistence of security forces and armed forces upon social engineering and the restructuring of social relations does not come out of nowhere. As we saw above, through Owens's observations, the production of part of social theory, and the emergence of social policy as such, not only had counterinsurgency objectives at their root, but were openly deployed according to the needs of pacification opera-tions: that is, political-military operations of population management. We can therefore observe methodological similarities between the different historical cases, the most important of which concerns the synergy of security and development. But we can also notice similar-ities in the ideological framework that underpins those operations. At the root of this particular military puzzle is the urgent need for a reshaping of the human terrain. Formerly articulated as the process of modernization of "developing" or "lagging" rural societies of the "Third World," this reshaping is nowadays articulated in the form of sustainable development and the resilience of fragile states or fragile cities. Today, as then, the notion of community lies at the heart of this ideological construction, either as the object of development or of policing, either in terms of community development or community policing. The restructuring of the social relations and space-times holding together these communities is therefore attempted through the aforementioned dialectic of the carrot and the stick. Yet we should perceive the carrot in its literal sense, long before we come to examine it, metaphorically, as the object that symbolizes development. Literally, as a biological necessity, as "food in people's mouths."

Fuck 'Em and Feed 'Em

The logic of community development as a preventive counterinsurgency strategy is not a Brazilian novelty, as we have seen already. The implementation of social programs and the allocation of funds and development packages as part of a broader public security agenda and as a method of managing security challenges is a motif consistently repeated since the end of World War II, during the period of decolonization, which saw the manifestation of both the "Third World question" as such, and the concept of international development/assistance as the solution to this question. The emergence of a broader counterinsurgency approach during that time, one that focused on the concepts of development and modernization, must be understood in this context. We therefore need to dwell on this environment longer to better understand how the food question arose as well. Under the strong influence of neo-Malthusian perceptions of world population growth and inadequate natural resources, Western cadres were terrified of the surplus populations of the periphery and their needs, as they were considered a source of potential political destabilization. It is clear that what was at stake during the Cold War era was not the propensity of these populations toward crime or their engagement with the flows of illicit economies, in the way we see it being problematized and represented in Rio today. Rather, what was at stake was the likelihood of uprisings and, even worse, of involvement with the communist bloc, as hunger and poverty were considered the most fertile ground for the seed of communism to grow. "Where hunger goes communism follows," as American aid experts would say at the time.[130] The containment of the communist threat was thus the main mission of the Western political and military cadres, meaning either the immediate suppression of guerrilla movements and uprisings that erupted in various parts of the capitalist periphery, or the pacification of surplus populations and their needs. Such pacification was to take place by preventively intervening and reshaping the social milieu in terms of social engineering.

And so, at a time when counterinsurgency/pacification is being established as a prominent and distinctive operational paradigm within military science, the issue of managing postcolonial surplus life arises in the form of a fundamental civilian-military mission. A mission that could only have been designed based on the physical and social characteristics of the fields for which it was intended. At the time, the laboratories of the capitalist periphery, as well as most of the rest of the world, still maintained a markedly agrarian character. What is called the "first" or the "developed" world, which was largely determined by a country's degree of industrialization and urbanization, was but one exception to the rule defined by rural cyclical time and its attendant forms of life. Organized efforts to understand these forms, from the theories of modernization and international aid policies to geopolitical analyses and counterinsurgency methodologies, were characterized by a conception of rurality as a regressive form of social organization: a homeostasis in the course of social development that had to be modernized. This understanding is central both to the brutal counterinsurgency operations carried out in various parts of the periphery and to a certain kind of global pacification and preventive counterinsurgency campaign launched at the same time, in order to pacify the needs of the populations of the periphery before they were pushed into the arms of communism. Manifested more in the form of development initiatives aimed at security, and less in the form of military operations, this campaign sought to reshape, inter alia, the rural landscape of the capitalist periphery, radically altering production processes, as well as the forms of life traditionally shaped through a close relationship with the land. Yet the effects of this developmental manifestation were not any less catastrophic, based, as it was, on the same logic as the destructive practices of counterinsurgency, regardless of whether this was the logic of the ideology of modernization from which it sprang, of the ways of problematizing and managing populations or, ultimately, of the technical means used.

The rurality of these societies, lying so far from the dominant models of development and modernization, was therefore inextricably linked to the issues of underdevelopment, poverty, and hunger. This had a decisive influence on the very establishment of a certain counterinsurgency approach at the time. Not only because of the rugged physical features with which rurality is identified—an operational parameter that obviously did not escape military theory and on which a large number of counterrevolutionary and counterinsurgency manuals were essentially constructed—but also because of its population and social particularities. That is because of the fact that pacification policies, whether expressed in terms of security or in terms of development, have been applied to specific and unfamiliar "human terrains" that had been bound to a rural way of life for centuries. As the rural character of a society is first determined by its attachment to the land and its direct relation to food production processes, it follows that this would attract the attention of civil-military planning and counterinsurgency operations in particular, as operations carried out primarily in the "human terrain." That is, on the land, on its people—the peasants— and on food. As Neocleous points out with regard to Vietnam, the emphasis there on the rural element was so closely intertwined with the pacification programs that these terms were used, in related terminology, as supplementary concepts.[131] What is of particular interest in the context of this analysis is the fact that food did not constitute a lesser parameter in the theories and practices of pacification. On the contrary, it has been employed systematically—sometimes as a method of exterminating the enemy, and other times as a means of population control and as a tool of social engineering, irreparably blurring the boundaries between biopolitics and thanatopolitics.

The idea of controlling food flows holds a particularly dark spot in the landscape of counterinsurgency and broader military practices. This is hardly surprising. After all, food has a key role in the bloody making of world history as shaped by wars, conquests, colonialism, and geopolitical antagonisms. The pivotal role of spices in medieval wars of conquest and in the "emergence of a closely integrated world trading system,"[132] the importance of sugar as a "colonial product in the growth of world capitalism" and the role of sugarcane plantations in the transatlantic slave trade and the establishment of colonies,[133] the predatory activity of American fruit companies and the so-called Banana Wars in the Caribbean and Central America,[134] the Green Revolution as a tool of Cold War strategy and a key pillar of the international anticommunist campaign,[135] the contemporary geopolitical significance of soybeans and other select food crops within the new grain-livestock-fuel agro-industrial complex,[136] and the emergence, today, of phenomena of neo-agro-colonialism through policies of land grabbing all testify to the fact that food has been at the forefront of the global geopolitical agenda for centuries.[137]

However, in addition to its strategic and geopolitical role, food has taken on a significant operational dimension. In the context of counterinsurgency and pacification, which are of particular interest to us here, food has become of critical tactical importance. This is because the center of gravity of counterinsurgency is, as we have seen, the population itself. The key position of the population on the counterinsurgency agenda lends the food question a terrifying operational potential, which becomes apparent if we observe how food has been used in a number of pacification operations: either in a repressive manner, that is, through familiar counterinsurgency/counterrevolutionary operations and the population control technologies these required; or in a preventive manner, that is, through developmental policies and security risk management policies similar to those described above. In both cases, the food question occupies a key position because the object and scope of counterinsurgency is to control the population and thus control population phenomena—food necessity being prevalent among them. Counterinsurgency, manifested as a sum of suppressive practices, has historically featured a gruesome set of techniques and methodologies used to control food needs and flows. The purpose of these techniques was to effectively cut off enemy access to food, and in order to achieve this, military cadres intervened in two different terrains: the human and the physical.

As we mentioned earlier, a population-centric perception of the enemy lies at the core of counterinsurgency logic. A perception, that is, that views the enemy through their relationship with a population. This relationship acquires material, political, and informational dimensions, among others. The population provides the guerrillas in the jungle and the rugged hills with the necessary supplies; it supports them politically in their struggle and keeps them apprised of the movements and the plans of the enemy. Food is central to the first part of this relationship and, as the history of war itself testifies, it is a privileged field of military intervention. By intervening in the materialities of this relationship, counterinsurgency forces can displace, exhaust, disrupt, or even exterminate guerrillas. As Riley Sunderland writes in reference to the British counterinsurgency operations in Malaysia, "The impact of food control on the guerrillas was great. In 1953, asked why they had become relatively inactive (the number of incidents having fallen from 5,727 in 1952 to 1,170 in 1953), a group of [surrendered enemy personnel] summed up the answer in one word, food. Food seeking has become a major objective, leaving the guerrillas little time or energy for planning or conducting other operations."[138]

From a more contemporary perspective, John Zambri highlights the fact that the success of an insurgency, and therefore of counterinsurgency in return, is up to whoever wins over the peasants. "Why is the peasantry so important?" asks Zambri. "For the insurgents the peasantry provides food, shelter, recruits, supplies, and most importantly, information on counterinsurgent forces. They are the bases that provide essential support functions." Therefore, "the population—the peasants—are the focus of support and legitimacy of the counterinsurgency solution and form the hub of counterinsurgency strategy."[139] That was even more critical during the Cold War era in particular, when a key tenet of US foreign policy was that "the most critical national security threat, present and future, would come from peasant-based 'subversive insurgency.'"[140]

Controlling a rural population largely meant controlling agricultural production and food flows. By directly controlling the population, the quantities of food available, and its circulation, counterinsurgency forces sought to cut off supply lines and material support to the guerrillas and deprive them of access to food. This would then force them to leave their bases making them easier targets. These food denial operations therefore raised not merely a logistical issue for the guerrillas but essentially, one of survival. As Sunderland points out, "When the counterinsurgent has effective control over the goods and people as well as wide, general control over the moving, stocking, and buying of food, he is able to use hunger as an offensive weapon against a specific group of guerrillas in a well-defined area."[141] This kind of control was exercised in a variety of ways and involved a detailed recording of what was produced, consumed, and distributed, which itself required the implementation of specific administrative control mechanisms and specific spatial and social surveillance techniques such as local population censuses and issuing of identity cards;[142] inventory of animals in the area;[143] isolation of populations from guerrillas using military checkpoints; barricades; traffic bans; and daily control of people's movements;[144] or forcible population displacement, often following the destruction of their settlements, and mass relocation to fenced-in settlements or concentration camps;[145] and house-to-house searches to locate food stocks.[146]

All of the above was therefore also aimed at controlling the total amount of available food and its circulation. The food needs of the constantly monitored populations were largely met through food distribution and rationing operated by the army itself. In many cases, this relationship of dependence and the inescapable necessity for food were employed as extortion techniques to force collaboration with counterinsurgency forces, as collaborators were issued special ration cards.[147] All this went on under the pretext that such counterinsurgency practices protected local populations from insurgents.[148] Social benefit policies for the monitored populations helped blur the boundaries between thanatopolitics and biopolitics, destruction, and "construction." Forcibly displaced populations became beneficiaries of social benefits. Damaged settlements were replaced by new monitored settlements. "Ignorance" gave way to "education."[149] The notorious Strategic Hamlet Program, implemented during the Vietnam War—before it was renamed the "rural community development program"—may perhaps be the best-known example of this practice. However, such practices were widely applied during a number of counterinsurgency operations by various forces, such as the Spanish army in Cuba, the US military in the Philippines, the French army during the Indochina war, and the British army during the Second Boer War, the suppression of the Mau Mau uprising in Kenya, and the anticommunist operations in Malaysia, which have since proved paradigmatic cases for food denial strategies.[150] The practice of forcibly resettling populations in enclosed and monitored settlements as a method of controlling food supplies and flows was consistently present in pacification operations, regardless of whether these settlements were called strategic hamlets, protected villages, new villages, agrovilles, or camps.

Interventions in the "human terrain" and the violent rearrangement of spatial and social relations were not, however, the only methods aimed at controlling food that were pursued through pacification programs. Another widespread and largely complementary practice was the intervention on the physical terrain, that is, directly on the land and the environment itself. This method is the epitome of destruction. Huge plots of land, crop fields, food stocks, and jungle and forests were systematically destroyed and animals were massively slaughtered, so that anything that could potentially be used as food by the guerrillas was wiped out. For this purpose, both mechanical and chemical means were used and the magnitude of the destruction was such that, in the early 1970s, there was talk of unprecedented ecological warfare, a practice that became known as ecocide, a term introduced in 1970 by the American professor Arthur Galston.[151] Perhaps the most well-known application of this logic was again demonstrated during the Vietnam War. Yet practices of direct intervention in the natural environment that were aimed at destroying crops, food stocks, food sources, and ultimately the very ability of the land to produce had already been tested out during previous counterinsurgency operations. During the Second Boer War, the British army employed a scorched-earth policy resulting in the "systematic destruction of crops and slaughtering of livestock, the burning down of homesteads and farms, and the poisoning of wells and salting of fields."[152] In addition, the British and the Australians employed similar practices in Malaysia, where they sprayed huge fields of crops with herbicides, destroying them with chemical defoliation.

Some years later, during the Vietnam War, these practices would be systematized to such an extent as to cause an outcry by the international community. In 1972, the International Commission of Inquiry into US Crimes in Indochina would report that "Indochina is today a testing ground for all the terrible means of destruction at disposal by the U.S. government."[153] Among them, it would single out "the use of herbicides and defoliants to destroy plant life under the code name Operation Ranch Hand—including plants giving cover or sanctuary to insurgents, food crops, and resources such as mangroves and nipa palms used for housing; the 'Rome Plow' program of massed bulldozers that flattened villages, farms, and trees, including hardwood forests and rubber plants" and the "carpet bombings by B-52 bombers and F-4 Phantom jets, supported by a stratified array of specialized aircraft, deployed for antipersonnel missions and to execute widespread craterization that rendered land useless for agriculture."[154] The purpose of these practices was twofold. On the one hand they were part of a typical food denial strategy "through crop destruction and wetland drainage." On the other hand, large territories were "cleared" of Viet Cong through the destruction of the natural environment and the cover this provided.[155]

The scale of the horror and destruction is readily revealed if we look at the figures for individual operations. In Operation Ranch Hand, between 1962 and 1971, about 19 million gallons of herbicides were used over 4.5 million acres of South Vietnam (12 percent of the country's total surface area), 11 million of which consisted of Agent Orange, a powerful chemical herbicide with "extraordinarily high concentrations of dioxin, the most toxic substance known to science."[156] On top of the incalculable consequences for the natural environment, the use of these chemicals caused serious health problems (malformations, cancers, genetic abnormalities, neurological problems, etc.) that are still evident today in the Vietnamese population, especially in the areas that had borne the brunt of the spraying.[157] In addition, the bulldozers of the Rome Plow program completely leveled approximately 2 percent of the total land area of South Vietnam, including entire forests, leaving behind bare, lifeless soil.[158] And finally, the mass bombardment operations had perhaps the biggest and most devastating impact on the environment. The 14.3 million tons of ammunition used during the period between 1965 and 1973, half of them delivered by air, left behind 20 to 23 million craters, covering an area of 423,000 acres.[159]

The above methods of control and destruction should not be perceived as instruments of an individual war but instead as forms of a broader geopolitical agenda concerning Western postwar hegemony. The issue of managing the surplus populations of the periphery was, as has been said, one of the key points of said agenda. An agenda that was not just about war zones but also parts of the so-called developing world more broadly. As colonial construction was rapidly deconstructed and the capitalist periphery was radically reshaped, the old colonial powers and the United States were trying to impose and set out specific directions for this remodeling. The above methodologies demonstrate that the food question has been a key parameter in this effort and the design of pacification operations in particular. They also show us that, despite counterinsurgency narratives about "winning hearts and minds" and protecting local populations, these operations, especially to the extent that they focused on the importance of food, were inherently

based on violence (on the violence engendered by biological necessity itself) and in planned mass destruction.[160] But this destruction
was not just a popular method of destroying the enemy. It was also a
prerequisite for a certain kind of "construction" and "development" in
the eyes of all those who were implementing plans for stopping the
communist threat in various parts of this planet at the time, either by
delivering development packages, testing new production techniques,
or implementing a broader policy of preventive counterinsurgency. It
was a prerequisite for the social engineering programs implemented to
reshape rurality and modernize the social milieu in many unfortunate
corners of the postcolonial world. Destruction-as-method must therefore be emphasized as a prerequisite for "construction," as we witness
the unfolding of outrageous arguments by all those who attempted—
and many are still attempting today—to hide their military plans and
political pursuits behind abstract calls for the protection of (surplus)
populations, behind charitable anxiety over poverty and hunger, and
behind theories of modernization of the capitalist periphery. In some
cases, and in this context, destruction has even been presented as a
self-evident fact in this context.

As put by a US Air Force sergeant who took part in the bombing
operation aimed at displacing populations during the Vietnam War,
"The villages got wiped out there, too, and everybody just picked up
their stuff and went somewhere else. Those aren't houses. They're just
huts."[161] Putting the term "house" next to "hut" constitutes a straight-
forward value judgment of the degree of modernization of the local
communities, and therefore of the need to overcome static and anachronistic forms of rural life, that would go so far as to legitimize their
total elimination. But this judgement does not comprise the individual
point of view of a single sergeant. As Owens points out, the option of
escalating the use of the US Air Force in the Vietnam War, and therefore
of mass bombings, was encouraged by Walt Rostow, among others, then
adviser to the Kennedy administration, who had also urged the latter
to extend the herbicide program in Vietnam, thus paving the way for
Operation Ranch Hand.[162] But Rostow was not a military man. He was
an internationally renowned economist who influenced the shaping of
the US strategy in the Vietnam War and more broadly, the planning of
American foreign policy at the time. As a staunch anticommunist and
supporter of the free market, he put forth one of the major theories of

modernization, which provided the basis for a key part of American foreign policy. At the core of this theory lie fundamental principles of an evolutionary interpretation of human societies, shared by those directly involved in the destruction of static forms of rural life but also by those who sought to modernize them.[163] This was several years before Rostow left his mark on US strategy in Vietnam and long before he was transformed from a development theorist into a bombing advocate, "as South Vietnam proved immune to modernization on the Western model."[164]

Conceptualizing and representing rurality in terms of social homeostasis must be understood in the context dictated by the alignment of social theories to evolutionary interpretations, which goes back to the late nineteenth century. Rostow's theory was not therefore strictly original, but it did exemplify the perception of the capitalist periphery as a dangerous backwardness in the course of "natural" and "linear" social evolution. In addition, it exemplified the need to place modernization at the very center of counterinsurgency/pacification and the transformation of development into a means of anticommunist struggle irrespective of whether this took place in war zones or not, or whether it was in the form of military operations or nation-building. "Nation building and COIN [counterinsurgency] converged during the Kennedy administration," writes Martin Clemis in that respect.[165] "Walt Rostow argued that modernization was the 'grand arena of revolutionary change.' Characterizing Communism as 'a disease' created by the postcolonial transition toward modernity and Communist insurgents as 'scavengers' of the modernization process, he believed that the United States has a 'special responsibility of leadership' in helping underdeveloped nations modernize. If Communism was, as Rostow and others believed, a disease of modernization, and wars of national liberation were the symptoms it produced, nation building and COIN were believed to be the cure."[166]

And so the issues of poverty and hunger and their relation to the uprisings that erupted around the world have been outlining the key pillars of a broader pacification program at least since the end of World War II. This program is aimed at managing and pacifying the growing needs of the surplus populations of the periphery, containing the global communist threat, and securing Western hegemony in Cold War antagonism. As Neocleous points out, Rostow and others were tasked early on with the mission "to provide an anti-Communist grand narrative of history around which a security strategy for the 'Third World' could be built. This narrative was modernization theory and the concept of development: the belief that 'underdeveloped' areas suffered from a fundamental lack, a fundamental incapacity which might be exploited as a political weakness by communism. Their 'development' or 'modernization' was to be their salvation and, concomitantly, was to be the First World's security."[167] To a large extent, this "modernization" was nothing but a program for the modernization of rurality itself, of the forms of rural life and (re)production that dominated most of the planet at that time. And this kind of modernization would be as disastrous as the means and methodologies used in the aforementioned battlefields.

Western cadres inevitably focused on the "agricultural question," which resurfaced during the decolonization period, as the rural populations (labeled as surplus) revealed by the deconstruction of old colonial structure, acquired geopolitical significance. As a result, they focused there based on evolutionary stereotypes imposed, at the time, by theories of modernization such as Rostow's. Following a crude reasoning that completely erased the social and historical complexity of the formation and function of individual rural societies, these theories proposed the idea of a linear evolution at the origin of which stood the concept of the village and at the end of it was the concept of the city. As Nick Cullather tells us, the concept of the village haunted developmental theories because it constituted the most widespread socio-spatial unit in the "developing" world and at the same time seeming closed unto itself and inaccessible to the logic of capital.[168] And at the center of these concerns was Asia—dotted with myriad small villages and already largely allied with the Communist Soviet Union and Communist China—which played home to the majority of the world's population. "Its rurality constituted the principal strategic problem for American planners" as Cullather writes about the continent, and it was there that several theories of rural modernization were tested.[169] Rurality, exemplified in the iconography of the village, was therefore located precisely at the starting point of this line. And, by and large, any attempts to interpret, evaluate, and deal with rurality employed tools fetched from the other end of this abstract evolutionary line—that is, the city.

Related theories have seen urbanization and its attendant phenomena as a means of problematizing rurality. Consistently linked to the degree of industrialization and together with other developmental parameters (hygiene, mortality rates, education, salary levels, etc.) it has been proposed as an indicator of the modernization of rural societies. But the city and urbanization were not confined to the narrow framework of a conceptual tool. In certain cases, they would also suggest a violent way of managing rurality itself, as the example of Vietnam reminds us again, which would manifest itself as forced movement along the evolutionary line proposed by modernization theories: a violent mass displacement of populations from the countryside to cities that would cause the rural world to shrink and therefore weaken the support provided to the insurgents by the population. As the influential American political scientist and adviser Samuel Huntington pointed out in 1968:

> In an absent-minded way the United States in Viet Nam may well have stumbled upon the answer to "wars of national liberation." The effective response lies neither in the quest for conventional military victory nor in the esoteric doctrines and gimmicks of counter-insurgency warfare. It is instead forced-draft urbanization and modernization which rapidly brings the country in question out of the phase in which a rural revolutionary movement can hope to generate sufficient strength to come to power. Time in South Viet Nam is increasingly on the side of the Government. But in the short run, with half the population still in the countryside, the Viet Cong will remain a powerful force which cannot be dislodged from its constituency so long as the constituency continues to exist. Peace in the immediate future must hence be based on accommodation.[170]

The number of people who were displaced to cities—around three million, according to Huntington's own estimates that year—testifies to the fact that his proposal was indeed implemented and that forced urbanization was used as a method of managing "dangerous" rurality, and as yet another weapon of war.[171] As Oliver Belcher points out, drawing from Mike Davis, "The connection between colonial counterinsurgency, forced displacement, and forced urbanization has many historical precedents, making the strategy ... 'one of the most ruthlessly efficient levers of informal urbanization.'"[172]

Whether employed as a model for problematizing and understanding rurality or as a method for its eventual eradication, urbanization and the notion of the city at large demonstrate that the microcosm of the village and the macrocosm of the unmapped and infinite global rurality were at the heart of geopolitical planning and comprised fundamental fields of intervention. The inflexibility of villagers' perceptions and traditions, the self-sufficiency and closedness of village life, as well as its scattered spatiality, so deeply immersed in the natural element, created the image of an introverted, impermeable, and inaccessible model of social organization. And the first attempts to describe this image were made through representations that testified to its (near) animalistic state. For example, a report entitled *Notes on Indian Agriculture*, published in 1952 by the Rockefeller Foundation, dealt with the possibilities of implementing agricultural modernization programs in India. The report reads: "The villages ... within a region ... are as uniform as so many ant hills. Indeed, from the air, where a number of villages may be seen simultaneously, they have the appearance of structures built by creatures motivated largely by inherited animal instincts, and devoid of any inclination to depart from a fixed hereditary pattern. The inheritance in this instance, of course, is social."[173]

Within such a representational context, modernization theories, both within and beyond the counterinsurgency framework, urgently required a response to rurality. The latter has been problematized as an object of social engineering and as a field that called for its immediate transformation. Among other means, this transformation was attempted through the implementation of community development programs;[174] rural land reform and redistribution programs;[175] efforts to change the farmers' modes of thinking, their motivations, psychology, and political awareness through training programs, financial incentives, and subsidies; the redesign of spatial relationships through the construction of model villages; and the introduction of mechanized high-productivity schemes in agricultural production. Both the social world of the villager and its productive context, which left much room for the introduction of new techniques/technologies, became fields of direct intervention. It was within this colossal venture of social engineering that the ground became fertile for another program, which had already left its mark on the field of agricultural production: the so-called Green Revolution.

To understand the importance of the Green Revolution we must first interpret it in the context of the development-security nexus.

The rationale on which it was founded was obviously not born out of any pure intentions to resolve the global food question, let alone the scientific vision shared by a faction of agronomists. On the contrary, it was yet another manifestation of US geopolitical goals. The Green Revolution was an organized response to the fears initially caused by the surplus populations of the periphery and, by extension, the post–World War II communist threat. The Green Revolution was based, as a narrative at least, on the rationale described above. On the rationale, in other words, in which hunger is the most fertile ground for the seed of communism to grow, and therefore must be urgently addressed. The Green Revolution was clearly a geopolitical tool. This was first confirmed by the person who is considered to have introduced the term, the US Agency for International Development administrator William Gaud. During a speech at the Society for International Development on March 8, 1968, and referring, as Raj Patel writes, to the results brought about by US charitable funding to promote the Green Revolution, Gaud argues: "These and other developments in the field of agriculture contain the makings of a new revolution. It is not a violent Red Revolution like that of the Soviets, nor is it a White Revolution like that of the Shah of Iran. I call it the Green Revolution."[176] It was a "Green Counter-Revolution," as David Rieff very aptly put it.[177]

The Green Revolution, as an exclusively American response to the global population question and its attendant food-related issues, did not come out of nowhere. Those responsible for its design had long had a leading role in other research fields such as public health, demography, and eugenics. Their aim was to promote their answers to the global population question. Having access to huge funds, maintaining close relationships with high government echelons and moving between philanthropy, research, and policy making, these agents were not mere peripheral actors nor did they simply propose potential "solutions," but rather imposed dominant ways of problematizing the population question and the policies required to address it. Giants in the philanthropy and research industries, such as the Rockefeller Foundation, considered the key mastermind behind the design of the Green Revolution, and the Ford Foundation, directly involved in its research and applications, set out guidelines, funded initiatives, and identified both the fields and models of its application. The institutional concern regarding the population question, which escalated during the period of decolonization, was linked, as we have seen, to broader concerns around global political destabilization and the spread of communism. In this context, the Green Revolution would become one of the most powerful tools in the implementation of a broader agenda that sought to enforce American hegemony during the Cold War, via both military and developmental means. The simultaneous establishment of a powerful national agency for international aid and a key pillar of US foreign policy, the USAID, would further promote the Green Revolution agenda. It did so by following the logic of managing surplus populations through international aid and, consequently, curtailing communist influence. The Green Revolution would soon make history as the most successful international aid program since the Marshall Plan.[178]

The Green Revolution is yet another manifestation of the strategic importance of the food question and agricultural modernization in the mid-twentieth century, and its use as a geopolitical tool that reached into areas regardless of armed conflict. It has been, in other words, the epitome of development and security, as well as a connecting link between "construction" and destruction. Behind the agricultural programs implemented in the context of the Green Revolution there were clear counterinsurgency objectives. But there was also the continued promotion of free-market logic and defense of specific financial interests, primarily those of the US. As we shall see below, these all came together to form a structural yet anticipated contradiction within the Green Revolution venture. A brief examination of certain typical chapters from its history should be enough to prove this. The Green Revolution was essentially inaugurated in 1941 in Mexico. The choice of time and place was not accidental. As Raj Patel explains, "The Rockefeller Foundation's decision to initiate a program in Mexico happened after a revolution, peasant uprising, and nationalization of resource wealth, and during a period of elite consolidation."[179] Further, an ambitious program of agricultural reform and land redistribution had just been implemented in the country. Even though this was directly challenging individual US financial interests, it was nevertheless read by Rockefeller Foundation executives as an opportunity to promote the logic of agricultural modernization. As an opportunity, in other words, to bring a large chunk of the country's "primitive" rural world into contact with new production techniques; the logic of entrepreneurship, market, and profitability; and another work culture and the achievements of industrialized civilization.[180] Fearing that Mexico, with its immediate geographical proximity to the US, would follow a leftist path, the Rockefeller Foundation decided to invest in an agricultural modernization program in the country, essentially following the policy of the US government and at the same time bypassing the corresponding Mexican policy. The Mexican Agricultural Program was developed in this context. It would subsequently be considered as a model for agricultural modernization and "the starting point of a worldwide agricultural transformation."[181] In essence, the Mexican Agricultural Program was a milestone in promoting the industrialization of agricultural production, with a focus on standardization and high yields. Soon enough, it would leave its own disastrous footprint.

Following on the "success" of the program in Mexico, and after a smaller-scale program was tested out in Colombia, the Green Revolution cadres chose to export their know-how to Southeast Asia, which, after the defeat of the nationalists in China in 1949, was faced with the "danger" of a communist outbreak. In addition to the Rockefeller Foundation's related initiatives, John D. Rockefeller III himself set up the Agricultural Development Council in 1953, which was "tasked with training rural scientists and finding solutions to the 'economic and human problems' associated with agricultural poverty in Asia."[182] The most critical field in the region was India, which had just been decolonized; together with Mexico, the two were most important examples in the implementation of the Green Revolution. In this political context, with a rapidly growing population and memories of the Bengal famine of 1943 still fresh, India was, in the eyes of Western politico-military cadres, a ticking time bomb. It was deemed necessary to modernize the country and this plan would constitute the driving force behind US policy in Asia. The Green Revolution contributed decisively here and was at the same time promoted as a way of managing the food pressure applied by the country's demographic explosion, as well as a method of preventive pacification of the population's needs with the aim of halting the communist threat.[183] India, however, was not the only politically and socially fertile field in Southeast Asia. The Green Revolution cadres simultaneously expanded their activities to the Philippines, which was considered one of the major bases of US influence in the broader region. The aim was to implement a model similar to the Mexican one. At the invitation of the local government, the Rockefeller Foundation established the International Rice Research Institute (IRRI) in 1961, in conjunction with the Ford Foundation and under the auspices of the State Department and the CIA. In the words of a Ford Foundation official, the institute was to function "as a potent weapon in the struggle against poverty and communism in Asia."[184] Perhaps the most well-known achievement of the IRRI was the production of a high yield hybrid variety of rice, codenamed IR-8, the so-called miracle rice. IR-8 would henceforth become the most visible mark of modernity on the ground.[185]

The "miracle rice" would soon travel to neighboring Vietnam, the war zone par excellence at the time. The USAID Accelerated Rice Program introduced both the first fifty tons in 1967 and, essentially, the Green Revolution itself. As Cullather points out, in the early stages of the Vietnam War the US policymakers described it "as a struggle for the control of rice."[186] Channeling the IR-8 there was therefore intended to increase overall rice production in the country, aiming to "win the hearts and minds" of local rural populations and to act as a symbol of the peace and prosperity that modern agricultural research would provide.[187] For the US cadres, IR-8 was much more than a rice variety. As a product of systematic agricultural research, it symbolized humankind's progress. Its arrival in Vietnam was an attempt to realize the "promise of a better life."[188] The presence of IR-8 signaled the end of the war; now, the mission was to win the peace, according to a White House official at the time.[189] So the thousands of tons of IR-8 distributed and produced in that field were a structural component of the pacification operations in the country. They were deployed as yet another weapon to enforce American hegemony. On the one hand this constituted the epitome of the "fuck 'em and feed 'em" doctrine. On the other hand, it emphasized the common root between development and war (or "construction" and destruction) within US geopolitical plans. "Rice is as important as bullets," argued Robert Komer, head of the infamous Civil Operations and Revolutionary—later Rural—Development Support program.[190] He was speaking in reference to the introduction of IR-8 in Vietnam, one of the few countries where "miracle rice" is still cultivated to this day.

The Green Revolution was to soon expand to other countries, including Brazil, always under these political conditions, as an expression of a broader anticommunist agenda. It would affect, in one way or another, food production processes at a global scale. And it would lay the groundwork for many of the gloomy phenomena that make up the normalities of the global agricultural landscape today. In short, the achievements of the Green Revolution would spread across the gray spectrum between war and "peace," demonstrating its critical geopolitical role. This parallel presence in war and non-war zones and the critical geopolitical importance of the Green Revolution within Cold War relationships is highlighted by USAID itself. As we read in the report entitled *USAID's Legacy in Agricultural Development: Fifty Years of Progress*, "The Cold War cast a shadow as USAID carried out stabilization and development alongside the military in Vietnam. At the same time, USAID provided key support to enable the Green Revolution."[191] Such accounts show that the boundaries between war and "non-war" zones on the map of geopolitical designs were, as we shall see in more detail below, altogether opaque. And we ought to understand this opacity through the genealogies of modernization practices, through the conceptual and ideological frameworks that supported the Green Revolution, and through the tactics and means this promoted in return.

Like other modernization theories of the time, the core principles of the Green Revolution were based from the outset on a Malthusian logic. In this case, concerns about rapid demographic transformations in the postcolonial world were expressed in terms of the finite ability of the earth to feed all these mouths, even more so because of the traditional and borderline "primitive" cultivation methods that dominated the larger part of the global periphery. Consequently, the instigators of the Green Revolution prioritized the increase of productivity, promoting the industrialization of agricultural production and related research. As John Perkins shows us in the case of India, the understanding of both overpopulation and prosperity were based on equations such as (population)/(resources) = (well-being).[192] As the actors involved in the planning of the Green Revolution found that they could not intervene to reduce the numerator in the fraction above, they decided to take steps to increase its denominator instead. They decided, in other words, to increase available resources. This would technically mean taking very specific actions. First, research would focus on producing high-yielding varieties and improved hybrid seeds (predominantly improved wheat and rice varieties) and on investing in technological innovations and in the application of industrialized cultivation methods. In addition, the plan for the modernization of production would promote, inter alia, the logic of monoculture farming: the massive use of pesticides, herbicides and fertilizers; the intensification of irrigation and the use of large irrigation projects; the promotion of credit and subsidies; land demarcation, land registry reform, and the determination of property rights and land titles; the creation of supply networks, roads, and other infrastructures; investment in rural research and education; and, more broadly, a complete change in the way traditional farmers thought and acted.[193] This would in turn promote the logic of entrepreneurship, integration into the market, and modes of self-perception in terms of human capital. In other words, it was a well-designed social engineering program that would radically transform the rural world and the field of agricultural production as a whole.

The Green Revolution marked the first time that such a large-scale "aid" program for rural development was implemented.[194] However, the program's course was far from uncharted or unfamiliar. The practices applied provocatively overlooked the fact that much of what is called surplus life on the planet had been the outcome of applying similar methods in the past. The new proposals were therefore reminiscent of many implemented already, which had been responsible for phenomena such as hunger and poverty, and which development experts now perceived to be "natural." However, hunger and poverty were obviously not natural phenomena but rather the result of centuries of capitalist accumulation, enclosures, colonial management, population displacement, the mechanization of agricultural production, and the violent conversion of farmers originally living in conditions of subsistence agriculture to land workers, small businessmen, or internal immigrants, who were forced to crowd against each other in swollen cities.[195] These practices not only changed the global rural scene but were also linked to a series of colossal social transformations and ultimately to the production of surplus life itself, through the conversion of rural populations into industrial/urban surplus populations. Populations rendered "surplus" by the fact that they could not be integrated into the flows of the capitalist economy. This had long been the case, for example, in England, the birthplace of industrial capitalism. As a pioneer of enclosures and accumulation processes, the country was the first to present serious symptoms of surplus life. By the nineteenth century, concerns about these surplus populations crowding in its cities were compounded by concerns over the so-called agricultural question; that is, about all those forces that were violently transforming life in the countryside. As Duffield writes, "Due to the increasing use of mechanization and growing livestock production, rural migrants were swelling the ranks of the urban unemployed, exacerbating unstable labor markets and exposing the limited amenities of the towns."[196] But this forced mass proletarianization of populations has unfortunately not been lost to history. On the contrary, it continues to determine the fate of the capitalist periphery today, and the Green Revolution has acted as an accelerator in this determining process.

And so, despite the fact that the disastrous consequences of agricultural modernization had long become evident, mid-twentieth century modernizers and "philanthropists" decided to further intensify and industrialize agricultural production. On the one hand, they believed this would afford them the opportunity to manage the geopolitical effects of accumulating surplus life on the planet, using development and productivity growth as technologies of security and preventive pacification. On the other, they pursued this growth through the logic of integrating increasingly larger parts of what they saw as an anachronistic rural world into the logic of entrepreneurship and the market, while at the same time providing profitable avenues for powerful actors in the agricultural sector, namely the agricultural and chemicals industries. This would be achieved by continuing the process of accumulation and enclosures, by normalizing rural landscapes and by exhausting their productive potential. This double aim therefore shaped the terms of a structural contradiction within the Green Revolution model. The effects of this contradiction are more visible than ever today, and they concern humanity as well as the natural environment. First, the practices of the Green Revolution have exacerbated existing social inequalities and most likely the issue of hunger itself, instead of helping solve it.[197] According to official evidence, the effects of hunger are still present despite this decades-long intensification of agricultural production. Today, it is estimated that around 820 million people worldwide suffer from chronic malnutrition, while over 2 billion people are estimated to be affected by "hidden hunger"; that is, from a lack of micronutrients.[198] These figures obviously serve to deconstruct the success story propagated by Green Revolution cadres, which, even then, relied on selective statistics and doctored figures, or on what Morten Jerven called the "political economy of data."[199]

To better understand this failure, we may focus on two points: First of all, as John Perkins aptly points out, the actors who planned the Green Revolution were concerned with the question of food production, not how this was to be distributed to the population. This means that, under conditions of constant food commercialization and the asymmetric ownership of land and the means of production alike, increasing production would only benefit those who owned these.[200] Class stratification and the particular characteristics of the societies in which the Green Revolution practices were implemented did not simply evade but were deliberately ignored by the institutions that designed the practices in question. It was a total redesign of the agricultural landscape that would not only serve to shield existing class relationships, but also sought to accentuate these. This is demonstrated if we examine, for example, the refusal by the cadres in charge to respond to popular demands for land redistribution in India and the Philippines, so as not to threaten the interests of agro-industries and large landowners;[201] their choice to promote specific crops and varieties produced in their research laboratories regardless of the eating habits of local communities; and, more generally, the proposals that were implemented—no matter whether these concerned subsidies or pesticides, fertilizers, seeds, and related technologies—that helped large and medium-sized farmers and landowners at the expense of small farmers, subsistence farmers, and the landless.[202] This brings us to the second point that needs to be highlighted, namely that the Green Revolution has essentially caused the production of additional surplus populations and thus the emergence of additional food problems, since it was directly responsible for the displacement of millions of people, mainly small farmers and their families.[203] This is clearly demonstrated by the example of Brazil, where as we shall see below, the policies of the Green Revolution led to the mass migration of rural populations from the countryside to urban centers, thereby contributing to informal urbanization and therefore to the production of an urban periphery with its own food issues. In short, the Green Revolution eventually exacerbated the very social inequalities it was supposed to solve.

But the adverse effects of the Green Revolution are not limited to exacerbating social inequalities or aggravating the food question.

It has also had an extremely destructive and most likely irreversible impact on the environment. The massive use of chemical pesticides and fertilizers, the promotion of water-intensive techniques and hybrid varieties that were thirsty for water, and the imposition of the logic of monoculture farming have all caused unprecedented environmental degradation and destruction. Soil erosion, flora poisoning, water resource depletion, and the shrinkage of biodiversity, among other losses, mark out the environmental footprint of such practices. All of the above have had an additional heavy impact on human health and on living beings on the planet as a whole. One could argue, in essence, that the implementation of modernization processes proved just as disastrous as the military operations mentioned earlier on. Not simply because "capitalism is always and everywhere engaged in a war of annihilation against every non-capitalist form that it encounters," as Neocleous rightly points out, drawing upon Rosa Luxemburg, but even more so because there was, in fact, a direct strategic and tactical conversation that occurred between the Green Revolution and counterinsurgency operations conducted by the US during that time.[204] And this destruction obviously did not occur in conditions of war but in conditions of supposed growth and prosperity. This is, on the one hand, the epitome of the logic of construction-as-destruction, a logic that lies at the core of modernization theories. On the other hand, it reaffirms in its own vicious way that war and capitalist development inherently share the same destructive root. As David Naguib Pellow puts it, in reference to the poisonous effects of the Green Revolution:

> Pesticides ... are created to enable production through the death of significant components of nature. Thus, through pesticide application, we are at once engaged in imagining the environment as a life-giving resource and as a force with which we are at war. This logic dictates that we must control and do violence to the ecosystem in order to make it work for us. This ideological framework is similar to those that support systems of social domination (slavery, militarism, patriarchy, classism, racism, and others) as well. The practice of harming the ecosystem around us in order to produce food for life-sustaining purposes should be cause for concern.[205]

Naturally enough, this shared destructive root is also to be found in the very means employed—that is, besides the common ideological and conceptual framework that supports the implementation of destruction in conditions of war and development alike. The chemical pesticides that were widely used for the needs of rural modernization, and have since then become a common and widespread agricultural practice, have been produced in part for the military industry. Some were designed in the laboratories of certain companies, as early as World War I, to be used explicitly as weapons of war, before being subsequently tested out in the field of agriculture. For example, organophosphates used as pesticides for crops, such as Parathion, were manufactured for the German military industry by Bayer Corporation, then owned by IG Farben.[206] Similar organophosphates developed after the 1930s as chemical weapons formed the basis for the manufacture of the herbicide glyphosate, which is the key ingredient of the well-known herbicide Roundup, sold for many years by Monsanto before being bought by Bayer.[207] Conversely, chemicals originally developed as herbicides and insecticides were subsequently turned into weapons of war. For example, the neurotoxic agent tabun was originally created by Bayer as an insecticide before it became "militarized" and considered suitable for use as a chemical weapon.[208] Similarly, the aforementioned Agent Orange was manufactured by the Dow Chemical Corporation (which is also the leading manufacturer of napalm incendiary bombs). Initially intended as an herbicide, it was then used en masse, as we saw, during the Ranch Hand operation in Vietnam. It was precisely this poisonous conversation between development and war that Galston also highlighted when he introduced the concept of ecocide. In doing so he showed that prior to being employed as a war tactic, ecocide had long been tested in the heart of the "developed" world as a tactic of (capitalist) development. As he stated characteristically, "It seems to me that the wilful and permanent destruction of environment in which a people can live in a manner of their own choosing ought similarly to be considered a crime against humanity, to be designated by the term ecocide. I believe that most highly developed nations have already committed autoecocide over large parts of their own countries."[209]

The agricultural modernization promoted by the Green Revolution meant, therefore, the implementation of a series of military means and tactics. That is why its effects were so devastating. Describing the material manifestations of the "agrarian war" that has been raging in Brazil for decades, Naiara Bittencourt and Alessandra Jacobovski write:

"From planting to harvest, strategies of war domination were imposed. Giant farm machinery, such as harvesters and sprinklers, were based on armored tanks. Chemical weapons were transformed into pesticides, herbicides, and fertilizers. Armor became equipment and protective clothing. Small reconnaissance aircraft are now used for aerial spraying. Even the barbed wire common in the Brazilian countryside comes from war barricades. And the sterility of modified seeds is a control tactic."[210]

Bittencourt and Jacobovski point out that the Green Revolution practices maintained a structural relationship with military technologies. Not just in terms of tactics but, as we saw earlier on, in terms of strategy and ideological content as well. Through the lens of food and in the light of the foregoing observations, we can now understand more deeply the interplay of destruction and "construction" as this plays out in the development and counterinsurgency agenda. The contemporary social and political history of food clearly shows that the Western cadres of governance and war have used similar strategic planning, similar ideological frameworks, and similar tactics in managing the food question and its security concerns alike. The poisonous dialectic of destruction and "construction" therefore blurs the boundaries between war and "peace." It is imprinted on the space-times of populations in ways that make it impossible to distinguish where a war zone ends and where a "non-war" zone begins. It proves that an agrarian war has been taking place with varying intensity, but on a global scale—and it couldn't have been otherwise.

The Green Revolution was yet another chapter in the violent history of enclosures and capitalist accumulation which, as Neocleous shows, constitutes a consistent separation of "people from subsistence on the land and its resources."[211] Plans for agricultural modernization, as a direct attack on the "anachronistic" and "unproductive" forms of rural life, meant a total redesign of the countryside, as we saw. This was of course met with local resistance.[212] Such a redesign could therefore only be realized through a close relationship with the security state and its darkest of mechanisms. Related proposals required the forcible imposition of certain spatial and social relationships, and this is how the redesign of the countryside turned into a field of social engineering, violence, and everyday warfare. And as Bittencourt and Jacobovski show us, this continues to be waged to this day. Referring to countries where the Green Revolution has been widely implemented, such as the

Philippines, India, Pakistan, Chile, and Brazil, Patel writes: "It is not accidental that these states shared a second common feature: they were all, at some point during the Green Revolution within their borders, dictatorships."[213] Brazil is perhaps one of the most striking examples. The Green Revolution reached the country relatively late, compared with Mexico or India. However, the industrialization of the country and its agricultural production had begun earlier, through the policies of Getúlio Vargas. Therefore, the Green Revolution first emerged in an environment that had already exhibited significant industrialization and modernization features. But what is also important is the geopolitical environment in which the Green Revolution was introduced into the country and, in particular, the role of the military government (1964–85) in promoting this.

From the early 1950s, the US civil-military cadres conceived Latin America as a territory that was, just like Southeast Asia, at serious risk of communist expansion. Already the revolution in Cuba and the rise of Fidel Castro to power formed a particularly threatening environment that was distressingly close to US territory. Subsequently, several guerrilla movements appeared in various Latin American countries, most of them in rural areas. This threat would have to be dealt with by using both developmental and military means. The US therefore decided to allocate several billion dollars to various Latin American governments in order to set up and strengthen key infrastructures and functions, including the agricultural sector. It is in this context that we witness the emergence of the so-called Alliance for Progress. This was, in effect, the development arm of US foreign policy in Latin America, implementing an ambitious social engineering program. At the same time, US involvement would naturally also take military form. The US military, in conjunction with USAID and the CIA, served as advisors and trained both police and military personnel (over 28,000 members of various armies).[214] Subsequently, and as security challenges shifted from rural to urban environments, the US military would promote the logic of "armed social work." In other words, it would push regular armies to undertake US-funded social programs in order to win the hearts and minds of local urban populations.[215] The anticommunist campaign further manifested itself through successive military coups. From 1962 to 1973, sixteen US-backed coups took place in Latin America, and by 1974 over half of the continent's countries were under military rule.[216]

We must therefore conceive the emergence of the Green Revolution in Brazil within the context of this geopolitical environment. That is, as a manifestation of US counterinsurgency development plans implemented jointly with the local military government As Oliveira points out, the Green Revolution was inextricably linked to the dictatorship and was promoted in the country as a tool of anticommunist policy, among other things. Military circles had been involved in agricultural policy since the mid-1950s, proving that the agricultural question was already performing crucial geopolitical functions in the country. Geopolitical functions linked to Brazil's relations with its neighbors (Bolivia, Argentina, Paraguay, and Uruguay) called for the occupation of unused land in the central and northern parts of the country and the expansion of commercial agriculture in those territories. Army generals serving at that time—the same who would lead the coup a few years later—were directly involved in this decision. A leading role was played by General Golbery do Couto e Silva, "who promoted the expansion of commercial agriculture for the territorial occupation of central and northern Brazil against threats of neighboring state incursions and rural communist uprisings."[217] Soon, however, the military's involvement in the design of national agricultural policy would increasingly look inwardly rather than toward any external threats.[218]

More precisely, land workers, who had not enjoyed the same labor rights as the industrial workers during the Vargas era (1930–45), began to organize themselves into Peasant Leagues, asking for better wages and better working conditions, resisting displacement and land grabbing, and demanding land redistribution.[219] Just days after the newly elected leftist president João Goulart announced the implementation of a radical agricultural reform in response to widespread rural discontent, the 1964 coup broke out. The coup masterminds, including Couto e Silva in a leading role, decided to overthrow Goulart and to take over the governance of the country. They placed agricultural production high up on their agenda from the outset, and the Green Revolution became one of their key tools. In addition to directly attacking the Peasant Leagues, and by extension the Communist Party that supported these, they also promoted the industrialization of agriculture, and supported the intensification and expansion of farming, especially in the regions of Cerrado and the Amazon, and they faithfully applied the Green Revolution model.[220] All this was obviously underpinned by their close ties with large agro-industrial conglomerates: ties that were to become even more overt when Couto e Silva took over as president of Dow Chemical for Latin America.[221]

The Brazilian military government was therefore a key regulator in the implementation of the Green Revolution in the country. However, the military government did not merely aim at promoting certain economic interests through this. It also aspired to respond to the productivity crisis that emerged in the middle of the last century in Brazil and other agricultural countries, and which was related, among other factors, to the intensification of agricultural production itself. As Oliveira puts it, "After all, communists were winning because landless peasants and poor workers were rising up against absentee or oppressive landlords and poverty wages, so unless agricultural productivity could be rapidly boosted and capitalist/state rule could be assured over the countryside, the international capitalist system—and the role of the US in leading it—were under grave threat of annihilation."[222] The Green Revolution in Brazil therefore played the familiar role of a preventive counterinsurgency policy. Through the modernization of agricultural production and the increase in productivity this would bring along, it attempted to address the growing food needs and manage the challenges posed by the demographic boom in the country, while overcoming the finite production capacity of traditional cultivation techniques. The key protagonists designing the Green Revolution, such as the Rockefeller Foundation and USAID, intervened in the Brazilian case as well.

The Rockefeller Foundation has had a strong presence in Brazil since the First World War, mainly in the fields of eugenics, hygiene, and public health, where it funded "programs aimed at 'the extermination of those considered degenerate.'"[223] In addition, the foundation was a key vehicle for US interests in the country. Maintaining close contact with the US government, the US military, the CIA, and large corporations, the foundation was directly involved both in the coup itself and the 1962 elections that preceded it. This shows that Goulart and his plans, in particular those related to the nationalization of oil, would undermine US interests in the country. Let us not forget that the foundation's vast wealth comes from the oil industry, and that it has maintained links to the largest oil companies, and to Standard Oil in particular. The foundation's activity during the military dictatorship was largely designed to exploit the country's land and natural resources.[224] For example, the Rockefeller Foundation funded the Summer Institute of Linguistics, an evangelical organization active in the Amazon region, which undertook the translation of the Bible into many local Indigenous languages. The institute essentially acted as a "scouting party that surveyed the Amazonian hinterlands for potential sources of opposition to natural resource exploitation," maintaining a steady presence in the Amazon and overseeing its natural resources.[225] In this context, it attempted to set up roadblocks to the dissemination of the "leftist" Liberation Theology among Indigenous peoples, undermining their social cohesion and initiating them into Western culture. In addition, the foundation was involved in drafting the "National Security Study Memorandum 200," which later on formed part of official US foreign policy. The key element of the memorandum was the concern of US cadres about the rapid growth of the population in thirteen "developing" countries, Brazil among them, and how this would affect the unhindered production and flow of available natural resources, which were, and continue to be, so essential for US capital. This would require population control measures and specific policies to secure land.[226]

Between the 1930s and the 1970s, the Rockefeller Foundation invested heavily in agricultural policy and in the formation of specialized agencies in particular. Some of these still exert enormous influence on the country's agricultural policy. For example, it invested in the development of the Luis de Queiroz Agricultural College of the University of São Paulo, and the state government's Agricultural Research Institute in Campinas. After the end of World War II, it founded the American International Association for Economic and Social Development, and the International Basic Economy Corporation, and its research institute. These institutions have substantially contributed to the acceleration of agricultural modernization in the country and by extension, to the implementation of the Green Revolution. Later on, the American International Association would conduct a large-scale survey in cooperation with USAID and the Brazilian Ministry of Agriculture to assess the sustainability of agro-industrial development in the Cerrado region. In the wake of the coup, writes Clifford Welch, the foundation intensified its activities in Brazil, as did the US government as a whole by launching, at the time, a large USAID mission to implement the broader Alliance for Progress policy in the country.[227]

USAID also played a leading role in the design of agricultural research and the industrialization of agricultural production in Brazil, most notably after the 1964 coup. Through USAID, the US government had been working with its Brazilian counterpart since 1961 to modernize the country in areas such as education, health and hygiene, agriculture, and public administration. Perhaps the most important USAID contribution to the agricultural sector was its direct involvement in the creation of the Brazilian Enterprise for Agricultural Research, known as Embrapa. Embrapa was established in 1973 by the military government's Ministry of Agriculture "as the core agricultural institution and the coordinator of a structured agricultural research system."[228] Embrapa is currently at the heart of the National System of Agricultural Research, a network comprising a multitude of universities, government research units, and federal and state funding agencies. It conducts a major part of the agricultural research in Brazil, while providing technical advice and know-how to farmers in forty-five research units across the country and has bilateral agreements with fifty-six countries and eighty-nine foreign institutions.[229] Its role is so crucial that Brazil's standing as one of the world's largest exporters of food today is considered to be due to Embrapa's agricultural research. USAID also supported, among other things, two public universities in Piracicaba and Viçosa, thereby strengthening agricultural science courses. Four decades later, both schools are regarded as major centers of agricultural knowledge production in Brazil and worldwide. In the 1960s and 1970s, USAID also promoted the exchange of Brazilian and US scientists in order to introduce the most advanced cultivation techniques to the country.

USAID's contribution to the industrialization of agricultural production in Brazil was therefore decisive. And it certainly does not stem from any genuine concern of US "philanthropists" over hunger or poverty. As said, USAID's development packages were part of a broader US geopolitical plan that sought to halt communist expansion in Latin American countries, while promoting the logic of the market and US financial interests. USAID's role in implementing agricultural policies is still central today, as Mark Langan shows us in relation to

Africa—even though such policies are no longer designed in the name of a "barbaric" industrial modernization, but are instead called for in the name of "sustainable development." There too the element of concern is unhindered access to natural resources, which is based on the promotion of agro-industrial activities and requires the implementation of land-grabbing practices under a politics of neocolonialism.[230] Indeed, the Brazilian model, which has been tested for decades, has been exported and applied today in various African countries in the context of a supposed "South-to-South cooperation." Embrapa is yet again playing a leading role in its implementation, as the Lula Institute emphasizes.[231]

But, clearly, USAID's presence in Brazil was not limited to the agricultural sector. As one of the key agents of US counterinsurgency, it was closely linked to the authoritarian regimes supported by the US. And this support has not only been expressed through programs of agricultural modernization and humanitarian aid, but also by modernizing local security forces and intensifying policing methods. Besides, the promotion of "growth" and the unhindered exploitation of natural resources required a "safe" environment in the wider region. And this was done, among other means, by letting USAID undertake the provision of security training both in Brazil and in other countries in the continent, a collaboration that naturally intensified following the 1964 coup. Both agricultural modernization and the modernization of public security were therefore two sides of the same counterinsurgency coin. Like in so many other Latin American countries, USAID's goal in Brazil was clear: "to inject financial and technical resources ... with the aim of stimulating modernization in the hope that this would weaken the appeal of revolution ... involving the stimulation of modernization, but also the financing and training of security forces, both military and police."[232] Especially when "Brazil had to remain the bulwark against communism in South America."[233]

The implementation of the Green Revolution and agricultural modernization in the country more broadly has left an extremely negative legacy. First of all, the industrialization of production has had a devastating effect on the natural environment itself. The use of herbicides and pesticides has caused enormous environmental degradation and destruction. Today, Brazil is considered one of the largest consumers of pesticides in the world. "Annual sales are around US$10 billion. In

2014, some 1,550 thousand tons were sold to Brazilian purchasers. This corresponds to around 7.5 kilograms of pesticides used per person in Brazil each year."[234] In 2018 rules regarding the use of certain pesticides, many of which had previously been banned in the European Union, were relaxed. The future looks bleak when considering that one of the members of the committee who approved this relaxation of the rules, Tereza Cristina Dias, took over the Ministry of Agriculture under the Bolsonaro administration. A prominent member of the country's agro-industrial lobby, Dias is nicknamed "the Poison Muse." In its first five months in power, the new administration approved the use of 197 pesticides.[235] All of this obviously leaves a devastating impact on the health both of the populations living in these areas and the consumers who purchase these agricultural and animal products.[236] In addition, the continued spatial expansion of the agricultural industry is responsible for the continual shrinkage of unique ecosystems, which are of vital importance to the country and the rest of the planet. The unstoppable deforestation of the Amazon and the continual occupation of its land by agricultural and livestock farms have an ecological impact on a global scale. In addition to the devastating impact on the region's flora and fauna, they also mark the rapid shrinking of the world's largest rainforest, which is believed to accelerate the already alarming signs of climate change.

Agricultural modernization also means that there is a permanent and ever-worsening war being waged, with thousands of victims. This agrarian war is waged first and foremost against Indigenous peoples, who see their land being destroyed and themselves displaced in order for the agro-industries to expand their activities. Since the time of the military government, their communities have been seen as an obstacle to the exploitation of specific regions and to development plans as a whole. The 1988 constitution included special protective frameworks for the country's Indigenous people, but today these legal frameworks are systematically disputed. Attacks on Indigenous populations have intensified, both from security forces and from armed groups and militias serving specific financial interests. For example, according to a Global Witness report entitled "At What Cost?," 2017 proved to be the world's bloodiest year for defenders of land and the environment alike. The Indigenous population paid the highest price, with 201 recorded murders. The agro-industrial sector (mainly the coffee, palm oil, and banana sectors) proved to be the most lethal, as it was involved in 46 of these murders. Sixty percent of all murders took place in Latin America, while "Brazil saw the most deaths ever recorded in any country," "with 57 people killed, 80% of them killed while protecting the natural riches of the Amazon."[237] Naiara Bittencourt and Alessandra Jacobovski speak of 65 deaths and 4 massacres in the same year and at least 1,536 clashes in 2016.[238] The situation is sure to deteriorate in the future, judging by Bolsonaro's announcements and by the fact that, on the first day of his presidency he decided to transfer responsibility for certifying Indigenous territories as protected lands from the National Indian Foundation to the Ministry of Agriculture.

This agrarian war is also waged against the landless or land-poor rural workers. Since colonial times, Brazil has been characterized by a terribly unequal distribution and occupation of land, a situation that remained unchanged even after its independence. This inequality has worsened over the years, as large landowners have increasingly appropriated land and expanded their holdings uncontrollably.[239] The aforementioned agricultural modernization policies and the Green Revolution in particular subsequently exacerbated this imbalance. On the one hand, large farm units and landowners benefited from these conditions by expanding their holdings and increasing their production.[240] On the other, the invasion of industrialization, which made manual farm work uncompetitive and unprofitable, led to a complete depreciation of the value of labor and further displaced large rural populations, virtually producing a new surplus population that was largely concentrated in the urban periphery.[241] In this context, the landless and poor farmers have been intensifying their struggles since the late 1970s, making land claims and gradually achieving the activation of agrarian reform and land redistribution programs.

Just a few figures will be enough for us to understand the significance and size of these struggles. Between 1988 and 2013, more than 9,400 land invasions and land occupations took place. As a result of these struggles, 770 million acres were transferred to approximately 1.25 million families as part of land redistribution initiatives.[242] This redistribution may have led to improvements at the local level, but it did not signal any substantial change in the imbalances that shape Brazil's overall rural landscape. And that is a testament to the power of the agro-industrial lobby in the country. Therefore, despite agricultural reform programs, the situation regarding land occupation has not changed substantially over the years. In addition, these rural struggles led to the mobilization of large-scale landowners and industrialists, who not only attempted to intervene at the institutional level to slow down and restrict land redistribution, but also acted in organized retaliation, forming militias and armed groups to protect their properties. According to official data, 1,208 murders of peasants and their senior representatives were recorded in this fifteen-year period demonstrating that "democratization" was accompanied by the escalation of an agrarian war that continues to this day.[243]

This war, like most wars, caused further mass population displacement. As we saw, within the competitive and asymmetric conditions created by the modernization of the countryside, new surplus populations were formed that were not only excluded from their means of survival and/or the local production process, but were also forced to migrate, seeking refuge primarily in urban centers. It is important to emphasize this because the processes of agricultural modernization and the Green Revolution as their structural component were more than just one of the key forces behind the acceleration of urbanization. As we have seen above in relation to the notorious "agricultural question," they were one of the main causes behind the formation of the urban periphery and informality in the way we know them to exist in Brazil today. In short, and looking specifically at the example of Rio, the favelas must be interpreted as a socio-spatial product of the Green Revolution as well.[244] Even though their history may be traced back to the late nineteenth century and their evolution runs throughout the first half of the twentieth century, the Green Revolution era undoubtedly signaled a tremendous spread of the phenomenon and, more broadly, an explosion of informal urbanization in the country, which was the outcome of the violence and urgency that forced millions of people to flee the countryside.

The country, of course, had been experiencing rapid urbanization since the Vargas era, when he implemented his plan to transform Brazil from a rural to an industrialized and urbanized country, and began the so-called Path to the West.[245] This plan would mean an increase in urbanization rates, which would already begin to manifest itself at the time in largely informal terms. As Oliveira points out, the agricultural modernization required by this "path" has massively displaced farmers and workers "from the countryside even faster than the import-substitution industrialization created employment opportunities in the cities, which began to mushroom with slums."[246] It is estimated that 3 million people moved to urban areas in the 1940s and 1950s, while the number more than doubled (7 million) in the following decade.[247] As a result, urbanization rates accelerated after World War II, but really skyrocketed in the 1960s and 1970s with the implementation of the Green Revolution.[248] According to data from the Brazilian Institute of Geography and Statistics (Instituto Brasileiro de Geografia e Estatística [IBGE]) and demographic censuses, there was a clear intensification of internal migration from the countryside to the cities in the 1960s and 1970s. During this time, a total of 31 million internal migrants fled to urban areas as a result of agricultural modernization.[249] Taking into account the indirect impact of migration as well, namely the children born to those who settled in the cities, it is estimated that between 1960 and the late 1980s some 43 million people moved from rural to urban areas.[250]

These moves obviously left a heavy mark on Rio as well. During the second half of the twentieth century, the total population of the metropolitan area of Rio nearly quadrupled. Much of this increase was absorbed in informal settlements within the city. Between 1960 and 1990, the population of favelas more than doubled according to the Brazilian Institute of Geography and Statistics. In the second half of the twentieth century, their growth rate was 2.5 times that of the rest of the city, which today hosts the largest population of favela inhabitants in Brazil, effectively accounting for one quarter of the total population that lives in favelas across the country.[251] The above figures show there was a huge population shift and a radical demographic transformation both locally and nationally within a very short time, in a country that in 1920 only measured a total of 27.5 million inhabitants.[252] As Martine and McGranahan point out, "Brazil went through a mechanical revolution, a chemical revolution and a demographic revolution, telescoping into a few years three processes that had each taken much longer to mature in rich countries."[253]

These figures clearly leave no doubt about the mark left by the Green Revolution in shaping Brazil's contemporary urban anthropo-geography. Yet if we placed them in the geopolitical context of the time, we would have the right to read this rapid urbanization not only as a vehicle and an indicator of the country's overall modernization but also as an (indirect) counterinsurgency methodology similar to that advocated by Huntington and applied, as we saw above, in the Vietnam War and elsewhere. Viewing these figures through the role that urbanization played in the counterinsurgency problematizations at the time, we might rightly assume that, from a certain point onward, the promotion of rural modernization in Brazil (and the Green Revolution in particular) may have been driven by similar intentions regarding the counterinsurgency function of urbanization. We might be right to assume, in other words, that the demographic explosion characterizing Brazilian cities and, by extension, the hundreds of thousands of people squeezed into Rio's informal settlements, was not a natural or accidental development. Instead, it was "allowed" to happen in order to move parts of the rural population out of the Brazilian countryside, at a time when communist armed resistance was making its presence felt in rural regions.[254] Even more so, since agricultural policies widened the gap between poor rural populations on the one hand and large landowners and agricultural industries on the other, forming an environment of social discontent and political grievances that could be exploited politically by the communists, even though this does not seem to have happened in the case of Brazil. This assumption can be further reinforced if we focus on the close relations Huntington himself had with the country's military government and especially if we consider the fact that his positions on urbanization-as-counterinsurgency had been formulated in 1968, only a few years before he met with representatives of the government of Emílio Garrastazu Médici in 1972, and in 1974 with General Ernesto Geisel. Together with Couto e Silva, Geisel then implemented the so-called "decompression" plan; that is, a plan to "liberalise" the regime, with Huntington himself in an advisory capacity.[255]

In short, Brazil's rapid urbanization may not have been merely an inevitable byproduct or accident on the way to modernization, but could also have been promoted as a tool of a broader counterinsurgency policy at the core of which lie, as we have seen, practices of population displacement and forced migration to cities. In any case, the accumulation of surplus life that formed the urban periphery would soon create its own challenges and its own fields of securitization. As Neocleous states in reference to Mexico's agricultural modernization policies, "the forcible dispossession of some two million farmers of their means of subsistence" would automatically turn them into immigrants and hence into a "security problem."[256] The theories of modernization would soon therefore reach their own limits. The city, as the spatial and ideological counterpoint to the village, once a symbol of the desirable end on the simplistic evolutionary continuum of developmental theories, would now (re)constitute a place of social tensions and challenges. The slums that in Huntington's eyes may have still seemed like a way to a better life for poor farmers, would soon force the cadres in charge to "reconsider the city's place at the top end of the developmental ladder."[257] Even more so after the urban riots and uprisings that have reached something of a peculiar urban normality since the Watts riots of 1965 onward.[258]

An important component of this urban question would henceforth concern the increased food needs and broader food insecurity of the populations of the urban periphery. This had already been highlighted by the prominent Brazilian physician and geographer Josué de Castro when he emphasized that in the rapid urbanization imposed by the logic of modernization and industrialization of the country, the dire food situation of poor urban populations constituted a major political issue.[259] Sooner or later governance cadres would therefore have to deal with the food needs of these populations. Obviously not out of a genuine interest in their hunger or suffering, but, as we have seen from the outset, because of their concerns about the explosive energy that may be released when these needs remain unfulfilled. After all, the ghost of food riots never ceased to haunt the plans of security and development experts. And as Foucault originally pointed out, this ghost has long had a certain relationship with the urban environment and its inhabitants. It is still present today, and perhaps now more than ever. "Hungry slum dwellers are unlikely to accept their fate quietly. For centuries, sudden hunger in slums has provoked the same response: riots," admits Paul Collier, a former director of the Development Research Group of the World Bank, with the well-known arrogance of high-ranking executives of organizations responsible for rural deregulation and the destruction of much of this planet.[260] And he acknowledges this in support of further strengthening all those practices that have been responsible for this very destruction.

The security risks posed by the accumulation of starving people in the cities therefore require another urgent cycle of productivity growth at all costs. All the more so today, when the combination of the rapid informal development of the cities of the Global South and the ongoing global food crisis, which is partly due to the steady rise in food prices and the dependence on centralized and largely globalized food distribution networks, makes the issue of the nutritional status of urban populations more complex and urgent.[261] Even though hunger and malnutrition are generally considered to primarily affect rural populations, poor urban populations in the periphery actually prove to be more vulnerable in times of crisis such as today's, as they are substantially more vulnerable to rising food inflation. This is because, on the one hand, they do not have sufficient purchasing power allowing them access to nutritious food, and, on the other, they do not produce food themselves and therefore "cannot cope with food price volatility and supply in the same way as rural populations."[262] As a result, this structural vulnerability completes, in the most ironic of ways, today's Green Revolution paradox: a "revolution" that was supposedly designed to boost agricultural productivity and lift the world's population out of the famine spectrum, has ultimately produced an urban surplus life that is condemned to continued food insecurity. A "revolution" promoted as a method for pacifying the surplus populations of this world has led to the production of additional surplus populations that are now subject to yet another pacification process.

Ecopacification: From Green Revolution to Green Governmentality

So we are right back where we started, back to the informal geographies of surplus life, back to the needs and security issues with which these cramped conditions are traditionally identified. As we saw earlier on, the relationship of food management to the (re)production of surplus populations is characterized by a structural antinomy in the pacification/counterinsurgency context. Not only is the food question central to their management but also to their own production. This antinomy shaped a large part of the postwar capitalist periphery. On the one hand, it did so through agricultural deregulation policies and the violent and irreversible transformation of the rural world, and on the other, through the rapid production of new urban surplus life with its own unsolvable food problems. This parallel movement is, as we have seen, perfectly visible in the case of Brazil, perhaps more so than anywhere else. This historic movement, both in Brazil and elsewhere in Latin America, may have entered a new phase as urbanization rates have fallen sharply. However, the issues that have shaped the course of this movement are still of critical importance. As we saw, the food question cannot be disconnected from the management of surplus life and from the issues of public security through which this life has been problematized throughout the ages. "Food in people's mouths," as Lula had argued from the outset, serves as a guarantee of public order. It functions as a prerequisite for social peace and, ultimately, as a means of population management. Our passage through the theories and practices of pacification/counterinsurgency has confirmed this position, and so it would now be meaningful to examine how the food question relates to the pacification program implemented in the city of Rio.

In late 2006, before the pacification operations began, Rio's Municipal Secretary for the Environment (Secretaria Municipal de Meio Ambiente [SMAC]) launched an ambitious urban agriculture program called Hortas Cariocas. Under this program, the municipality decided to create urban gardens in various areas of Rio, among them certain favelas selected following a census and a Pereira Passos Institute survey on "per capita income in areas with land available for horticulture."[263] According to Adrian Hearn, with regard to the favelas, the aims of this initiative were social integration and the improvement of nutritional health indicators in those areas. This was to be achieved, on the one hand, by creating jobs in local communities and, on the other, by giving local residents the opportunity to access organic and better-quality food. Under this program the Municipal Secretary for the Environment was to provide the people working in the gardens an amount equal to half the minimum wage, derived from funds collected from petroleum rights and municipal fines, under the condition that they offer half of their production to schools, kindergartens, and poor families.[264] They were also allowed to sell the remainder of their production in local markets.

This program gradually garnered attention and was advertised as one of the municipality's more successful initiatives. This was not only due to its scale—forty gardens of different sizes have been created since 2006, not all of them equally successful.[265] It also had to do with the fact that the program was linked to the broader agenda of sustainable development in which, as we shall see below, the city of

Rio plays a central role. However, what lends the program additional importance, and what is of particular interest to us, is the fact that from a certain point onward, it fell under the auspices of the pacification program. It is therefore important to dwell briefly on the parameters of this integration in order to reexamine how food, and the question of its production in particular, becomes part of public security policy. The context of the "securitization" of the food question may change significantly in this particular case, in comparison to the Cold War framework discussed above. However, it is important to highlight the role of food, and its production in particular, in the design and implementation of a pacification program, in order to reveal both the similarities and differences between the two frameworks and to focus on broader issues that ultimately do not only concern the city of Rio. At first glance, the interest of security cadres in an urban agriculture project would appear somewhat inexplicable. In practice, however, it turned out that urban gardens, as part of a wider urban revitalization program, worked well with pacification operations. In order to better understand how this happened we have to read it in light of the notion of sustainable development, which as we shall see, constitutes not only one of the dominant ways in which human existence acquires meaning in the biosphere today, but also a discourse of truth that redefines social engineering practices in the context of so-called green governmentality. In other words, in the context of an agenda that introduces the environmental parameter and the demand for environmental protection into population management technologies.[266]

In June 2012, and while the pacification operations were in full swing, Rio hosted the United Nations Conference on Sustainable Development. This conference remains an important event in relation to the city's own public security policies: not only did it require increased policing and military involvement to safeguard the smooth conduct of the conference but also, as a mega-event in itself, it served as a unique testing ground for the FIFA World Cup and the Olympic Games that were to follow in 2014 and 2016 respectively. In this way, it contributed to Rio's effort—and that of the country as a whole—to secure global visibility and a stronger branding by proving that Rio is a safe city.[267] Yet the importance of this conference also lies in the debate on sustainable development, since this is exactly where the current development agenda of the international community was set.

As Eduarda de La Rocque and Petras Shelton-Zumpano point out, "Rio de Janeiro has become one of the leaders of local governments in the global South for discussions on sustainable development."[268] More concretely, the proceedings of this conference resulted in the "Post-2015 Development Agenda" and gave birth to the so-called Sustainable Development Goals (SDGs). This is a list of seventeen goals pertaining to economic development, social inequality, social prosperity, and environmental degradation, set by the United Nations as a target to be accomplished by all national governments by 2030.

This conference is the most recent stop, for the time being, on a course originally plotted in 1972 when the United Nations Conference on the Human Environment took place in Stockholm. Its aim was to establish limits on the dominant developmental policies of the time in terms of their environmental impact.[269] We could claim that this was the official starting point for the debate on sustainable development, at least in the way it is formulated in the international governmental agenda, given that sustainability discourse had already emerged, in different ways, in the 1960s and 1970s, through the activity of radical environmental movements and intellectuals. This was followed by a systematic effort which essentially gave shape to the sustainable development agenda. For example, the World Commission on Environment and Development, otherwise called the Brundtland Commission, was established in 1983. The outcome of this commission was the publication, four years later, of *Our Common Future*, widely known as the "Brundtland Report." It was followed by the United Nations Conference on Environment and Development held in Rio in 1992 (also known as the Rio de Janeiro Earth Summit), the UN Conference on Environment and Development held in Johannesburg in 2002, also known as Rio+10, and finally the aforementioned 2012 conference in Rio, also known as Rio+20.

In short, two conferences have been held in Rio while Johannesburg's conference had a sequential Rio reference in its title. This all shows that the city plays a central role in shaping the sustainable development agenda, to the extent that Joseph Huber speaks of "the Rio process."[270] This term however, as Lynley Tulloch and David Neilson point out, does not merely confirm Rio's pivotal position within this agenda. It further demonstrates that, through the last three conferences, its neoliberalization has been attempted and achieved.

In short, the "Rio Process" has gradually shifted the debate from a direction that perceived sustainability as a critique of the economy, to a direction that now entrusts the market with the task of resolving the environmental impasses it creates itself, no matter how paradoxical that might sound. Commenting on the interaction of sustainability with neoliberalism, Brad Evans and Julian Reid write: "While sustainable development, in particular, deploys ecological reason to argue for the need to secure the life of the biosphere, neoliberalism prescribes economy as the very means of that security."[271] Ultimately, this interaction reveals the confusion inherent in the very notion of sustainable development. Within this discourse, it is difficult to ascertain whether the priority is the sustainability of the planet or the sustainability of development itself. As Serge Latouche rightly points out: "Sustainable development (or 'durable' as we call it in France) is an oxymoron. It is a contradiction in terms and, in fact, appears as a terrifying or miserable word. At least with 'un-sustainable' (non-durable) development, we could maintain the hope that this lethal process would have had an end."[272]

It is therefore not a coincidence that, the more the debate on sustainable development spreads, the more this paradox is highlighted. The so-called paradox of sustainable development brings forth the antinomy inherent in the notion itself: within the capitalist system and the logic of competitiveness and profitability on which this rests, the notion of development cannot be dissociated from the continued consumption of natural resources and the continuous production of pollutants/waste and therefore from environmental degradation.[273] This antinomy is even visible in the formal definition of sustainable development proposed by the "Brundtland Report," to the extent that the economy—in the form of development—is presented as an inescapable element of the way we understand the natural world itself. According to this definition, sustainable development is defined as "development that meets the needs of the present without compromising the ability of future generations to meet their own needs."[274] However, as Evans and Reid write, commenting on the theoretical direction that the "Brundtland Report" inaugurates, "Proponents of sustainable development did not claim to question the value of economic development in and of itself, but they did aspire to offer a framework for the re-regulation of the economy in alignment with the needs and interests of the biosphere."[275] This privileging of the economy was gradually validated within the official governmental agenda. As Mark Langan points out, the adoption of SDGs by the international community marks the transition to a phase where economic development becomes a priority.[276] The SDGs took the place of the so-called Millennium Development Goals (MDGs), which were agreed upon by all members of the United Nations at the Millennium Summit held in New York in September 2000, with the ambition of defining the development agenda until 2015. However, as Langan observes, while the MDGs focused on humanitarian issues (at least in theory) the SDGs directly raised the issue of economic development instead.[277]

In essence, this choice directly and actively involves the notions of the market and of entrepreneurship in the process of solving social and environmental problems. In the words of Rob Krueger and David Gibbs, "The market, properly defined, incentivized, and reflecting real costs of development, is the most desirable institution for delivering human prosperity and ecological integrity. Here market-produced values are surrogates for the value of 'environment.'"[278]The notion of sustainability is therefore gradually being deprived of its character as a critique of development, which it had been essentially associated with in the 1960s and 1970s, and becomes instead part of a broader redesign and "greening" of the economy, which was based on the dominance of the neoliberal model. Radical ecological principles were therefore stripped of their political content and incorporated into neoliberal policies, which since the 1980s have called for continued promotion of market and competitiveness on one hand, and the drastic shrinking of the welfare state and reduction of social spending on the other. Both of these approaches are relevant to the advancement and implementation of the sustainable development agenda, particularly in the countries of the Global South. Sustainability presupposes the creation/expansion of a business enabling environment and a market-driven economy, especially in places that still maintain forms of subsistence economy. At the same time, it reflects the neoliberal critique of state and state intervention, namely the state modernization policies of the Cold War. As we shall see, these focused on the self-reliance of local populations and the boosting of the private sector and market logic.[279]

While sustainable development has been adopted as a central policy framework of the international community, it is not in fact a practice that runs horizontally across all corners of this world. Rather, it concerns primarily the countries of the "developing" world and describes a specific relationship between them and the "developed" world. In other words, it helps reproduce and exacerbate the long-standing divisions between the two worlds, if we may call them so. Evidently following in the footsteps of the broader notion of development, sustainable development renews the relations of domination that make up the colonial context. In short, it is only an updated and "greener" form of the West's attempt to reshape the "developing" world based on western criteria and with a view to integrating it into a market economy. Such reshaping initially required the "developing" world to be problematized through western perceptions (e.g., about poverty, prosperity, and social progress). It then advanced the logic of economic development as the solution to any social problems. As Subhabrata Bobby Banerjee puts it, when describing Arturo Escobar's approach, "development first created the notion of poverty ... then 'modernized' the poor, transforming them into the 'assisted.' This set in place new modes of relations and mechanisms of control under the clarion call of 'development.' Development proceeded by constructing problems, applying solutions and creating 'abnormalities,' such as the 'illiterate,' the 'underdeveloped,' the 'landless peasants' who would later be treated and reformed."[280]

The notion of sustainable development follows this logic, introducing current environmental stakes into the debate. Hence the fact that the promotion of the sustainable development agenda was perceived by the countries of the Global South as a new form of colonization and as the imposition from above of a global environmental discourse that trampled over local cultural idioms and systems of knowledge, essentially imposing a homogeneous perception of nature that quantifies and ultimately turns it into a "natural asset."[281]

Sustainability discourse began to gain traction at a time when there was much criticism, both on the part of social movements and the academic community, of the western model of postwar development that was imposed on "developing" countries, due to its social and environmental impact. However, the criticism and opposition to this state-controlled development model did not originate solely in these movements or among those who displayed political sensitivity to neocolonial policies and the plight of the periphery. They also originated among certain liberal cadres and, more specifically, in neoliberal circles. On the one hand the ambition of development theorists, such as Rostow, to gradually transform the capitalist periphery into a Western-style consumer society that would attain the standard of Western life led to colossal social upheavals when implemented. Along with these came fears for the disruption of social cohesion and public security. On the other hand, the constraints placed on development by the sustainability agenda were convenient for those who challenged state-led modernization and nation-building policies, demanding the curtailing of state involvement in development plans as these were implemented at various points in the periphery.

Within these cycles, the ambition to equate the "developing" with the "developed" world by improving production and consumption indices ran counter to the awareness of the world's finite resources and the realization that the "developing" world could not, in the end, enjoy the luxuries and amenities of the western way of life. This realization is repeated today more than ever, in the shadow of global demographic spread in countries in the Global South and climate change. But the rise to predominance of the neoliberal model meant much more than the mere realization of this finitude. On the one hand, it signaled the rejection of protective regulatory frameworks, opening up more avenues for uncontrolled market expansion. It meant, in other words, that an increasing part of the "developing" world would continue to be the object of predatory exploitation, with large corporations and international financial organizations engaging in land grabbing, the privatization of natural resources, the relocation of polluting units, even the acquisition of emissions, and the export of waste to the periphery, among other things. An economic model, in short, that is anything but sustainable. On the other hand, as Duffield points out, the sustainable development agenda would suit neoliberal cadres and would provide an excellent opportunity to recast the demand for "less state,"[282] now based on the importance of the communities' self-reliance and their ability to secure the preconditions for their survival, reproduction, and their own well-being.[283]

The neoliberal advancement of sustainable development therefore demanded the withdrawal of the state and hence of any chances of establishing some kind of social protection—even if the creation of a social state was admittedly not among the intentions of state-led development theorists either. In this way, it simply affirmed the gap between the "developed" and the "developing" world, as defined by the presence or absence of social protection/welfare institutions. It affirmed, in other words, the gap between insured and uninsured populations.[284] Within this context, the theory of sustainable development largely crystallizes the predominance of the neoliberal agenda, which promotes the model of a subject that manages alone the risks of their existence in this life,[285] and by extension their exposure to the disastrousness of this world.[286] This is why the notion of sustainability is so closely linked to the notion of resilience, yet another buzzword of the modern age that perfectly condenses the impact of neoliberalism on the subject's perception and production.[287] Within this context, the surplus populations of the capitalist periphery are therefore called upon to face the challenges of daily life without the expectation of social protection frameworks, sometimes only supported by some form of financial aid or self-help policy that will provide the incentives needed for them to become at best (small) business owners and the opportunity of their integration into the flow of the market, like in the Green Revolution example. In the words of Duffield,

> Sustainable development reflects a neoliberal political agenda that shifts the burden of supporting life from states to people. It is a population, however, reconfigured in risk-management terms as social entrepreneurs or active citizens, in this case operating at the level of the household, community and basic needs. Development interventions create opportunities for such entrepreneurs to prove themselves by bettering their individual and collective self-reliance. Sustainable development is a security technology that attempts to contain the circulatory effects of non-insured surplus life by putting the onus on potential migrants to adjust their expectations while improving their resilience through self-reliance in situ.[288]

The debate on sustainable development is therefore more complex and pertains to much more than the environmental implications of each development model. This complexity, which primarily concerns power relations and subject production processes, largely manifests itself in the simplistic "North/South" geopolitical axis but also in every field where the toxic dialectic of development/underdevelopment applies, as evidenced by the increasingly widespread debate on the sustainability of cities today. The so-called urban periphery, in the form of pockets of "underdevelopment" within the city, is constantly being problematized through the conceptual tools of sustainability—and so are its surplus populations. The case of Rio in particular offers relevant correlations and provides a paradigmatic application of this logic. As mentioned, the city plays a leading role in shaping the sustainable development agenda. But how does this agenda return to, and how is it imprinted upon the city's daily space-times? The Rio+20 conference established the global agenda for sustainable development until 2030. The conference's decisions influenced the municipality's policies in a number of ways. At the initiative of the mayor at the time, Eduardo Paes, the city decided to chart the "2013–2016 Strategic Plan," which was also to be implemented by 2030. The plan largely incorporated key points of the sustainable development agenda.[289] These points are located within what Eduarda de La Rocque and Petras Shelton-Zumpano call the "Sustainable Development Strategy of the Municipal Government of Rio."[290] This helps us understand more concretely how environmental issues are directly intertwined with governance, security, and the market. As the two authors point out, the municipality's "sustainable" policy did not merely adopt the three key pillars of sustainable development—economic, social, and environmental—as these had already been outlined by the Brundtland Commission in 1987. It incorporated, in addition, good governance, which was the fourth pillar proposed in *The Future We Want*, the document produced by Rio+20.[291]

Through their roles as Pereira Passos Institute executives (president and technical advisor specifically for the Rio+Social program), La Rocque and Shelton-Zumpano give a detailed overview of the implementation of the sustainability agenda through the municipality's policies and through the institute's involvement. The institute, as mentioned above, was a key pillar in the design and implementation of the pacification program. Reading through the municipality's so-called "Sustainable Development Strategy," we are able to see first of all how the roles of the market and the private sector were prioritized in achieving sustainability. References to the private sector, multisector partnerships, and public-private partnerships are to be found numerous times throughout the detailed account of this strategy. As the two authors put it, the fourth pillar of sustainable development concerns "good governance, not only of public administration but also of the alliances established between people, governments, civil society and the private sector."[292] However, this "strategy" reveals another thing as well. By focusing on the pillar of "good governance" it links the sustainable development agenda to public security. "Good governance requires peace and security," write La Rocque and Shelton-Zumpano; and this is when the UPPs make their appearance, too.[293] As paradoxical as it may sound, the pacification program is not merely described as a required component of so-called good governance but also as one of the prerequisites for achieving sustainable development in itself. Through the municipality's "Sustainable Development Strategy" we are then able to comprehend that the issue of urban revitalization in the name of sustainability and green development presupposes the involvement of security forces; regardless of whether this involvement is expressed in terms of police-military occupation or manifested through the more sophisticated forms of armed social work. The "aggressive formalization" program of social and spatial relations (market promotion, land use regulation, standardization of informal livelihood and social reproduction, and a broader enclosure policy) as described above, was therefore enriched with green meanings, in keeping with the spirit of our times.

The pacification program contributed to the promotion of the sustainability agenda in the way this was perceived by government cadres. That is to say, it underscored the role of the market. In essence, it created an appropriate and safe environment for the advancement of social and business innovation and for the arrival of public and private services that allowed the "reintegration" of the favelas into "democratic society," as Cabral put it above.[294] This "shock of order," to recall the official term used by Paes himself, was achieved not only through the use of weapons, but also thanks to the involvement of social scientists, social workers, and NGOs. In some cases, in addition to providing social services and greening different aspects of everyday life, these actors consciously or unconsciously created the conditions necessary for the integration of informal forms of livelihood and social reproduction into the sphere of the formal economy.[295] This integration was nothing but the opening of a new market and the discovery of a new land for the private sector, thereby confirming the neoliberal shift of the sustainability agenda outlined above.

The World Bank report, which was incidentally compiled by the Sustainable Development Sector Management Unit of the Latin American and Caribbean Regional Office, reads: "Today virtually every large regional, national or multinational company present in Rio has some type of activity in UPP areas.... From the largest banks to telecom companies, Coca-Cola, and cosmetics brands, the private sector has now realized that with the pacification, investments in these communities mean building access to new consumer markets. In addition, they have started to see in these areas the potential of training workers for the booming sectors of the economy, such as tourism, industry, and services, which are in high demand for more human capital."[296]

This is also confirmed by the policy of the Brazilian Service for the Support of Micro and Small Business (Serviço Brasileiro de Apoio às Micro e Pequenas Empresas [SEBRAE]), the principal body of the federal and state government policies with regard to the creation and development of businesses, which "created a special division for those favelas in which the UPP had succeeded."[297] The foregoing shows that one goal, if not the most fundamental, of the pacification operations was to turn the favelas into a field of economic exploitation. To open up, in other words, these once "introverted" places to the market and to facilitate conditions for companies and businesses to either enter, or be established there.

This logic could be said to have structural similarities to the preceding debate regarding the agricultural modernization of the capitalist periphery. Despite the fact that a shift from modernization to sustainable development is readily discernible at the discursive level, one of the key issues in both examples remains the integration of any "periphery" into the market, whether this means the invasion of business, the forced relocation of subjects from conditions of subsistence or informal economy to the sphere of formal economy, or the advancement of entrepreneurship and the transformation of community members into (micro)entrepreneurs. There are additional similarities to be noted in the formulation of this issue. In the discourse regarding the pacification of favelas, we may trace a conceptual axis, similar to the one based on the village/city dichotomy, and which constituted the measure by which modernization theories evaluated a community's degree of development. More specifically, one may argue that the favelas are being problematized as a certain kind of "village" within the urban environment. A "village" based both on the degree of state and market presence and on the quality of the environment and related infrastructures. The latter testify to the degree of under-development in ecological terms, in the sustainability context. The terminology used to refer to different aspects of the city also attests to this fact. The two different terms used for the formal (*asfalto*, or asphalt) and informal (*morro*, or hillside) city do not simply reflect the city's unique physical terrain.[298] They are furthermore based on the division between village and city and on the differences between urban and rural topography. And this terminological distinction is not limited to spatial and topographical characteristics. It is also articulated in anthropogeographic terms and it is linked to the predominantly rural past of the people living in the favelas. This relates to both the first phase of the formation of the favelas, largely composed of those formerly enslaved on Brazilian plantations who immigrated to Rio after the abolition of slavery in 1888, and to the phase that coincided with the Green Revolution. Its practices forced, as we saw already, a large proportion of rural populations, mostly from northeastern Brazil, to migrate from the countryside to Rio's urban periphery.[299]

In the case of the Rio pacification program, as in the examples of the implementation of agricultural modernization, the aim is the problematization and management of this peculiar (urban) "rurality." Such "rurality" had to be transformed at the first opportunity through community development initiatives and through its link to the opera-tions of the market. Through an intensive social engineering program, that is, based on the development-security nexus; or, to be more precise, on the sustainable development-pacification nexus. As David Nally and Stephen Taylor put it in relation to the practices of the Green Revolution, "strategies designed to orientate social exchanges away from subsistence living and toward commercial practices formed an integral part of counter-insurgency planning."[300] In the case of Rio, this social reform may not be attempted today in the name of (industrial) modernization but rather in the name of sustainable development or, in Huber's words, ecological modernization.[301] However, the logic of market expansion as well as the orientation of "social exchanges away from subsistence living" and informal forms of life "toward commercial practices" remain paramount. The only real difference between the two is phrasing. The appeal to sustainability and environmental sensitivity is but a new wrapping for an old and familiar logic. This is the logic of enclosures, commercialization, and market expansion; only this time, it comes with "green" packaging.

The case of the private electric power company Light is probably the most characteristic one here. The entering of the UPPs into certain favelas was followed by Light technicians tasked with removing illegal connections, called *gatos*, which are widespread in the favelas, and installing modern meters and legal connections instead. This development meant that many residents who had been accessing electricity informally would be subject to "bloated" bills from now on, to the extent that many were eventually forced to settle elsewhere.[302] In other words, the process of formalizing the provision of a utility led not only to a sharp increase in the cost of living, but to population displacement as well. Indeed, in some cases the formalization of electricity access served that exact purpose, as witnessed by the example of the favela Rio das Pedras.[303] Obviously, the replacement of illegal connections is justified on the basis of lost revenue for the company—"favela gatos cost Light an estimated US$200 million in lost revenue per year," writes Erika Robb Larkins.[304] It is interesting however to see how the sustainability discourse was used to support this particular enclosure. First, arguments were made about the ecological footprint of total energy consumption through illegal connections. It was assumed that the formalization of electricity access would force consumers to realize, due to their increased bills, the real importance of energy consumption. This would therefore lead them to adopt a more "responsible" consumption behavior. In short, it would lead them limit their needs given that they would no longer be able to cover the exorbitant bills.[305] Obviously, as far as the company was concerned, the issue was not the "ecological footprint" per se, but the (dis)ability of consumers to bear its financial cost. But this was hidden behind the familiar argument about the supposed "ecological ignorance" of the poor, who therefore have to be trained in energy austerity and prove resilient to this. As Evans and Reid rightly put it, "Alleviating threats to the biosphere requires improving the resilience of the poor, especially, because it is precisely the poor that are most 'ecologically ignorant' and thus most prone to using 'eco-system services' in nonsustainable ways. Thus ensuring the resilience of the biosphere requires making the poor into more resilient kinds of subjects, and making the poor into more resilient subjects requires relieving them of their ecological ignorance."[306]

The sustainability parameter manifested itself in yet another way, particularly with the active involvement of the consumers themselves. In five favelas (Santa Marta, Rocinha, Chácara do Céu, Babilônia, and Chapéu Mangueira and Cruzada S. Sebastião) Light implemented the Light Recicla program, which offered a discount on electricity bills in exchange for recyclable materials collected by the consumers themselves.[307] Naturally, this plan was designed in order to mitigate the residents' dissatisfaction with the overbilling of a utility they had previously accessed via illegal connections and without paying bills. As a result, even though Light was responsible for the financial burden imposed upon the daily lives of thousands through the formalization of connections, it simultaneously presented itself as generous and inventive, offering "opportunities" for discounts on bills while at the same time marketing the program as an exemplar of "social innovation" and corporate social responsibility. This discursive trick is evident, for example, in the description of this program by Caral Cipolla, Patricia Mello, and Ezio Manzini. As they write, "Light Recicla was designed to support people living in pacified favelas in Rio de Janeiro who were in the process of obtaining legal access to energy."[308] Here Light Recicla is presented as "support" to consumers, but clearly "legal access to energy" was neither a natural phenomenon nor a matter of choice, since it was imposed in the context of pacification, that is, the presence of armed security forces.

"Under the framework of the pacification strategy," write Cipolla, Mello, and Manzini, "commercial companies and favela residents are establishing new relationships. Light Recicla aims to define a new mode of collaboration between the energy company, Light, and its customers that addresses this new set of social relations."[309] The use of appropriate terminology, therefore, helps describe a condition that has been violently imposed from above as collaboration and as a new set of social relations. However, even such a cheap switch serves to confirm that the object of pacification operations is to reshape social relations on the basis of the market. The Light Recicla program therefore constitutes another social engineering tool, this time toward the direction of green governmentality, and a typical example of market expansion in the name of sustainability, confirming "the emergence of new market-based relationships within the pacification process."[310] But Light's involvement in the sustainability agenda was not limited to this program. For example, it participated "in the creation of a multi-sector participatory governance mechanism called Travessias for the community-led management of sports facilities in favelas."[311] It did so within the framework of the municipality's "Sustainable Development Strategy," jointly with the state of Rio, the Pereira Passos Institute–Rio, and other stakeholders. As part of this initiative, Light funded a "community-managed sports facilities project," demonstrating its social sensibilities and its "faith" in "inclusive governance and community participation," two concepts that had already been advanced at the discursive level by the pacification program itself. As La Rocque and Shelton-Zumpano point out, these concepts are "among the most important objectives and methods of Rio+Social."[312]

The focus of the "Sustainable Development Strategy" on multi-sector partnerships is, as mentioned, emphatic, and accurately demonstrates the role of the market and the private sector in the implementation of sustainable development. These types of partnerships (multisector partnerships and public-private partnerships) have been proposed as effective governance tools within the sustainability agenda. They were also one of the key Rio+Social methodologies. As we mentioned above, UPP Social, the developmental arm of the pacification program, was renamed Rio+Social and was considered to be the flagship project of the Pereira Passos Institute. First of all, the very decision to change the name of UPP Social to Rio+Social appears to be far from incidental. Quite the opposite: the resemblance of the new name to the Rio+20 conference seems to indicate an attempt to link the pacification program to the broader sustainable development agenda, which is probably justifiable if we also consider the relationship between Rio+Social and UN-Habitat. After all, it makes sense for a program that claims to work in the direction of community development to want to distance itself, even if in name only, from a policing program and to engage with the more "positive" notion of sustainability instead. In any case, the only sustainability Rio+Social contributed to seems to be that of the market and certainly of pacification itself.[313] Despite having been promoted as the developmental part of the pacification program and as the body that would take over the implementation of the third stage of the "clear-hold-build" triptych referred to earlier on, the "developmental" adjective ultimately referred to economic, rather than community, development. As Luiza Fenizola from the Catalytic Communities NGO points out, if the residents of the favelas ever came into contact with anything relating to the Pacifying Police Units, it was the armed and security forces and not the social programs that were advertised as being under the auspices of UPP Social / Rio+Social.[314] Similarly, Sebastian Saborio writes, "It is not clear which actions have been undertaken to effectively implement new social policies. As a result, no significant policies in healthcare, education or concerning basic needs have followed the implementation of the UPP."[315]

At the same time, things are clearer when it comes to the issue of economic development, as witnessed by the example of Light, which according to the World Bank report "was one of the most benefitted with the new markets."[316] The decision to promote the logic of multisector partnerships proves that businesses and the notion of the market in general would become an indispensable tool for achieving sustainability and therefore, an essential component toward the solution of environmental problems in the periphery. So within this particular sustainable development–pacification nexus, and by taking advantage of the neoliberal turn in the sustainability agenda, Rio+Social also undertook some initiatives regarding the question of food (in) security. This undertaking is, on the one hand, linked to the fact that the official sustainability agenda, as defined by Rio+20 and formulated in *The Future We Want*, also focuses on the question of food security, while at the same time making special reference to the importance of sustainable agriculture.[317] On the other hand, it is linked to the accumulation of surplus life in the urban periphery, which, as we have seen above, raises its own urgent food questions. In this context, Rio+Social together with UN-Habitat decided to support the aforementioned Hortas Cariocas program.[318] This decision can probably be explained by the fact that the program in question had already yielded results within some of the favelas and established relationships with community members. Consequently, it would be an appropriate basis for the municipality's "Sustainable Development Strategy," in order to show to the international community that steps were already being taken on the question of food (in)security, as formulated in the Rio+20 agenda. However, (and this is what interests us in this debate) in Hortas Cariocas the pacification program was to find another way to advance urban revitalization plans that required the reshaping of spatial and social relations in the favelas, this time in terms of green governmentality.

As mentioned above, Hortas Cariocas was supported by Rio+Social, the "social" arm of the pacification program, and therefore furthered the UPP mission in a certain way. During a personal communication with Julio Barros, the mastermind behind the design and implementation of Hortas Cariocas, this relationship was initially concealed. In a related question, Barros claimed that there was no relationship between Hortas Cariocas and the pacification program. Only after a second question, and after realizing that we had information about this relationship at our disposal, did Barros admit that Hortas Cariocas was in fact supported by Rio+Social and UN-Habitat in some ways. He went on to say, however, that this relationship impeded rather than facilitated the work of Hortas Cariocas. This was because the two entities, for reasons of communication policy, were more interested in publicizing the program and demanding the publication of relevant reports rather than practically supporting the project.[319] In any case, the pacification program used Hortas Cariocas. We will now highlight how it was used, with the understanding that urban agriculture projects are considerably multifaceted and have obvious positive effects, which are not necessarily undermined by the overall strategy behind them. In short, it is not our intention to question the positive impact of urban gardens and urban greening in general on aesthetic, psychological, or environmental levels, let alone judge the people who work and make a living through these projects. Rather, the intent here is to demonstrate the relationship of these gardens to pacification operations and to show how the food question strategically reemerges within the pacification/counterinsurgency agenda.

First of all, the Hortas Cariocas program is not a novelty. It essentially forms part of a wider global contemporary trend—found not only in the urban periphery—that promotes urban agriculture in the context of urban sustainability, institutionally or otherwise. Despite not being the only initiative in this vein to have been introduced in Rio's favelas, it is still the only program that formed part of the municipality's official policy. In the case of Rio, several such initiatives emerged. For example, Favela Orgânica—a food reuse company founded by Regina Tchelly, a resident of the favela Babilônia, created a few small gardens in the Babilônia and Chapéu Mangueira favelas and advanced the concept of the reuse of food that was produced in them.[320] More specifically, it promoted the use of parts of fruits and plants that would otherwise be thrown away, creating a list of special recipes and aspiring to educate favela inhabitants on how to cook with these "leftovers." This training is provided by female Babilônia residents who work for the business part-time. The company has become increasingly popular in Brazil and beyond, and is considered an exemplar of social entrepreneurship in the spirit of sustainable development.[321] Another relevant example is Rio's Sustainable City project, which was also active in the Babilônia favela. This was a short-term public-private partnership initiative that focused on training volunteers in micro-entrepreneurship and agroecological food production on the rooftops of their homes. The initiative has since been replicated in other communities and was promoted as a corporate-sponsored social entrepreneurship project. More precisely the project was "developed as part of Rio's Sustainable City program, executed by the Brazilian Business Council for Sustainable Development and financed by the Souza Cruz tobacco company."[322] Finally, the organization Green My Favela created a series of small-scale gardens in a number of Rocinha neighborhoods (e.g., Valão, Cachopa, and Porto Vermelho), in some cases in collaboration with the Hortas Cariocas program.[323] It was also involved in the Manguinhos favela by participating in the cultivation of part of the urban garden created by Hortas Cariocas, which is the largest urban vegetable garden in Latin America today.[324]

The above examples show a tendency toward urban agriculture that is not, however, exclusive to Rio. Urban agriculture, particularly in terms of agroecology, is being proposed around the world as a way of resolving a number of critical urban issues, such as food (in)security and environmental upgrading and restoration by urban greening.[325] This is all the more important today when the acceleration of informal urbanization in the countries of the Global South and the exacerbation of the symptoms of climate change have created an urgent situation threatening the sustainability of cities. Urban agriculture essentially forms part of a broader trend that promotes the creation of so-called green infrastructures in cities, such as parks, urban gardens, trees, and so forth.[326] The creation of green infrastructure has a number of obvious positive impacts on the environment, society, and health. Among other things, it contributes to addressing environmental challenges such as air pollution, rising temperatures, and flooding; it has a psychotherapeutic effect and it helps improve and maintain health both through better food quality (when it comes to urban agriculture) and improved environmental conditions, and finally establishes sites of socialization and social interaction.

However, along with the positive impact of green infrastructures, there is a growing critical debate today as to how they may be involved in processes of gentrification and the production of "environmental privilege," urban inequalities, and more general issues of social inclusion.[327] Through this debate we come to understand that greening the city may mean radical fluctuations in land value and real estate prices and a valorization of specific areas that not only does not guarantee social inclusion, but rather operates under an "exclusionary displacement."[328] This can occur either intentionally, that is, in the context of a planned process where green initiatives are followed by gentrification, what is today called green or eco-gentrification.[329] Or it may occur unintentionally, that is, as an undesirable side effect of a well-intentioned, even participatory, process of creating green infrastructures. So the issue of urban greening cannot be assessed independently of its overall social impact and its specific role in urban renewal plans. Especially in the case of Rio, the initiative to create urban gardens should be evaluated in the context of both the promotion of the neoliberal version of the sustainability agenda, and the pacification operations as a program of social engineering and urban redesign.

A major objective of this redesign was therefore to limit informal housing and illegal land use. This was done in a number of ways, including building walls around favelas to limit illegal building and expansion of housing at the expense of the city's natural environment and the forced relocation and demolition of the homes of many favela inhabitants, under the pretext of either the unsuitability of the ground on which they had been built or the protection of areas of natural interest.[330] However, in both cases the policy of enclosures, evacuations, and demolitions was heavily criticized, as it was alleged to have been based on the strategic gentrification of certain neighborhoods bordering affluent areas, under a policy of controlling poor communities that did not include residents in the decision-making process.[331]

As part of this land use restoration strategy, some urban gardens also appeared in areas that had previously been used informally. Through this practice, the municipality would seek to expand its presence in the favelas, on the one hand, by implementing the sustainable development agenda specifically in terms of urban greening, and on the other, by limiting informal housing and formalizing land uses. In short, some urban gardens were created to suit the needs of the pacification program, one of which was to address urban informality as such. That is to say, they were part of the wider plan to "reoccupy" the "ungoverned territories" of the favelas, whose targets were not just the drug gangs, but also informal land uses and informal forms of life in those areas, as dictated by the "shock of order" doctrine. Behind the concept of environmental restoration, therefore, lay a process of formalization of land uses. That is to say, a process of land reuse under the conditions of state control and the formal economy. It is indicative that Lea Rekow, founder of Green My Favela, refers not only to the concept of "environmental restoration" but also to "land use restoration."[332] This connection is also confirmed by Barros himself, who argues that the municipality is using Hortas Cariocas to curb illegal land uses, informal housing, and the occupation of land.[333] Similarly, in another interview, Barros stated: "The municipal government wants to achieve several goals through our project, including reducing social inequality and slowing the illegal occupation of land."[334]

In the case of the Manguinhos garden, which is essentially the showcase for the Hortas Cariocas, we see an example of how such "illegal occupation of land" is being problematized and dealt with. "The Production Unit in Manguinhos is located in the Vila Turismo community, near the train station. A place formerly known as Rio de Janeiro's biggest 'cracolândia,' marked by the consumption of crack, insalubrity and violence, it now houses the largest urban garden in Latin America, with more than 300 flowerbeds, of which 177 are already in production."[335] Another example is to be found in Rocinha. More specifically, in the case of the garden created in the Laboriaux neighborhood, land use rights were approved by the State Department of Human Rights and Social Assistance (Secretaria de Estado de Assistência Social e Direitos Humanos [SEASDH])—the "social" arm of UPP at the time, as described by Rekow.[336] The garden was located in an area that had been cleared of residents, and neighboring buildings had been demolished. However, population displacement may not only be a result of planning but also a subsequent side effect of the increase in land values brought about by the creation of gardens in particular areas. In the case of Manguinhos, for example, property prices in the vicinity of the local garden increased by 50 percent, which may have forced some residents to relocate.[337] This case merely validates in its own way a broader trend observed in the areas where the UPPs were operating, namely the increase in land values, real estate prices, and cost of living in general.[338] If we can learn something, then, from these examples, it is the fact that "'green' development agendas have been driving new forms of displacement and 'environmental/ecological gentrification' in the Global South."[339]

The strategic position of urban gardens within the pacification program also manifested itself tactically. In some cases, UPPs were proven to be a prerequisite for promoting urban greening. As Rekow puts it, "Within the favelas, UA [urban agriculture] investments have been small, nevertheless, food security initiatives remain one of the few programs that have been facilitated in some way by the presence of the UPP."[340] For example, the garden at Manguinhos could only be created after UPPs were encamped in the area. As Barros describes it, "The project started with the implementation of the UPP that made it possible for us to be entering there, and circulating with tranquility," something that he also confirmed during our personal communication.[341] Moreover, in the case of Favela Orgânica, the UPPs were behind the implementation of the project itself. More specifically, for the purposes of launching this initiative, Tchelly attended a UPP-sponsored workshop.[342] This functional relationship is also evident in Rekow's research on the gardens that were created with the participation of Green My Favela. Despite her criticisms of the public security policies in Rio, her decision to describe the functioning of these green infrastructures through their interrelationships with the security landscape in the particular areas and the dynamics of UPPs in them is remarkable. And unless it is simply unfortunate, her decision denotes that these initiatives were perceived as part of a broader debate on pacification in the favelas.

There is an ongoing debate on the importance of greening within conflict zones today that Rekow seems to follow.[343] More specifically, her research attempted to demonstrate the link "between gardening and its relationship to territorial conflict inside fragile informal urban contexts," by evaluating green infrastructures even in terms of conflict resolution.[344] Evaluating, in other words, gardens not only as a means of environmental restoration but also as a method of securing social peace, through which "gardens take the place of weapons."[345] Almost all of the urban gardens mentioned by Rekow were created after the invasion of UPPs in the areas concerned.[346] Her research aims to highlight the challenges created by this simultaneous movement, especially in the complex and dynamic environments shaped by the everyday microphysics of power in the favelas. It is also indicative that UPPs were present in most of the favelas in which Hortas Cariocas installed gardens, with the possible exception of the examples found in Maré (see, for example, the favelas Morro da Formiga, Morro do Salgueiro, Chácara do Céu, Manguinhos, Morro do Borel, Morro do São Carlos, Rocinha, and Cidade de Deus).[347]

In any case, sustainable development initiatives have proven to be fully consistent with the objectives of pacification operations. As Rekow argues, "Urban revitalization through sustainable economic development is foundational to the neoliberal goals the UPP facilitates."[348] This is confirmed, in a sense, through the example of urban gardens. Promoting sustainable development here also meant promoting entrepreneurship and the market, just as neoliberal logic dictates. If one looks at the discourse accompanying the creation of the gardens in question, one will notice that a particular repertoire keeps being repeated: that despite a rhetorical emphasis on participatory spirit, community involvement, and social movements, these cases do not necessarily relate to social movement politics, self-organization, or horizontality. Instead, they are linked to an agenda promoting micro-entrepreneurship and a specific business model.[349] For example, in the case of Manguinhos, "a municipal policy guaranteeing demand from public schools created an enabling operational environment, within which Julio [César Barros] activated links between community, state, and market. Residents' horticultural skills and desire to generate income aligned with the government's attempt to provide alternatives to the narcotics trade through subsidized gardening positions. The prospect of becoming independent suppliers into private farmers markets appealed to the community, coinciding with the state's interest in private business development."[350]

In other words, and as Hearn puts it, "Julio secures government inputs on the condition that he encourages private business development."[351] The logic of promoting a business model through Hortas Cariocas was also confirmed during a personal visit to the Manguinhos garden. The Municipal Secretary for the Environment executive who gave the guided tour mentioned that the goal of the program was not just to provide jobs to community members, but to create entrepreneurs, to provide them with support and incentivize them to then start their own businesses. The point is for them to learn how to set up companies, following their structure, spirit, and hierarchy—for example by having specific roles within them such as president, manager, secretary, and so forth.[352]

Similarly, if we look at the language used by Rekow we will notice that gardens are described in terms of social entrepreneurship, sustainable economic development, social capital, and productivity.[353] It is a language similar to that used to describe more broadly the need to create a "business enabling environment" in the favelas, which as we have seen was one of the main goals of the pacification program. Despite the obvious and substantial differences—differences in means, techniques, scale, geography, demography—one could argue that food and its production are problematized in these cases in terms similar to those found in the policies of the Green Revolution. The promotion of entrepreneurship as a social engineering tool and as a method of reshaping social and spatial relationships is prominent in both examples. As has been said above with regard to the sustainability agenda, the objective of these urban-agricultural initiatives was not just to green the urban periphery but to facilitate a more general move toward a market-driven society. In essence, we observe the application of a fundamental motif of the Green Revolution, this time not on "poor peasants" and the surplus populations of the capitalist `periphery, but on the informal proletariat and the surplus populations of the urban periphery. Like in the case of the older laboratories of the Green Revolution, the objective is twofold; first, for the urban "farmer" to enter the market and second, and this is a more radical goal, for market logic to enter the urban "farmer."[354]

These initiatives, which aim to turn the urban poor into microentrepreneurial urban farmers, build on the old logic of reformative philanthropy, which seeks to reshape the perceptions and behaviors of the poor, and which, as Nally and Taylor show us, is simply a securitization tool: that is, a tool that helps manage the security risks posed by surplus life. However, this particular logic not only attempts to help the poor in terms of charity (and here lies the difference between the English terms *charity* and *philanthropy*, according to Nally and Taylor) but also to reform them by helping them help themselves and "be actively enrolled in the process of securing their own salvation."[355] In other words, to help them stand on their own two feet and turn them into entrepreneurs in their own right in order to integrate them into the capitalist system and the free market. This logic in many ways is reminiscent of the one used in community development programs, which as Cullather shows us, were implemented during the Green Revolution in both Indian villages and American slums. And this is because "the 'blighted' slum and rural village both represented zones of poverty and social stagnation that were alike illegible to the state"; not only illegible but also dangerous, as we saw above with regard to geopolitical objectives of agricultural modernization.[356]

To this end, the logic of self-help was also employed in order to manage the risks posed by the accumulation of surplus life. Already from the time of the pioneers of philanthropy, such as Andrew Carnegie and John D. Rockefeller Sr., this logic aimed at managing the tensions and crises created by the capitalist system due to the inequalities it generated and the asymmetric accumulation of wealth through a "strategic practice of gift giving," to reform it, not in order to destroy it, but rather to save it.[357] This required reforming the perceptions of the poor themselves. With some initial financial support and specific incentives, the poor would be initiated into a process of perceiving themselves as human capital. They would extricate themselves, in other words, from the stagnation and inertia of their own poverty in order to embrace the logic of entrepreneurship, which requires innovative initiatives, investments, maneuvering, and risk-taking, always within a constraining, risk-prone environment. It is precisely this "entrepreneurial rationality" that dominates the neoliberal agenda, continually educating the subjects in a managerial ethos and ultimately capitalist logic itself, just as our tour guide in the Manguinhos garden described. After all, as Dardot and Laval remind us, "The first commandment of the entrepreneur's ethics is 'help thyself' and that in this sense it is an ethic of 'self-help.' It will rightly be said that this ethic is not new; that it forms part of the spirit of capitalism from the start."[358] This logic was consistently present both in the fields of the Green Revolution as well as a number of pacification operations, precisely because they both focused on the issue of community development and they were both social engineering programs. It is also present today within this peculiar sustainable development-pacification nexus as developed in Rio's urban periphery, allowing us yet another glimpse into how "'self-help' enters into the sphere of strategic calculation."[359]

The remarks above are in no way intended to call into question the positive impact of urban gardens and green infrastructure within the city as a whole. Their environmental, aesthetic, psychological, and nutritional contributions, especially in crowded environments such as favelas, appear to be unquestionable. However, these observations show something more: that urban agriculture should be evaluated within specific contexts, in order to understand its particular position in the production of urban space and the debate on urban inequality and the right to the city more broadly. They further confirm that the food question, and its production in particular, consistently comprises an object of securitization, and it further comprises a key parameter in the planning of pacification operations and population governance policies as a whole. The foregoing examples appear to play a key role in a particular urban agenda. Behind the beautiful green foliage and inspirational islands of life and leisure, we may encounter ongoing processes of destruction, land grabbing, population displacement, and the imposition of market logic. In short, these examples should also be understood as part of an agenda that is based, on the one hand, upon a very specific problematization of sustainability and, on the other, is partly linked to a pacification program, which is nothing more than a program of social engineering and violent "socio-cultural adaptations,"[360] an agenda that is ultimately shaped in terms of green governmentality. As a result, these examples should be understood by focusing "on how regimes of truth are made, how strategies of regulation are formed, and how human subjectivities are enacted with reference to the environment."[361] Our journey through the sustainable landscapes of Rio's urban gardens has therefore provided us with an opportunity to understand how the food question is reintroduced in the pacification/counterinsurgency agenda by tracing its complexities and by following the biopolitical thread that unfolds during the transition from Green Revolution to green governmentality.

NOTES

1   Lula quoted in Maria Helena Moreira Alves and Philip Evanson, *Living in the Crossfire: Favela Residents, Drug Dealers, and Police Violence in Rio de Janeiro* (Philadelphia: Temple University Press, 2011), 170.

2   Food Security Information Network, *Global Report on Food Crises 2018* (FSIN, 2018), 2, https://www.fsinplatform.org/sites/default/files/resources/files/GRFC_2018_Full_report_EN_Low_resolution.pdf.

3   Food Security Information Network, *Global Report on Food Crises 2018*, 2.

4   Gustavo de L.T. Oliveira, "The Geopolitics of Brazilian Soybeans," *Journal of Peasant Studies* 43, no. 2 (2016): 15.

5   Food Security Information Network, *Global Report on Food Crises 2018*, 11.

6   The danger that lies behind this outward movement can be better understood in light of the renowned narrative of "state of nature," i.e., a basic conceptual construction employed by some political philosophers in order to establish and legitimize the concept of state sovereignty. According to this narrative, human societies require the intervention of an external monitoring/regulatory authority. Otherwise, human coexistence would turn into a "war of all against all" since, according to Thomas Hobbes, "man is a wolf to men." The state therefore exists in order to head off the impetuosity of natural needs and instincts of self-preservation, to regulate human relationships, and to prevent the animalistic from invading the political, and the political from slipping into the animalistic. Should this happen, as Hobbes argued, the state would reach its breaking point. See Giorgio Agamben, *Homo Sacer: Sovereign Power and Bare Life*, trans. Daniel Heller-Roazen (Stanford: Stanford University Press, 1998), 63–64.

7   Giorgio Agamben, *State of Exception*, trans. Kevin Attell (Chicago: University of Chicago Press, 2005), 22–23.

8   Hannah Arendt, *On Revolution* (London: Penguin Books, 1990), 61–62.

9   Hannah Arendt, *The Human Condition* (Chicago: University of Chicago Press, 1958).

10 Frédéric Gros, *The Security Principle: From Serenity to Regulation* (New York: Verso, 2019), 24.

11 Agamben, *Homo Sacer*, 9–13; Arendt, *Human Condition*.

12 Maria Christou, "I Eat Therefore I Am: An Essay on Human and Animal Mutuality," *Angelaki* 18, no. 4 (2013): 64–65.

13 Arendt, *Human Condition*, 28, 32.

14 Agamben, *State of Exception*, 26.

15 Santi Romano quoted in Agamben, *State of Exception*, 27.

16 Mark Neocleous, *Critique of Security* (Edinburgh: Edinburgh University Press, 2008), 18.

17 This dual legal function of necessity, both as a legislative/lawmaking "tool" and as the suspension of law is well described by the Latin maxim *necessitas legem non habet* on which Agamben focuses. This maxim "is interpreted in two opposing ways: 'necessity does not recognize any law' and 'necessity creates its own law.'" Agamben, *State of Exception*, 24.

18 Walter Benjamin, "Critique of Violence," in *Walter Benjamin: Selected Writings*, vol. 1, *1913–1926*, trans. Marcus Bullock and Michael Jennings (Cambridge, MA: Belknap Press, 2002), 252. Benjamin writes: "Lawmaking is powermaking, assumption of power, and to that extent an immediate manifestation of violence" (248).

19 Arendt, *Human Condition*, 113.

20   Arendt, *Human Condition*, 113.
21   Arendt, *Human Condition*, 113.
22   Michel Foucault, *Security, Territory, Population: Lectures at the Collège de France, 1977–78*, trans. Graham Burchell (New York: Palgrave Macmillan, 2007), 30.
23   See Paul Collier, "The Politics of Hunger: How Illusion and Greed Fan the Food Crisis," *Foreign Affairs* 87, no. 6 (2008): 70.
24   Arendt, *On Revolution*, 59.
25   Patricia Owens, *Economy of Force: Counterinsurgency and the Historical Rise of the Social* (Cambridge, UK: Cambridge University Press, 2015), 121. See also Arendt, *On Revolution*, 59.
26   The title of this section is borrowed from "A Brighter and Nicer New Life: Security as Pacification" by Mark Neocleous.
27   According to Corey Robinson, "Brazil is demonstrating to the world that it can craft a national security strategy that deals with its external threats while simultaneously addressing its internal security issues so it can negotiate more legitimately with other established democracies in matters of international affairs and foreign policy. A formalized national defense strategy is important for Brazil since its constitution still allows the military to step in when law enforcement cannot provide effective internal security." Robinson, "Order and Progress? The Evolution of Brazilian Defense Strategy," (postgraduate thesis, Naval Postgraduate School, 2014), 25.
28   José Mariano Beltrame quoted in Marcus Ferreira Larsen, "Pacifying Maré: The Militarisation of Urban Policing in Rio de Janeiro," (postgraduate thesis, University of Copenhagen, 2016), 4.
29   Constance Malleret, "The End of 'Pacification': What Next for Rio de Janeiro's Favelas?" PhD diss., University of Essex, 2018, https://repository.essex.ac.uk/26930/1/1807428_Dissertation.pdf; Maíra Siman and Victória Santos, "Interrogating the Security-Development Nexus in Brazil's Domestic and Foreign Pacification Engagements," *Conflict, Security & Development* 18, no. 1 (2018): 61–83; Tomas Salem, "Security and Policing in Rio de Janeiro: An Ethnography of the Pacifying Police Units," (postgraduate thesis, UiT Arctic University of Norway, 2016), 2, 102, https://www.researchgate.net/publication/315669322_Security_and_Policing_in_Rio_de_Janeiro_An_Ethnography_of_the_Pacifying_Police_Units; Elizabeth Leeds, "What Can Be Learned from Brazil's 'Pacification' Police Model?" WOLA, March 11, 2016, https://www.wola.org/analysis/what-can-be-learned-from-brazils-pacification-police-model; Robert Muggah, "The State of Security and Justice in Brazil: Reviewing the Evidence," Working Paper Series No. 4, Brazil Initiative, Elliott School of International Affairs (2016), 10, https://pdfs.semanticscholar.org/8d6e/2d4e331bd0db37713411bb8f086e00116b14.pdf.
30   Gareth A. Jones and Dennis Rodgers, "The World Bank's World Development Report 2011 on Conflict, Security and Development: A Critique through Five Vignettes," *Journal of International Development* 23, no. 7 (2011): 10, http://eprints.lse.ac.uk/38462.
31   Due to the federal nature of Brazil and under the current constitution, public security policy is not determined by the central government but by each state instead. It may be the first time such an emergency measure has been implemented by any federal government since the dictatorship. However, this is not the first time the army has taken to the streets of Rio. According to Manoela Miklos and Tomaz Paoliello, "Over the last decade, the state of Rio has appealed to the Armed Forces 12 times" ("Militarization of Public Security in Rio, and Around

the World," *Open Democracy*, October 4, 2017, https://www.opendemocracy.net/en/democraciaabierta/militarization-of-public-security-in-rio-and-around.

32   As Patricia Owens shows in *Economy of Force*, counterinsurgency theory has many things in common with social theory, as they both aim to understand the causes behind social resistance and political violence, in order to comprehend the social milieu in which they wish to intervene. It is essentially nothing but a special political-military response to the Social Question.

33   Mark Neocleous, "A Brighter and Nicer New Life: Security as Pacification," *Social & Legal Studies* 20, no. 2 (2011): 198.

34   See the French colonial school, and in particular Joseph Gallieni and Hubert Lyautey's theory of pacification war (Owens, *Economy of Force*, 156; Etienne de Durand and Octavian Manea, "Reflections on the French School of Counter-Rebellion: An Interview with Etienne de Durand by Octavian Manea," *Small Wars Journal*, March 3, 2011, 5, https://smallwarsjournal.com/blog/journal/docs-temp/686-manea.pdf); the British experience during the Second Boer War (Owens, *Economy of Force*, 155, 177); and the theory of Charles Callwell and Charles Gwynn, who essentially represent the early British counterinsurgency doctrine (Sergio Miller, "The Simple Truth? Securing the Population as a Recent Invention," *Small Wars Journal*, May 30, 2012, https://smallwarsjournal.com/jrnl/art/the-simple-truth-securing-the-population-as-a-recent-invention); and finally US counterinsurgency theory and practice, as has surfaced during the American Occupation of the Philippines (Owens, *Economy of Force*, 162–72) and US involvement in the so-called Banana Wars (Oliver Belcher, "The Afterlives of Counterinsurgency: Postcolonialism, Military Social Science, and Afghanistan 2006–2012," [PhD diss., University of British Columbia, 2013], 36–37, https://open.library.ubc.ca/media/download/pdf/24/1.0165663/1).

35   Jones and Rodgers, "World Bank's," 10.

36   David J. Kilcullen, *Out of the Mountains: The Coming Age of the Urban Guerrilla* (New York: Oxford University Press, 2013), 236.

37   Robert Muggah and Albert Souza Mulli, "Rio Tries Counterinsurgency," *Current History* 111, no. 742 (2012): 64.

38   US Department of the Army, *Insurgencies and Countering Insurgencies*, FM 3-24/MCWP 3-33.5 (Washington, DC: Department of the Army, 2014), 1–2, glossary-3, https://fas.org/irp/dodder/army/fm3-24.pdf. The shift in the definition of insurgency is evident if we look at the corresponding definition proposed by the previous edition of this manual: US Department of the Army, *Counterinsurgencies*, FM 3-24, MCWP 3-33.5 (Washington, DC: Department of the Army, 2006), 1–1, glossary-5, https://www.thenewatlantis.com/wp-content/uploads/legacy-pdfs/20090202_COINFieldManual2006.pdf.

39   This is what Sergio Cabral, the governor of Rio for 2007–14, called "gang-dominated favelas," quoted in GlobalSecurity.org, "Favela War," accessed March 13, 2020, https://www.globalsecurity.org/military/world/war/favela-war.htm.

40   Richard Norton, "Feral Cities," *Naval War College Review* LVI, no. 4 (2003): 97–106; Robert Muggah, "A Manifesto for the Fragile City," *Journal for International Affairs* 68, no 2 (2015): 23. According to the definition put forth by Robert Lamb, an ungoverned area is "a place where the state or the central government is unable or unwilling to extend control, effectively govern, or influence the local population, and where a provincial, local, tribal, or autonomous government does not fully or effectively govern, due to inadequate governance capacity, insufficient political will, gaps in legitimacy, the presence of conflict, or

restrictive norms of behavior" ("Ungoverned Areas and Threats from Safe Havens: Final Report of the Ungoverned Areas Project," [Washington, DC: Office of the Under Secretary of Defense for Policy, 2008], 6). For a critical interpretation of the term "ungoverned spaces" see Jennifer M. Hazen, "Understanding Gangs as Armed Groups," *International Review of the Red Cross* 92, no. 878 (2010): 378–81.

41   Kristian Williams, "The Other Side of the COIN: Counterinsurgency and Community Policing," in *Life During Wartime: Resisting Counterinsurgency*, ed. Kristian Williams, Will Munger, and Lara Messersmith-Glavin (Edinburgh: AK Press, 2013), 95.

42   Kilcullen, *Out of the Mountains*, 126.

43   Vanda Felbab-Brown, *Shooting Up: Counterinsurgency and the War on Drugs* (Washington DC: Brookings Institution Press, 2010); Michael Freeman and Hy Rothstein, introduction to *Gangs and Guerrillas: Ideas from Counterinsurgency and Counterterrorism*, ed. Michael Freeman and Hy Rothstein (Monterey, CA: Naval Postgraduate School, 2010), 1, https://www.hsdl.org/?view&did=6229; Muggah and Mulli, "Rio Tries Counterinsurgency"; Claudio Ramos da Cruz and David H. Ucko, "Beyond the Unidades de Polícia Pacificadora: Countering Comando Vermelho's Criminal Insurgency," *Small Wars & Insurgencies* 29, no. 1 (2018): 3–33.

44   Kilcullen, *Out of the Mountains*, 126.

45   Russell W. Glenn et al., "'People Make the City,' Executive Summary: Joint Urban Operations Observations and Insights from Afghanistan and Iraq" (Santa Monica, CA: RAND Corporation, 2007), xviii, 57, https://www.rand.org/pubs/monographs/MG428z2.html; Jamison Jo Medby and Russell W. Glenn, *Streetsmart: Intelligence Preparation of the Battlefield for Urban Operations* (Santa Monica: RAND Corporation, 2002), 35, 45, https://www.rand.org/pubs/monograph_reports/MR1287.html.

46   David J. Kilcullen, *Counterinsurgency* (Oxford: Oxford University Press, 2010), 9, 10, 45.

47   John Nagl, foreword to *Counterinsurgency Warfare: Theory and Practice*, by David Galula (London: Praeger Security International, 2006), ix.

48   Owens, *Economy of Force*, 23, 31, 157, 232, 279.

49   David H. Petraeus, "Reflections on the 'Counterinsurgency Decade': *Small Wars Journal* Interview with General David H. Petraeus, by Octavian Manea," *Small Wars Journal*, September 1, 2013, 2, https://smallwarsjournal.com/jrnl/art/reflections-on-the-counterinsurgency-decade-small-wars-journal-interview-with-general-david; Roberto J. González, "Embedded: Information Warfare and the 'Human Terrain,'" in Network of Concerned Anthropologists, *The Counter-Counterinsurgency Manual or, Notes on Demilitarizing American Society* (Chicago: Prickly Paradigm Press, 2009), 97–113.

50   Ralph Peters, "The Human Terrain of Urban Operations," *Parameters* 30, no. 1 (2000): 4.

51   Owens, *Economy of Force*, 23, 31, 157, 232, 279. Owens specifically writes: "With the exception of the Boer concentration camps, in which large numbers of women and children were detained, Europeans gave little thought to administering populations in the midst of fighting. However, with the imperial upheavals of two world wars, the military and political organization of anti-colonial resistance vastly improved, providing insurgents with a popular base of support" (*Economy of Force*, 177).

52   As the US counterinsurgency manual states, "another important factor in analyzing economic activity is the informal economy. In weak states, understanding

the informal economy is key to providing a full understanding of an operational environment" (US Department of the Army, *Insurgencies and Counter Insurgencies,* 2–6).

53 Mark Duffield, *Development, Security and Unending War: Governing the World of Peoples,* (Malden, MA: Polity Press, 2006), 13.

54 Neocleous, "Brighter and Nicer," 202.

55 Saskia Sassen, "When the City Itself Becomes a Technology of War," *Theory, Culture & Society* 27, no. 6 (2010): 46.

56 Felbab-Brown, *Shooting Up,* 5.

57 Erika Robb Larkins, *The Spectacular Favela: Violence in Modern Brazil* (Oakland: University of California Press, 2015), 146.

58 This is also demonstrated linguistically if we take into account, for example, the discourse over pacification in the favelas, which clearly refers to "pacified favelas" (World Bank, "Bringing the State Back into the Favelas of Rio de Janeiro: Understanding Changes in Community Life after the UPP Pacification Process," October 2012, http://documents.worldbank.org/curated/en/255231468230108733/pdf/760110ESW0P12300RioodeoJaneiroo2013.pdf); Esther Werling, "Rio's Pacification: Paradigm Shift or Paradigm Maintenance?" Humanitarian Action in Situations Other than War (HASOW) Discussion Paper 11, August 2014, https://igarape.org.br/wp-content/uploads/2016/04/Rio%E2%80%99s-Pacification-.pdf; Muggah and Mulli, "Rio Tries Counterinsurgency"). After all, as David Galula tells us, the verb *to pacify* points toward populations and their land (*Pacification in Algeria, 1956–1958* [Santa Monica: RAND Corporation, 2006], https://www.rand.org/content/dam/rand/pubs/monographs/2006/RAND_MG478-1.pdf).

59 US Department of the Army, *Insurgencies and Counter Insurgencies,* 1–9.

60 Patrick Donley, "Economic Development in Counterinsurgency: Building a Stable Second Pillar," *Joint Force Quarterly,* no. 81 (2016): 103.

61 Duffield, *Development,* 2.

62 Duffield, *Development,* 24.

63 Austin Long, *On "Other War": Lessons from Five Decades of RAND Counterinsurgency Research* (Santa Monica, CA: RAND Corporation, 2006), 22, https://www.rand.org/content/dam/rand/pubs/monographs/2006/RAND_MG482.pdf.

64 Long, *On "Other War,"* 52.

65 Mark Duffield, *Development,* 4. Here we can agree with Neocleous, who discerns security and accumulation (and not security and development) at the very point where liberal ideology constitutes itself (*War Power, Police Power* [Edinburgh: Edinburgh University Press, 2014], 13–14). At the root of liberalism and the "liberal problematic of security" referred to by Duffield lies not the notion of freedom and an interest in securing "the essential processes of life" "in the name of people, rights and freedom" (*Development,* 4) but the notion of security. And this, long before it took the form of human security, made sure it was expressed in terms of security of capitalist accumulation. In other words, there is nothing really paradoxical in what Duffield calls the "paradox of liberalism" (*Development,* 7, 177, 225).

66 Stilhoff Jens Sörensen and Fredrik Söderbaum, "Introduction: The End of the Development-Security Nexus?" *Development Dialogue,* no. 58 (2012): 10.

67 Duffield, *Development,* 19.

68 US Department of the Army, *Insurgencies and Counter Insurgencies,* 1–10.

69 Mark Neocleous, George Rigakos, and Tyler Wall, "On Pacification: Introduction to the Special Issue," *Socialist Studies* 9, no. 2 (2013): 1.

70   In this respect, the account of a Special Police Operations Battalion patrol
      leader is typical: when asked by journalist Ben Anderson about the pacifica-
      tion program, he admitted this was a military occupation and not an operation
      based on public consent. See "Afghan Money Pit and the Pacification of Rio,"
      VICE News, September 12, 2016, (see 20:15), https://video.vice.com/en_us/video/
      afghan-money-pit-and-the-pacification-of-rio/578426c19e5b33a85b4cd8a2.

71   Walter Souza Braga Netto quoted in Juliana Cesario Alvim Gomes and Andrés
      del Río. "Military Justice, Intervention and Human Rights in Brazil," *openDem-
      ocracy*, July 5, 2018, https://www.opendemocracy.net/en/democraciaabierta/
      military-justice-intervention-and-human.

72   Gomes and Del Río, "Military Justice."

73   Lise Alves, "Rio to Remove Half of Police Pacifying Units from Favelas," *Rio
      Times*, April 27, 2018, https://riotimesonline.com/brazil-news/rio-politics/
      rio-to-remove-half-of-police-pacifying-units-from-favela-communities.

74   Anna Jean Kaiser, "Rio Governor Confirms Plans for Shoot-to-Kill Policing Policy,"
      The Guardian, January 4, 2019, https://www.theguardian.com/world/2019/jan/04/
      wilson-witzel-rio-police-security-shoot-to-kill; Júlia Dias Carneiro, "Violence
      in Rio: Public Security Expert Warns of a 'Retreat from Rights,' Return to Old
      Policies of Confrontation," *Rio on Watch*, March 29, 2019, http://www.rioonwatch.
      org/?p=52373.

75   Siman and Santos, "Interrogating," 73. In fact, from 2008, when the program
      was launched, until 2014 there was a drastic reduction in homicides and killings
      by the police. Yet, there has been an increase in disappearances over the same
      period, as Rio State representative Marcelo Freixo admits (VICE News, "Afghan
      Money Pit," at 21:25). The above obviously cast doubt on the reliability of the data
      published during that time, forcing many to consider that one statistic corrected
      the other in the context of a creative accounting (VICE News, "Afghan Money
      Pit," at 22:00). Since 2014 both the total number of homicides and the overall
      numbers of killings involving police have increased again.

76   Neocleous, "Brighter and Nicer," 193.

77   Michel Foucault, *Society Must Be Defended: Lectures at the Collège de France 1975–76*,
      trans. David Macey (New York: Picador, 2003), 268;

78   Werling, "Rio's Pacification," 5; Larkins, *Spectacular Favela*, 149; US Department
      of the Army, *Counterinsurgency*, 5–18; US Department of the Army, *Insurgencies
      and Counter Insurgencies*, 9-1; Williams, "Other Side of the COIN," 94.

79   Carla Cipolla, Rita Afonso, Bonno Pel, Roberto Bartholo, Édison Renato Silva,
      and Domício Proença Júnior, "Coproduced Game-Changing in Transformative
      Social Innovation: Reconnecting the 'Broken City' of Rio de Janeiro," *Ecology
      and Society* 22, no. 3 (2017): 4.

80   Describing the third phase of the pacification program (unit establishment),
      Sergio Cabral writes: "It occurs when military police officers, specially trained
      for the exercise of the proximity policing, arrive definitively at the community
      contemplated by the pacification program, preparing it for the arrival of other
      public and private services that allow it to be reintegrated into democratic soci-
      ety" ("Decreto No. 42787 de 06/01/2011," *Normas Brasil*, January 7, 2011, https://
      www.normasbrasil.com.br/norma/decreto-42787-2011-rj_158962.html).

81   James Dobbins et al., *The Beginner's Guide to Nation-Building* (Santa Monica:
      RAND Corporation, 2007), xxxvi, https://www.rand.org/pubs/monographs/
      MG557.html.

82   John Zambri, "Counterinsurgency and Community Policing: More Alike than

Meets the Eye," *Small Wars Journal*, July 8, 2014, https://smallwarsjournal.com/jrnl/art/counterinsurgency-and-community-policing-more-alike-than-meets-the-eye. As Long points out, pacification should be understood as an intensified version of community policing (*On "Other War,"* 53).

83   Williams, "Other Side of the COIN," 84, 95.

84   This relationship is described by Beltrame (see Alves and Evanson, *Living in the Crossfire*, 141), who challenges all those who argue that the logic of community policing (should) work against the policy of confrontation, those citing the model of the Police Group for Special Areas (Grupamento de Policiamento de Áreas Especiais [GPAE]), namely the special community policing units developed in the Rio Favelas in 2000, among them.

85   Siman and Santos, "Interrogating," 61–83.

86   Neocleous, *War Power*, 13.

87   The logic of interventions that were to "improve" the function and organization of local communities through the involvement of the military was not, however, a postwar phenomenon. The US, French, and British armies had long been involved in social engineering programs and development initiatives. In the context of late colonialism, "military commanders would then oversee various forms of 'liberal improvement' to facilitate the extraction of raw materials and the opening up of the territory to trade. Building roads and markets, canals and schools were viewed as the means to liberal improvement just as the labouring classes were improved by various forms of social intervention back home" Owens, *Economy of Force*, 22.

88   Nick Cullather, *The Hungry World: America's Cold War Battle against Poverty in Asia* (Cambridge, MA: Harvard University Press, 2010), 8. However, David Rieff rightly points out that the issue of hunger had been understood as a matter of security and political stability long before the advent of modernization theories ("Where Hunger Goes: On the Green Revolution," *The Nation*, February 17, 2011).

89   Cullather, *Hungry World*, 41.

90   Duffield, *Development*, 160.

91   Siman and Santos, "Interrogating," 74.

92   World Bank, *Bringing the State Back*, 38.

93   Siman and Santos, "Interrogating," 73.

94   Eduarda de La Rocque and Petras Shelton-Zumpano, "The Sustainable Development Strategy of the Municipal Government of Rio de Janeiro," (paper presented at the Citizen Security in Brazil: Progress and Challenges seminar at the Woodrow Wilson International Center for Scholars in Washington, DC, March 28, 2014), 5, https://www.rio.rj.gov.br/documents/91329/893c5a46-c32f-441e-a4d2-914e5a512925.

95   Patricia Owens, "From Bismarck to Petraeus: The Question of the Social and the Social Question in Counterinsurgency," *European Journal of International Relations* 19, no. 1 (2011): 141–50.

96   Sebastian Saborio, "The Pacification of the Favelas: Mega Events, Global Competitiveness, and the Neutralization of Marginality," *Socialist Studies* 9, no. 2 (2013): 139.

97   Ramos da Cruz and Ucko, "Beyond the Unidades," 60.

98   Siman and Santos, "Interrogating," 73–74.

99   Tudobeleza, "End of the UPP Is Nigh," *Deep Rio*, December 18, 2017.

100 Erika Robb Larkins, "A Different Kind of Security: The Need for Appropriate

Healthcare Policies in Rio de Janeiro's Favelas," *LSE Research Online*, 2015, http://eprints.lse.ac.uk/63051.

101 Larkins, *Spectacular Favela*, 146.

102 According to the Catalytic Communities website (https://catcomm.org), "as part of the PAC I, four favelas in Rio received over R$600 million in investments, and as part of PAC II there are upgrades currently underway in over 20 additional favelas in the city."

103 Alves and Evanson, *Living in the Crossfire*, 6. PRONASCI was a suite of ninety-seven subprograms that addressed both the security forces themselves and specific favelas/communities. It provided for, inter alia, the training of security personnel on human rights and community policing practices, subsidies to low-paid police officers for training seminars and for the purchase of housing, construction of police gyms, and social security services and health services for security forces, community initiatives in the favelas in order to facilitate intervention in the communities and reduce incidents of violence—see, for example, the Women of Peace initiative (Mulheres de Paz)—and new employment programs like the Project for the Protection of Youths in Vulnerable Territories (Programa de Proteção de Jovens em Territorio Vulnerável [PROTEJO]). According to the then national secretary for public security, Ricardo Balestreri, this was the largest program of its kind on the planet (see Alves and Evanson, *Living in the Crossfire*, 127–29, 142–48, 165–66). PRONASCI effectively ended in 2011, at the time of the Rousseff administration.

104 For a detailed outline of the projects implemented in Rocinha under PAC see Meg Healy, "Brazil's Political Crisis Threatens Essential Upgrading Works in Rocinha," *Rio on Watch*, June 8, 2016, https://www.rioonwatch.org/?p=28887.

105 Alves and Evanson, *Living in the Crossfire*, 29.

106 Healy, "Brazil's Political Crisis."

107 Larkins, *Spectacular Favela*, 152–53.

108 Larkins, *Spectacular Favela*, 19.

109 Cabral, "Decreto no. 42787 de 06/01/2011."

110 World Bank, *Bringing the State Back*, 37.

111 Owens, "Bismarck to Petraeus," 152–54.

112 At this point, it would be interesting to see how community policing apologists would attempt to formalize various informal forms of social reproduction (e.g., illegal connections to public utility networks or illegal land use) if not by intimidation, violence, and coercion.

113 Mark Duffield, "The Liberal Way of Development and the Development-Security Impasse: Exploring the Global Life-Chance Divide," *Security Dialogue* 41, no. 1 (2010): 68.

114 Mark Duffield, "Global Civil War: The Non-Insured, International Containment and Post-Interventionary Society," *Journal of Refugee Studies* 21, no. 2 (2008): 147.

115 Duffield, *Development*, 182–83.

116 Larkins, *Spectacular Favela*, 151.

117 Neocleous, *War Power*, 30.

118 Dobbins et al., *Beginner's Guide*, xxiii.

119 US Department of the Army, *Counterinsurgency*, A-7. See also the identical wording proposed by Kilcullen: "Counterinsurgency is armed social work: an attempt to redress basic social and political problems while being shot at" (*Counterinsurgency*, 43).

120 Kilcullen, *Counterinsurgency*, 43.

121 These descriptions are reminiscent of American General Charles Krulak's notorious notion of the "Three Block War," born after the rather unpleasant American experience of Mogadishu in 1993. In Krulak's words, "In one moment in time, our service members will be feeding and clothing displaced refugees—providing humanitarian assistance. In the next moment, they will be holding two warring tribes apart—conducting peacekeeping operations—and, finally, they will be fighting a highly lethal mid-intensity battle—all on the same day … all within three city blocks. It will be what we call the 'three block war'" (quoted in US Department of the Army, *Urban Operations*, FM 3-06 [Washington, DC: Department of the Army, 2006], https://fas.org/irp/doddir/army/fm3-06.pdf). This notion describes the role of the armed forces in a way effectively resembling armed social work. What it does not show are the reasons behind the presence of these forces in those three city blocks in the first place.

122 Siman and Santos, "Interrogating," 63.

123 David Galula, *Counterinsurgency Warfare: Theory and Practice* (London: Praeger Security International, 2006), 66.

124 Carl von Clausewitz, *On War*, trans. Michael Howard and Peter Paret (Oxford: Oxford University Press, 2007), 13.

125 Glenn et al., "People Make the City," 30.

126 Andrew Birtle, *US Army Counterinsurgency and Contingency Operations Doctrine 1860–1941* (Washington, DC: US Army Center for Military History, 2009), 92.

127 Owens, *Economy of Force*, 279.

128 Owens, *Economy of Force*, 279.

129 Birtle, *US Army Counterinsurgency … 1860–1941*, 5.

130 Rieff, "Where Hunger Goes."

131 See, for example, terms such as "rural construction/pacification" or "pacification/rural development" (Neocleous, "Brighter and Nicer," 197).

132 Paul Freedman, "How the Search for Flavors Influenced Our World," *YaleGlobal Online*, March 11, 2003. https://archive-yaleglobal.yale.edu/content/search-flavors-influenced-our-world.

133 Sidney W. Mintz, *Sweetness and Power: The Place of Sugar in Modern History* (New York: Penguin Books, 1986), 7, 37–38.

134 Mark Oliver, "The Banana Wars: How the U.S. Plundered Central America on Behalf of Corporations," September 14, 2017, https://allthatsinteresting.com/banana-wars; Roberto González, Hugh Gusterson, and David Price, "Introduction: War, Culture, and Counterinsurgency," in *The Counter-Counterinsurgency Manual: Or, Notes on Demilitarizing American Society*, by Network of Concerned Anthropologists (Chicago: Prickly Paradigm Press, 2009), 15.

135 Cullather, *Hungry World*; John Perkins, "The Rockefeller Foundation and the Green Revolution." *Agriculture and Human Values* 7, no. 3–4 (1990): 6–18; John Perkins, *Geopolitics and Green Revolution: Wheat, Genes, and the Cold War* (New York: Oxford University Press, 1997); Raj Patel, "The Long Green Revolution," *Journal of Peasant Studies* 40, no. 1 (2013): 1–63.

136 Oliveira, "Geopolitics of Brazilian Soybeans."

137 Matheus Hoffman Pfrimer and Ricardo César Barbosa Jr., "Neo-Agro-Colonialism, Control over Life, and Imposed Spatio-Temporalities," *Contexto Internacional* 39, no. 1 (2017): 3–33.

138 Riley Sunderland, *Resettlement and Food Control in Malaya* (Santa Monica, CA: RAND Corporation, 1964), 64, https://www.rand.org/pubs/research_memoranda/RM4173.html.

139 John Zambri, "Peasant Roles in Insurgency and Counterinsurgency: A Brief Historical Analysis." *Small Wars Journal*, June 17, 2017, 3, https://smallwarsjournal.com/jrnl/art/peasant-roles-in-insurgency-and-counterinsurgency-a-brief-historical-analysis.

140 Cullather, *Hungry World*, 91.

141 Sunderland, *Resettlement and Food Control*, 73.

142 Galula, *Counterinsurgency Warfare*, viii, 66, 82; Roger Trinquier, *Modern Warfare: A French View of Counterinsurgency*, trans. Daniel Lee (London: Praeger Security International, 2006), 30, 62, 70, 71; Frank Kitson, *Low Intensity Operations: Subversion, Insurgency, Peace-Keeping* (Dehra Dun: Natraj Publishers 1992), 107; Long, On *"Other War,"* 54, 72–73.

143 Trinquier, *Modern Warfare*, 30, 62, 70–71.

144 Galula, *Counterinsurgency Warfare*, 56, 66, 83, 85; Owens, *Economy of Force*, 233; Andrew J. Birtle, *US Army Counterinsurgency and Contingency Operations Doctrine 1942–1976* (Washington, DC: US Army Center for Military History, 2006), 393.

145 Owens, *Economy of Force*, 155, 198, 236, 264.

146 Sunderland, *Resettlement and Food Control*, 77; Owens, *Economy of Force*, 181–82.

147 Galula, *Counterinsurgency Warfare*, 71; Owens, *Economy of Force*, 187; David C. Gompert et al., *War by Other Means: Building Complete and Balanced Capabilities for Counterinsurgency* (Santa Monica, CA: RAND Corporation, 2008), 91, https://www.rand.org/pubs/monographs/MG595z2.html.

148 Owens, *Economy of Force*, 155, 246; Zambri, "Peasant Roles," 3, 4, 6, 8; Galula, *Counterinsurgency Warfare*, 16, 61, 65, 70, 83; Miller, "Simple Truth."

149 Owens, *Economy of Force*, 132, 150, 162, 177, 208, 237.

150 Sunderland, *Resettlement and Food Control*; Gompert et al., *War by Other Means*, 91; Owens, *Economy of Force*, 163, 181.

151 Felicity D. Scott, *Outlaw Territories: Environments of Insecurity/Architectures of Counterinsurgency* (New York: Zone Books, 2016), 172, 175; David Zierler, "Against Protocol: Ecocide, Détente, and the Question of Chemical Warfare in Vietnam, 1969–1975," in *Environmental Histories of the Cold War*, ed. J.R. McNeill and Corinna R. Unger, (New York: Cambridge University Press, 2010), 237.

152 Excerpt from Wikipedia entry "Second Boer War concentration camps." See also Owens, *Economy of Force*, 155.

153 Scott (*Outlaw Territories*, 172) quotes an extract from Swedish Prime Minister Olof Palme's speech during the United Nations Conference on the Human Environment, which began in Stockholm just one day after the proceedings of the commission: "The immense destruction brought about by indiscriminate bombing, by large-scale use of bulldozers and herbicides is an outrage sometimes described as ecocide, which requires urgent international attention."

154 Scott, *Outlaw Territories*, 175.

155 Owens, *Economy of Force*, 233.

156 David Naguib Pellow, *Resisting Global Toxics: Transnational Movements for Environmental Justice* (London: MIT Press, 2007), 159; see also Thomas D. Pilsch, "Operation Ranch Hand," accessed March 13, 2020, https://www.cc.gatech.edu/~tpilsch/AirOps/ranch.html; Zierler, "Against Protocol," 232–36; Scott, *Outlaw Territories*, 180.

157 See also the Al Jazeera documentary "Children of Agent Orange," September 28, 2011, https://www.aljazeera.com/program/people-power/2011/9/28/children-of-agent-orange.

158 Scott, *Outlaw Territories*, 181.

159 Scott, *Outlaw Territories*, 175, 180; Greg Bankoff, "A Curtain of Silence: Asia's

Fauna in the Cold War," in *Environmental Histories of the Cold War*, ed. J.R. McNeill, and Corinna R. Unger (New York: Cambridge University Press, 2010), 216–17.

160 As Owens (*Economy of Force*, 37) points out, "Populations are forced to collaborate through the dictate of violent necessity, becoming objects of social administration rather than political agents or subjects."

161 Nick Cullather, "'The Target Is the People': Representations of the Village in Modernization and U.S. National Security Doctrine," *Cultural Politics* 2, no.1 (2006): 35. "Entire villages" adds Owens (*Economy of Force*, 232), "were levelled with ploughs and bulldozers; homesteads were burned down to signal to people that they would never be able to return."

162 Zierler, "Against Protocol," 233.

163 In Owens's (*Economy of Force*, 219) account, this theory supported the existence of specific "stages of economic growth" in the course of social evolution. "All societies ... developed along an evolutionary path through objective and observable stages. These stages progressed from traditional society to one in which the 'preconditions' of modernity take root, to 'take-off,' then 'maturity,' all culminating in the pinnacle of growth and development: the stage of 'high mass-consumption.'"

164 Owens, *Economy of Force*, 236.

165 Clemis quoted in Belcher, "Afterlives of Counterinsurgency," 39.

166 Clemis quoted in Belcher, "Afterlives of Counterinsurgency," 39.

167 Neocleous, *Critique of Security*, 171.

168 Cullather, "Target Is the People." 29–36.

169 Cullather, "Target Is the People," 30. See also Cullather, *Hungry World*, 2.

170 Samuel Huntington, "The Bases of Accommodation." *Foreign Affairs* 46, no. 4 (1968): 652.

171 Huntington, "Bases of Accommodation," 649. Mike Davis, (*Planet of the Slums* [New York: Verso, 2006], 57) challenges that figure, raising the number of displaced people to five million. Citing historian Marilyn Young, he writes: "the urban share of South Vietnam's population soared from 15 percent to 65 percent, with five million displaced peasants turned into slum-dwellers or inhabitants of refugee camps."

172 Belcher, "Afterlives of Counterinsurgency," 161.

173 Perkins, "Rockefeller Foundation," 11.

174 Cullather points out that although community development in 1956 had been recognized by the United Nations as its official term for describing rural modernization initiatives, in the Vietnam War it "was about to acquire a second life as a counterinsurgency strategy" and it perhaps reached its most militarized form through the Strategic Hamlets (*Hungry World*, 91).

175 The fact that agricultural reform and land redistribution programs were used as a geopolitical tool testifies to the fact that they were promoted by the West as long as Cold War rivalries were in full force. After the collapse of the Soviet bloc, the idea was abandoned. As James C. Scott points out, "When it was a bipolar world, the US and the West were interested in land reform in places where the land distribution was wildly unequal. After 1989, the IMF and the World Bank have never talked about land reform again" (P. Schouten, "Theory Talk #38: James Scott on Agriculture as Politics, the Danger of Standardization and Not Being Governed," *Theory Talks*, May 15, 2010, https://www.files.ethz.ch/isn/155099/Theory%20Talk38_Scott.pdf, 7)

176 Patel, "Long Green Revolution," 5.

177 Rieff, "Where Hunger Goes."
178 Cullather, *Hungry World*, ix, 234; Rieff, "Where Hunger Goes." According to Warren Weaver, director of the Natural Science Program at the Rockefeller Foundation and one of the main masterminds of the Green Revolution agenda, "The problem of food has become one of the world's most acute and pressing problems; and directly or indirectly it is the cause of much of the world's present tension and unrest.... Agitators from Communist countries are making the most of the situation. The time is now ripe, in places possibly over-ripe for sharing some of our technical knowledge with these people. Appropriate action may now help them to attain by evolution the improvements, including those in agriculture, which otherwise may have to come by revolution" (quoted in Perkins, "Rockefeller Foundation," 11).
179 Patel, "Long Green Revolution," 10.
180 This attempt to "familiarize" farmers with the logic of production and profit was arguably yet another chapter in the long and violent history of the colonization of these lands. As Neocleous (*War Power*, 71, 73) explains, what lay at the core of the theoretical framework supporting the colonialists' presence in South America and the expropriation of the land of the Indians was the concept of *waste*, and *waste land* in particular. The absence of the concept of land ownership among Indigenous peoples led Western law theorists to argue that the natives did not know how to use the land and were therefore "wasting" it. In other words, "the colonizing impulse simply assumed the 'Indian,' like the peasant, to be incapable of occupying and improving land as private property, and hence left everything to waste." This waste of land, inconceivable for the West, practically legitimized its colonization. According to the logic of Emer de Vattel, a prominent theorist of international law, "Things which are 'uncultivated' or 'untilled' become open to appropriation in order that they may not be wasted" (Neocleous, *War Power*, 71).
181 Cullather, *Hungry World*, 43–44.
182 David Nally and Stephen Taylor, "The Politics of Self-Help: The Rockefeller Foundation, Philanthropy and the 'Long' Green Revolution," *Political Geography* 49, no. 3 (2015): 57.
183 As Perkins ("Rockefeller Foundation," 7) points out, in Mexico, the other major field of the Green Revolution, there were no corresponding concerns about the growth of the national population.
184 Patel, "Long Green Revolution," 14.
185 Cullather, *Hungry World*, 160.
186 Cullather, *Hungry World*, 173.
187 "Miracle rice became the visible mark of a pacified landscape" writes Cullather (*Hungry World*, 177). For the use of IR-8 in the Vietnam War see Cullather, *Hungry World*, 173–78.
188 Cullather, *Hungry World*, 172.
189 Cullather, *Hungry World*, 173.
190 Robert Komer quoted in Cullather, *Hungry World*, 174.
191 USAID, *USAID's Legacy in Agricultural Development: Fifty Years of Progress* (Washington, DC: USAID, 2016), xiv, https://www.usaid.gov/agriculture-and-food-security/document/usaids-legacy-agricultural-development-50-years-progress.
192 Perkins, "Rockefeller Foundation," 13.
193 According to the USAID Mission in India, "chemical fertilizers accounted for

the largest part of Green Revolution production increases" (*USAID's Legacy*, 115). Patel is categorical on the importance of subsidies: "The Green Revolution would not have succeeded without subsidies" ("Long Green Revolution," 16).

194 David Nally, "The Green Revolution as Philanthropy," *HistPhil*, April 18, 2016, https://histphil.org/2016/04/18/the-green-revolution-as-philanthropy.

195 Neocleous, *War Power*, 56, 67, 86; Oliveira, "Geopolitics of Brazilian Soybeans," 15; Rieff, "Where Hunger Goes".

196 Duffield, *Development*, 20.

197 Perkins, "Rockefeller Foundation," 6; Patel, "Long Green Revolution," 24.

198 Theda Gödecke, Alexander J. Stein, and Matin Qaim, "The Global Burden of Chronic and Hidden Hunger: Trends and Determinants," *Global Food Security* 17 (2018), 21, https://www.sciencedirect.com/science/article/pii/S2211912417301578.

199 Patel, "Long Green Revolution," 6, 13.

200 This has been acknowledged even by USAID itself (*USAID's Legacy*, 30). See also Patel, "Long Green Revolution," 2, 18–26.

201 Patel, "Long Green Revolution," 13, 15. Within a broader counterinsurgency logic, the solution to the food problem may have been promoted as a key target. However, the choice of US civil-military cadres to shield local class relations was clear. As Birtle (*US Army Counterinsurgency ... 1860–1941*, 102) puts it, with the "indulgent" view of an army historian speaking about US counterinsurgency operations in Cuba and the Philippines a few decades earlier, "In economic matters, the Army's activities were both shaped and limited by the standards of laissez-faire capitalism, while its respect for private property, one of the most sacrosanct of American tenets, prevented officers from dabbling in schemes of land redistribution and agrarian reform that might have helped redress some of the deepest social and economic inequities of the islands."

202 Patel "Long Green Revolution," 18–26; Nally and Taylor, "Politics of Self-Help," 57. See, for example, the Mexican Agricultural Program's focus on the mass production of wheat which, although less popular than corn in Mexico, was preferred because the means of its production had already been tested in the US. Or the promotion of maize in India which, despite the fact that it accounted for only about 3 percent of its total production, was preferred because the relevant research and production framework had already been tested and established in Mexico (Patel, "Long Green Revolution," 9, 12).

203 The irony here is that the Green Revolution may also have contributed to the global population growth that terrified its cadres so much. As Perkins ("Rockefeller Foundation," 15) points out in relation to the case of India, "A deep irony attends the issue of overpopulation on the subcontinent, because it was concern that population growth rates caused political instability that shaped the Rockefeller Foundation's plans. Yet unequal distribution of increased agricultural productivity may be a major contributory factor to India's continued high population growth rate. Development that does not result in a more egalitarian society may create an underclass of people for whom more children are the only source of economic security, however meager. Given the Malthusian pall that hung over the Foundation's planning in the 1940s and 1950s, it would be ironic indeed that the Foundation's responses to overpopulation might have created the very situation its officers most dreaded."

204 Neocleous, *War Power*, 56.

205 David Naguib Pellow, *Resisting Global Toxics: Transnational Movements for Environmental Justice* (London: MIT Press, 2007), 149.

206 Pellow, *Resisting Global Toxics*, 159.

207 Naiara Bittencourt and Alessandra Jacobovski, "Agrotóxicos como arma química: a permanente guerra agrária no Brasil," Terra de Direitos, May 5, 2017, https://terradedireitos.org.br/acervo/artigos/artigo-agrotoxicos-como-arma-quimica-a-permanente-guerra-agraria-no-brasil/22695.

208 Pellow, *Resisting Global Toxics*, 159; Wayne Biddle, "Nerve Gases and Pesticides: Links Are Close," *New York Times*, March 30, 1984, https://www.nytimes.com/1984/03/30/world/nerve-gases-and-pesticides-links-are-close.html; Sarah Everts, "The Nazi Origins of Deadly Nerve Gases," *Chemical & Engineering News* 94 no. 41 (2015): 26–28, https://cen.acs.org/articles/94/i41/Nazi-origins-deadly-nerve-gases.html.

209 Arthur Galston quoted in Zierler, "Against Protocol," 237.

210 Bittencourt and Jacobovski, "Agrotóxicos."

211 Neocleous, *War Power*, 56, see also 65.

212 Patel, "Long Green Revolution," 3, 10, 27; Cullather, *Hungry World*, 175.

213 Patel, "Long Green Revolution," 17.

214 Andrew J. Birtle, *US Army Counterinsurgency and Contingency Operations Doctrine 1942–1976* (Washington, DC: US Army Center for Military History, 2006), 298.

215 Birtle, *US Army Counterinsurgency … 1942–1976*, 300–304.

216 Birtle, *US Army Counterinsurgency … 1942–1976*, 302.

217 Oliveira, "Geopolitics of Brazilian Soybeans," 4–5.

218 Oliveira, "Geopolitics of Brazilian Soybeans," 6.

219 Oliveira, "Geopolitics of Brazilian Soybeans," 5.

220 In essence, the Amazon's deforestation, which is currently a matter of international concern, stems from the military government's agricultural modernization policies. In addition, the expansion of agricultural activities to the Cerrado region had begun earlier, under the Vargas administration. As Geraldo Barros points out, it was a brutal process against Indigenous peoples and immigrants from the northeast ("Brazil: The Challenges in Becoming an Agricultural Superpower," in *Brazil as an Economic Superpower? Understanding Brazil's Changing Role in the Global Economy*, ed. Lael Brainard and Leonardo Martinez-Diaz (Washington, DC: Brookings Institution Press, 2009), 85.

221 We can testify to the appalling resemblance between this particular situation and reality in the country following the election of Bolsonaro and the close ties his administration maintains with the agro-industrial lobby. Philip Fearnside, "Why Brazil's New President Poses an Unprecedented Threat to the Amazon," *YaleEnvironment360*, November 8, 2018, https://e360.yale.edu/features/why-brazils-new-president-poses-an-unprecedented-threat-to-the-amazon.

222 Oliveira, "Geopolitics of Brazilian Soybeans," 4–5.

223 *BrasilWire*, "David Rockefeller and a Dark Legacy in Brasil—A Critical Obituary," *BrasilWire*, March 20, 2017, http://www.brasilwire.com/david-rockefeller-legacy-in-brasil.

224 This became evident when Nelson Rockefeller became coordinator of the Office of Interamerican Affairs (*BrasilWire*, "David Rockefeller").

225 Carmelo Ruiz, "Wycliffe and the CIA: The Summer Institute of Linguistic Connection SIL and the CIA," Akha Heritage Foundation, accessed March 14, 2020, http://www.akha.org/content/missiondocuments/wycliffecia.html.

226 *BrasilWire*, "David Rockefeller."

227 Clifford A. Welch, "Rockefeller and the Origins of Agribusiness in Brazil: A Research Report," Rockefeller Archive Center, 2014, https://www.issuelab.org/resources/27973/27973.pdf.

228 Barros, "Brazil: The Challenges," 97.

229 Isadora Ferreira, "From Famine to Feast in Brazil," *Frontlines* (November/ December 2011): 7, https://2012-2017.usaid.gov/sites/default/files/frontlines/ FL_NOVDEC11%20%281%29.pdf; Barros, "Brazil: The Challenges," 97.

230 Mark Langan, *Neo-Colonialism and the Poverty of "Development" in Africa* (Cham, CH: Palgrave Macmillan, 2018), 54, 65. In regard to the policies of land grabbing under today's neo-agro-colonialism see Pfrimer and Barbosa, "Neo-Agro-Colonialism."

231 Brazil's presence in Africa's agricultural landscape and its geopolitical implications constitute a separate and important chapter in this debate. See indicatively Oliveira, "Geopolitics of Brazilian Soybeans," 11–15; Marcus Power, *Geopolitics and Development* (New York: Routledge, 2019).

232 Rodrigo Patto Sá Motta, "Modernizing Repression: USAID and the Brazilian Police," *Revista Brasileira de História* 30, no. 59 (2010): 236. Certain gentrification efforts made during the military government, in which USAID was actively involved and which required the demolition of favelas, should also be positioned within the context of this modernization.

233 Oliveira, "Geopolitics of Brazilian Soybeans," 5.

234 Of all the pesticides available in the country, the two most widely used are glyphosate and 2,4-D (one of the key components of Agent Orange), which, as we saw above, are directly related to the military industry (Human Rights Watch, "'You Don't Want to Breathe Poison Anymore': The Failing Response to Pesticide Drift in Brazil's Rural Communities," 29, 37, https://www.hrw.org/sites/default/ files/report_pdf/brazil0718_web.pdf.

235 Brasil de Fato, "Bolsonaro Administration Approves 197 Pesticides in Five Months," May 22, 2019, https://www.brasildefato.com.br/2019/05/22/bolsonaro-administration-approves-169-pesticides-in-five-months. Resistance to the use of pesticides can lead to killings, as witnessed by the case of José Maria Filho, who was killed in 2010 in Limoeiro do Norte because he brought up the issue of spraying in the area. See Human Rights Watch, "You Don't Want," 38; Paulo Prada, "Fateful Harvest: Why Brazil Has a Big Appetite for Risky Pesticides," Reuters, April 2, 2015, https://www.reuters.com/investigates/special-report/brazil-pesticides.

236 It is important at this point to add another dimension to the relationship between the Green Revolution and public health. The Green Revolution should be understood not only as an imposition of a specific productive logic but also as the long-term promotion of a particular nutritional culture, which contributes in its own way to contemporary food insecurity phenomena. The modernization of agricultural production meant, as we have seen, the promotion of certain high-yielding varieties, the expansion of monoculture farming, and the focus on a limited range of agricultural products. This would gradually leave its mark not only on production but also on consumption, as it shaped global eating habits based on the ever-increasing availability of a limited number of foods and therefore the deterioration of dietary diversity. Therefore, the increasing dependence on a narrow range of foods has prompted the rapid spread of a dietary homogeneity and food culture that is ultimately based on specific energy-dense foods (i.e., animal products, plant oils, and sugars) over cereals, pulses, and vegetables, thereby contributing to a new epidemic of noncommunicable diseases such as diabetes, heart disease, and certain forms of cancer (Colin K. Khoury et al., "Increasing Homogeneity in Global Food Supplies and the Implications

for Food Security," *PNAS* 111, no. 11 (2014): 4001, 4004, https://doi.org/10.1073/pnas.1313490111); Andrew Jacobs and Matt Richtel, "How Big Business Got Brazil Hooked on Junk Food," *New York Times*, September 16, 2017, https://www.nytimes.com. A development that is particularly visible today in Brazil, and in its urban populations in particular.

237 Global Witness, *At What Cost? Irresponsible Business and the Murder of Land and Environmental Defenders in 2017*, July 24, 2018, 8, 10, 21–24, https://www.globalwitness.org/en/campaigns/environmental-activists/at-what-cost.

238 Bittencourt and Jacobovski, "Agrotóxicos."

239 Michael Albertus, Thomas Brambor, and Ricardo Ceneviva, "Land Inequality and Rural Unrest: Theory and Evidence from Brazil," *Journal of Conflict Resolution* 62, no. 3 (2018): 568–70.

240 George Martine and Gordon McGranahan, "Brazil's Early Urban Transition: What Can It Teach Urbanizing Countries?" *International Institute for Environment and Development* (2010), 13, https://www.iied.org/10585iied; Alain de Janvry and Eisabeth Sadoulet, "A Study in Resistance to Institutional Change: The Lost Game of Latin American Land Reform," *World Development* 17, no. 9 (1989): 1397–1407; Patel, "Long Green Revolution," 18–26. The policy of subsidies and subsidized loans by the state contributed to this expansion. This policy aimed at industrializing agricultural production, promoting Green Revolution technologies (specialized farm equipment, fertilizers, pesticides, etc.) and increasing productivity (Bernardo Mueller and Charles Mueller, "The Political Economy of the Brazilian Model of Agricultural Development: Institutions versus Sectoral Policy," *Quarterly Review of Economics and Fin*ance, no. 62 (2016): 15, 17); Barros, "Brazil: The Challenges," 85, 99; Patel, "Long Green Revolution," 16–17, 21, 26).

241 Paulino, "Agricultural, Environmental and Socio-Political," 139; Cristóbal Cay, "Latin America's Exclusionary Rural Development in a Neo-Liberal World." Paper presented at the meeting of the Latin American Studies Association (LASA), Guadalajara, Mexico, April 17–19, 1997, 9–12, http://biblioteca.clacso.edu.ar/ar/libros/lasa97/kay.pdf.

242 Albertus, Brambor, and Ceneviva, "Land Inequality," 558, 562, 571; Mueller and Mueller, "Political Economy," 15.

243 Albertus, Brambor, and Ceneviva, "Land Inequality," 558, 569, 585.

244 This position was supported by Lucineia Freitas (member of Campanha Permanente Contra os Agrotóxicos) during the panel entitled "Agronegócio, dominação e resistência no campo" (December 13, 2018), as part of the Semana da Soberania Alimentar na Maré, (Maré, Rio de Janeiro, December 9–15, 2018). See also Cullather, *Hungry World*, 68.

245 Barros, "Brazil: The Challenges," 81, 83; Oliveira, "Geopolitics of Brazilian Soybeans," 4–5.

246 Oliveira, "Geopolitics of Brazilian Soybeans," 5.

247 Martine and McGranahan, *Brazil's Early Urban Transition*, 14.

248 Martine and McGranahan, *Brazil's Early Urban Transition*, 10, 12.

249 Martine and McGranahan, *Brazil's Early Urban Transition*, 13, 14.

250 Fausto Brito, "The Displacement of the Brazilian Population to the Metropolitan Areas," *Estudos Avançados* 20, no. 57 (2006): 222; Lea Rekow, "Fighting Insecurity: Experiments in Urban Agriculture in the Favelas of Rio de Janeiro," *Field Actions Science Reports*, no. 8 (2015): 3, http://factsreports.revues.org/4009.

251 Janice Perlman, *Favela: Four Decades of Living on the Edge in Rio de Janeiro* (New York: Oxford University Press, 2010), 51–53, 55.

252 Brito, "Displacement," 222.
253 Martine and McGranahan, *Brazil's Early Urban Transition*, 13. As Barros also writes, "Brazil's share of the rural population fell from 64 percent of the total in 1950 to 44 percent in 1970 and to 19 percent in 2000. That has meant that since World War II, every decade has seen about 10 to 15 million people in Brazil leave rural areas and move to urban centers" ("Brazil: The Challenges," 91).
254 It should be noted that armed resistance in Brazil has largely followed a more urban direction than in examples from neighboring countries. Contrary to Che Guevara's teachings and "foco theory," which in its original conception focused on rural areas, Brazilian revolutionaries preferred to organize within the urban terrain. From a certain point onward, however, armed communist cells also appeared in rural areas, such as in the Amazon state and in the Araguaia River region, while poverty and the dismal living and working conditions in the northeast of the country were deemed fertile ground for popular uprisings and insurgencies. See Alan S. Craig, "The Internal Enemy: Insurgency in Brazil," GlobalSecurity.org, March 8, 1985, https://www.globalsecurity.org/military/library/report/1986/CAS.htm; Thamyris F.T. Almeida, "Araguaia: Maoist Uprising and Military Counterinsurgency in the Brazilian Amazon, 1967–1975," (postgraduate thesis, University of Massachusetts Amherst, 2015), https://scholarworks.umass.edu/cgi/viewcontent.cgi?article=1241&context=masters_theses_2. The whole debate on the counterinsurgency role of urbanization in Brazil may therefore be viewed in this context.
255 Ankober, "Is Huntington the Source of Our Mess?" De Birhan Media, August 11, 2010; John Hugh Crimmins, "Document 97: Telegram 1850 from the Embassy in Brazil to the Department of State," in *Foreign Relations of the United States, 1969–1976, Volume E-11, Part 2, Documents on South America, 1973–1976*, ed. Adam M. Howard, Sara Berndt, Halbert Jones, and James Siekmeier (Washington, DC: USGPO, 2015), https://history.state.gov/historicaldocuments/frus1969-76ve11p2/d97; Anthony W. Pereira, "Samuel Huntington and 'Decompression' in Brazil"; Samuel Huntington, "How Countries Democratize," *Political Science Quarterly* 106, no. 4 (1991–92): 595.
256 Neocleous, *War Power*, 86. See, relatedly, the devastating effects of the MAP in Mexico, which among other things forced millions of farmers to migrate to urban slums or other countries (Cullather, *Hungry World*, 68).
257 Cullather, *Hungry World*, 242.
258 Cullather, *Hungry World*, 242; Nick Cullather, "Development Doctrine and Modernization Theory: The Decline of Modernization Theory," American Foreign Relations, accessed March 13, 2020, https://www.americanforeignrelations.com/A-D/Development-Doctrine-and-Modernization-Theory-The-decline-of-modernization-theory.html.
259 Barros, "Brazil: The Challenges," 84. Similarly, as Almeida points out, the Communist Party of Brazil stressed in an issue of *A Classe Operária*, printed in 1972 (that is, at the heart of the Green Revolution) that "the mass exodus of landless *camponeses* to the cities decreased the number of peoples engaged in subsistence farming and increased the demand for food in urban centers" ("Araguaia," 25).
260 Collier, "Politics of Hunger," 67, 70. I would like to thank Alexis Gazis for his help in accessing this source.
261 Informal urban settlements host nearly one billion people today—that is, about a quarter of the global urban population (UN-Habitat, *The Challenge of Slums:*

Global Report on Human Settlements (London: Earthscan 2016), 13–14, 51, 57). This figure will almost certainly increase as it is estimated that 2.5 billion people will be added "to the world's urban population by 2050, with almost 90% of this growth happening in Asia and Africa" (United Nations, Department of Economic and Social Affairs, Population Division, "World Urbanization Prospects: The 2018 Revision," https://population.un.org/wup/Publications/Files/WUP2018-KeyFacts.pdf.

262 To quote from NutriCities, "Community Brief #1": "Constantly rising food prices drastically affect people's purchasing power and their potential for access to nutritional food .... Food insecurity refers to the lack of secure access to suffi-cient amounts of safe and nutritious food for normal growth and development and an active and healthy life. Food insecurity is therefore not only related to the question of the physical lack of food. In the majority of cases—and in cities in particular—subnutrition and malnutrition are associated, among others, with the poorest populations' insufficient purchasing power to buy safe and nutritious food." This is a common characteristic among favela inhabitants today. For exam-ple, according to research conducted in 2018 by the Minhocas Urbanas collective in Maré's neighborhoods, a large proportion of its residents are not fed properly because of their financial difficulties (personal communication, December 18, 2018, in Maré).

263 Adrian H. Hearn, "Beanstalks and Trust in Chinese and Brazilian Food Systems," *Journal of Latin American Geography* 17, no. 2 (2018): 99.

264 From a personal communication with one of the program managers during a visit to the garden of Hortas Cariocas in Manguinhos favela on December 17, 2018.

265 Hearn, "Beanstalks," 101.

266 Stephanie Rutherford, "Green Governmentality: Insights and Opportunities in the Study of Nature's Rule," "Progress in Human Geography" 31, no, 3 (2007): 291–307; Stephanie Rutherford, "Environmentality and Green Governmentality" in *The International Encyclopedia of Geography*, ed. Douglas Richardson, Noel Castree, Michael F. Goodchild, Audrey Kobayashi, Weidong Liu, and Richard A. Marston (John Hoboken, NJ: Wiley, 2017).

267 Luiza Fenizola from the Catalytic Communities NGO, personal communication, December 20, 2018.

268 La Rocque and Shelton-Zumpano, "Sustainable Development Strategy," 2.

269 As mentioned above, the ecocidal practices of the US in Vietnam also came under close scrutiny by the international community in this conference.

270 Joseph Huber quoted in Lynley Tulloch and David Neilson, "The Neoliberalisation of Sustainability," *Citizenship, Social and Economics Education* 13, no.1 (2014): 32–33.

271 Evans and Reid, *Resilient Life: The Art of Living Dangerously* (Malden: Polity Press, 2014), 70, 82.

272 Serge Latouche, "Sustainable Development as a Paradox" (paper given at the Baltic Sea Symposium of the Religion, Science, and the Environment Movement, June 3, 2003), 10, http://www.rsesymposia.org/themedia/File/1151679499-Plenary2_Latouche.pdf.

273 Latouche, "Sustainable Development"; Rob Krueger and David Gibbs, "Introduction: Problematizing the Politics of Sustainability," in *The Sustainable Development Paradox: Urban Political Economy in the United States and Europe*, ed. Rob Krueger and David Gibbs (New York: Guilford Press 2007); Dan A. Tarlock, "Ideas Without Institutions: The Paradox of Sustainable Development," *Indiana Journal of Global Legal Studies* 9, no. 1 (2001): 35–49.

274 "Brundtland Report" cited in Tulloch and Neilson, "Neoliberalisation of Sustainability," 33.

275 Evans and Reid, *Resilient Life*, 73.

276 Langan, *Neo-Colonialism*, 177–82.

277 Langan, *Neo-Colonialism*, 177, 179.

278 Krueger and Gibbs, "Introduction," 2.

279 Duffield, *Development*, 55, 67–70; Evans and Reid, *Resilient Life*, 74; Rutherford, "Green Governmentality," 295.

280 Subhabrata Bobby Banerjee, "Who Sustains Whose Development? Sustainable Development and the Reinvention of Nature," *Organization Studies* 24, no. 1 (2003): 150.

281 Tarlock, "Ideas Without Institutions," 35; Rutherford, "Environmentality," 2; Rutherford, "Green Governmentality," 295; Banerjee, "Who Sustains," 144, 146, 157–60.

282 Duffield, *Development*, 67–70.

283 Evans and Reid, *Resilient Life*, 77.

284 Duffield, *Development*, 55, 68–69; Evans and Reid, *Resilient Life*, 33, 74–77.

285 Pierre Dardot and Christian Laval, *The New Way of the World: On Neoliberal Society* (New York: Verso, 2013), 164–65, 172, 190; Maurizio Lazzarato, *The Making of the Indebted Man: An Essay on the Neoliberal Condition* (Los Angeles: Semiotexte, 2012), 51, 93, 143.

286 Evans and Reid, *Resilient Life*, 79.

287 Evans and Reid, *Resilient Life*, 79; Mark Neocleous, "Resisting Resilience," *Radical Philosophy*, no. 178 (2013) 1–7; Maria Kaika, "'Don't Call Me Resilient Again!': The New Urban Agenda as Immunology … or … What Happens when Communities Refuse to Be Vaccinated with 'Smart Cities' and Indicators," *Environment and Urbanization* 29, no. 1 (2017): 89–102; Sörensen and Söderbaum, "Introduction."

288 Duffield, *Development*, 69. The promotion of the logic of the lesser state and the shifting of "responsibility" to the subjects themselves does not obviously originate in the trust in the emancipatory potential of agency and self-organization as would be the case, for example, if we viewed these from the perspective of social antagonism. Self-reliance has long been the outcome of the lived experience of the communities of the periphery and of all those living in a subsistence economy. But the emergence of self-reliance within neoliberal discourse begins elsewhere. It is founded on a constitutional prioritization of populations and "the expectation that those excluded from the feast—the international surplus population thrown off by a globalizing search for progress—will be satisfied with basic needs and homeostasis"; an expectation that, as Duffield points out, "is, at best, unrealistic and, at worst, racist in its implications" (*Development*, 70). Such prioritizing is not surprising. On the contrary, it is a structural element of the neoliberal logic and testifies to the prevalence of the belief in the "survival of the fittest," as articulated by Herbert Spencer in the mid-nineteenth century, which, as Pierre Dardot and Christian Laval claim, constitutes a decisive turning point in the course of liberalism itself (*The New Way of the World: On Neoliberal Society* [New York: Verso, 2013], 32–36).

289 Obviously, the spread of sustainable development discourse and its practical application to municipal policies does not signify the absence of conventional development models in the operation of the city. This is made evident by the fact that during the period when sustainability discourse was being formulated, the city and the country at large were preparing for two mega-events that were

moving along a typical direction of development that was far from sustainable, despite having been advertised as sustainable events. Reality has deconstructed these propaganda constructs, revealing that, at the core of the two events lay an impossible sustainability, as expected (see James Armour Young, "Rio Has Broken Its Promise of an Environment-friendly Olympics," VICE News, August 1, 2016, https://news.vice.com/en_us/article/kz99wz/rio-has-broken-its-promise-of-an-environment-friendly-olympics. See also Ruby Russell, "Going for Green: No Medals for the Rio Olympics' Environmental Legacy," Deutsche Welle, August 23, 2016, https://www.dw.com/en/going-for-green-no-medals-for-the-rio-olympics-environmental-legacy/a-19495318; Autumn Spanne, "Brazil World Cup Fails to Score Environmental Goals," Scientific American, June 19, 2014, https://www.scientificamerican.com/article/brazil-world-cup-fails-to-score-environmental-goals. In short, one may observe the simultaneous promotion of two different developmental paradigms/models in Rio. This does not seem to be a paradox, or at least it is not greater than the paradox that already existed at the heart of the very notion of sustainable development.

290 La Rocque and Shelton-Zumpano, "Sustainable Development Strategy."

291 Sustainable Development Solutions Network, *An Action Agenda for Sustainable Development* (SDSN, June 6, 2013), 1, 34, https://unstats.un.org/unsd/broaderprogress/pdf/130613-SDSN-An-Action-Agenda-for-Sustainable-Development-FINAL.pdf.

292 La Rocque and Shelton-Zumpano. "Sustainable Development Strategy," 2.

293 La Rocque and Shelton-Zumpano, "Sustainable Development Strategy," 5.

294 Carla Cipolla, Patricia Mello, and Ezio Manzini, "Collaborative Services in Informal Settlements: Social Innovation in a Pacified Favela in Rio de Janeiro," in *New Frontiers in Social Innovation Research*, ed. Alex Nicholls, Julie Simon, and Madeleine Gabriel (New York: Palgrave Macmillan, 2015), 128–42; Cipolla et al., "Coproduced Game-Changing"; Isabella Nunes Pereira, Roberto Bartholo, Édison Renato Silva, and Domício Proença, "Entrepreneurship in the Favela of Rocinha, Rio de Janeiro: A Critical Approach," *Latin American Research Review* 52, no. 1 (2017): 79–93.

295 The activity of NGOs in the favelas constitutes a whole separate issue. It is indicative that about a hundred NGOs are currently registered in the Maré area alone. In the case of Brazil, their proliferation, which took place in the 1990s, is a symptom of the country's democratization effort after the fall of the dictatorship. But it is also linked to the strong interest now widespread among both the international community and the business world in the countries of the Global South, which promotes funding in the field of social services and social responsibility (Timo Bartholl, personal communication, December 12, 2017). The proliferation of NGOs is, after all, a broader phenomenon related to the promotion of the humanitarian industry within the post–Cold War agenda of international interventions and is obviously not novel to Brazil or Rio. As Duffield points out, it was exactly in the 1990s that a clear change in the functioning of NGOs was observed, which led to closer cooperation with governments, international community actors, and military forces to the extent that it directly challenged the "nongovernmental" designation (*Development*, 26–29, 66, 131–32). In other words, NGOs have gradually become an extension of individual government planning and a tool of governance. "The NGO movement is no longer outside the state: it has reinvented itself as intrinsic to its reconstruction and power projection," writes Duffield (*Development*, 29).

296 World Bank, *Bringing the State Back*, 100.

297 I. Pereira et al., "Entrepreneurship in the Favela," 79, 81.

298 *Asfalto* means asphalt. The use of the term *morro*, which means hill, has to do with the fact that many favelas have spread to the city's hills, and it also suggests a relationship with Morro da Providência, Rio's first favela.

299 Both of these phases left their mark on the racial composition of the favelas. As Perlman writes, "a much higher proportion of Rio's total black population lives in favelas than do whites" (*Favela*, 170). This mix of rurality and "Blackness" is steadily fueling stereotypical perceptions of the favela inhabitants, starting from colonial representations of the Other and the constitutional devaluation of the Black population, since their arrival as slaves and continuing to the pacification operations.

300 Nally and Taylor, "Politics of Self-Help," 57.

301 Joseph Huber, "Towards Industrial Ecology: Sustainable Development as a Concept of Ecological Modernization," *Journal of Environmental Policy & Planning* 2, no. 4 (2000): 269–85.

302 Saborio, "Pacification," 139. World Bank, *Bringing the State Back*, 95–96.

303 Tyler Strobl, "Inexplicable Sky-High Electric Bills Threaten Rio das Pedras, Escalate Fear of Eviction," *Rio on Watch*, January 25, 2018, https://www.rioonwatch .org/?p=41384.

304 Larkins, *Spectacular Favela*, 153.

305 World Bank, *Bringing the State Back*, 93. See also Cipolla, Mello, and Manzini, "Collaborative Services," 134.

306 Evans and Reid, *Resilient Life*, 34–37.

307 Cipolla, Mello, and Manzini ("Collaborative Services," 132) describe the operation of the program as follows: "Light Recicla was designed as a complex service resulting from the combination of two services: delivery of electricity and collection of recyclable materials. The parent company—Light—itself managed the delivery of electricity. Meanwhile, a Light partner operated the collection of recyclable materials. Electricity was delivered in the standard way except for the payment system: citizens were requested to bring recyclable materials to dedicated collection points, where the value of these materials was converted into credits towards a discount in their next electricity bill. Customers played an active role in the Light Recicla service: they collected the rubbish, washed it, separated it and brought it to the Collection Point, where the rubbish was weighed and the appropriate discount calculated and recorded in the system to appear on the next bill."

308 Cipolla, Mello, and Manzini, "Collaborative Services," 131.

309 Cipolla, Mello, and Manzini, "Collaborative Services," 128.

310 Cipolla, Mello, and Manzini, "Collaborative Services," 128.

311 La Rocque and Shelton-Zumpano "Sustainable Development Strategy," 6.

312 La Rocque and Shelton-Zumpano "Sustainable Development Strategy," 6.

313 Siman and Santos, "Interrogating," 73.

314 Personal communication, December 20, 2018.

315 Saborio, "Pacification," 139.

316 World Bank, *Bringing the State Back*, 92.

317 Rio+20, *The Future We Want: Outcome Document of the United Nations Conference on Sustainable Development*," United Nations, 2012, 30–32, https:// sustainabledevelopment.un.org/content/documents/733FutureWeWant.pdf.

318 Hearn, "Beanstalks," 99.

319 Personal communication, December 11, 2018. This observation is certainly not

surprising. Instead, it affirms the general governmental tendency to address individual social and environmental issues through frameworks, policies, and methodological tools based on technocratic language, reports, indicators, and numbers, ultimately seeking a "greening by numbers and indicators," in Maria Kaika's apt description ("Don't Call Me Resilient," 2).

320 Rekow, "Fighting Insecurity," 2.

321 The case of Favela Orgânica provides us with a typical example of how resilience discourse perceives the adaptability and ingenuity of the people of the periphery. Tchelly is presented as the paradigmatic self-made entrepreneur who innovates, maneuvers, and capitalizes on the material difficulties of life in the favelas (Shannon Sims, "Regina Tchelly: Bringing Good Food to Rio's Hilltop Favelas," *Ozzy*, October 2, 2014; Peter Basildon, "Regina Tchelly: A Favela Food Fight," *Fine Dining Lovers*, March 30, 2015, https://www.finedininglovers.com/stories/regina-tchelly-food-in-favelas; Sandro Carneiro, "Regina Tchelly: The Affective Gastronomy of the Slum," *Believe Earth*, accessed March 13, 2020, https://believe.earth/en/regina-tchelly-the-affective-gastronomy-of-the-slum. It is not just the relation of the notion of innovation to the making of the entrepreneurial self, as this is constitutionally promoted in the neoliberal logic of entrepreneurial individualism, that finds its legitimacy in her case (Dardot and Laval, *New Way*, 117–19). What also gains legitimacy is the connection between sustainability and entrepreneurship, through which austerity is perceived as wisdom (Gauri Shankar Gupta, "The Paradox of Sustainable Development: A Critical Overview of the Term and the Institutionalization Process," *Periodica Polytechnica Social and Management Sciences* 25, no. 1 [2017], 6; and (environmental) destruction as a field of opportunity (Evans and Reid, *Resilient Life*, 78–82). The enthusiastic media discourse surrounding Tchelly is the epitome of the modern resilience agenda; it reveals a fully adaptable subject who views the constraints of their environment as opportunities. As Evans and Reid put it, "We teach how to fish in spite of the polluted waters" (*Resilient Life*, 33).

322 Rekow, "Fighting Insecurity," 3.

323 Rekow, "Fighting Insecurity," 3; Lea Rekow, "On Unstable Ground: Issues Involved in Greening Space in the Rocinha Favela of Rio de Janeiro," *Journal of Human Security* 12, no. 1 (2016): 52–73, https://doi.org/10.12924/johs2016.12010052.

324 Hearn, "Beanstalks," 99; Julio Cesar, "Hortas Cariocas," *Towards the Human City*, accessed March 13, 2020, https://towardsthehumancity.org/initiatives/hortas-cariocas-rio-de-janeiro; Rekow "Fighting Insecurity," 5.

325 Elizabeth Royte, "Urban Farming Is Booming, but What Does It Really Yield?" *Ensia*, April 27, 2015, https://ensia.com/features/urban-agriculture-is-booming-but-what-does-it-really-yield; Ibrahim Game and Richaela Primus, "Urban Agriculture," 2015, https://sustainabledevelopment.un.org/content/documents/5764Urban%20Agriculture.pdf; Dagmar Haase et al., "Greening Cities—To Be Socially Inclusive?: About the Alleged Paradox of Society and Ecology in Cities," *Habitat International*, no. 64, (2017): 41–48.

326 Haase et al., "Greening Cities," 42.

327 Haase et al., "Greening Cities"; Nathan McClintock, "Cultivating (a) Sustainability Capital: Urban Agriculture, Eco-Gentrification, and the Uneven Valorization of Social Reproduction," *Annals of the American Association of Geographers* 108 no. 2 (2017): 579–90; Nathan McClintock, Jason Sauer, and Marissa Matsler, "Green Gentrification and Urban Agriculture," January 1, 2018, in Future Cities podcast 5, MP3 audio, 46:56, https://sustainability.asu.edu/urbanresilience/news/archive/

future-cities-podcast-episode-5-green-gentrification-urban-agriculture; Isabelle Anguelovski, "From Toxic Sites to Parks as (Green) LULUs? New Challenges of Inequity, Privilege, Gentrification, and Exclusion for Urban Environmental Justice," *Journal of Planning Literature* 31, no. 1 (2015): 23–36.

328 Haase et al., "Greening Cities."
329 Kenneth A. Gould and Tammy L. Lewis, *Green Gentrification: Urban Sustainability and the Struggle for Environmental Justice* (New York: Routledge, 2017), 2; McClintock, "Cultivating," 1; McClintock, Sauer, and Matsler, "Green Gentrification."
330 Perlman, *Favela*, 28–29; Rekow, "Unstable Ground," 64.
331 Rekow "Unstable Ground," 56, 62, 64.
332 Rekow, "Fighting Insecurity, 1.
333 Personal communication, December 11, 2018. See also Rekow, "Fighting Insecurity," 4.
334 Quoted in Hearn, "Beanstalks." 99.
335 Érika de Mattos O'Reilly, "Agricultura Urbana: Um Estudo de Caso do Projeto Hortas Cariocas em Manguinhos, Rio de Janeiro," (graduation project, Federal University of Rio de Janeiro, February 2014), 49, http://monografias.poli.ufrj.br/monografias/monopoli10009377.pdf.
336 Rekow, "Unstable Ground."
337 Personal communication with garden manager, Manguinhos, December 17, 2018.
338 Jonathan Watts, "The Rio Favela Transformed into Prime Real Estate," *The Guardian*, January 23, 2013, https://www.theguardian.com/world/2013/jan/23/rio-favela-real-estate; World Bank, *Bringing the State Back*, 16, 96, 106–107; I. Pereira et al., "Entrepreneurship in the Favela," 80–81. This is also confirmed by Fenizola (from personal communication held on December 20, 2018). Also, as written by I. Pereira et al. ("Entrepreneurship in the Favela," 81), SEBRAE's initiative to create a special section in favelas in which pacification operations were successful "has led to the increase of local businesses and triggered processes of gentrification."
339 Kaika, "Don't Call Me Resilient," 3.
340 Rekow, "Fighting Insecurity," 1.
341 Julio César Barros quoted in O'Reilly, "Agricultura Urbana," 49.
342 Rekow, "Fighting Insecurity," 2.
343 See Keith G. Tidball and Marianne E. Krasny, eds., *Greening in the Red Zone: Disaster, Resilience and Community Greening* (London: Springer, 2014); Keith G. Tidball and Marianne E. Krasny, "From Risk to Resilience: What Role for Community Greening and Civic Ecology in Cities?" in *Social Learning Towards a Sustainable World: Principles, Perspectives, and Praxis*, ed. Arjen E.J. Wals (Wageningen: Wageningen Academic Publishers, 2007), 149–64.
344 Rekow, "On Unstable Ground," 58.
345 John Parnell, "Sustainability in the Favelas: Swapping Guns for Gardens," *Climate Home News*, June 13, 2012, http://www.climatechangenews.com/2012/06/13/sustainability-in-the-favelas-swapping-guns-for-gardens. The use of urban greening as a method of achieving social peace is not a new practice. Germany offers us a striking historical example when, after the revolution of 1848 and at a time when the submission of the working class was a major issue for the state, the latter established the institution of "small gardens" (*Kleingärtner*) within the urban environment. This institution, primarily concerned as it was with the sphere of social reproduction, was further linked to the concepts of family, work ethics, homeland, and ownership as opposed to the habits of the workers who

frequented bars or fraternized with sex workers. The aim was to discipline the working class in order to ultimately "eliminate tensions and divisions between different classes." This reference to the German "small gardens" is not an attempt to draw direct parallels to the policy pursued in the favelas. The two processes, and the historical subjects in the two examples, have very different characteristics. However, both are underpinned by the logic of urban greening as a method of social engineering and conflict resolution. See also the article "Randale! Bambule! Hamburger Schule!" *Dérive*, no. 11 (April–June 2003): 25–27.

346 Rekow "Fighting Insecurity"; Rekow, "Unstable Ground."

347 See O'Reilly, "Agricultura Urbana," 38.

348 Rekow, "Fighting Insecurity," 1.

349 This was also confirmed during a communication with a person involved in community work in Morro da Formiga that took place following the panel entitled "Desafios agroecológicos nas periferias urbanas: Práticas e perspectivas" (December 12, 2018), during the Semana da Soberania Alimentar na Maré. Referring specifically to the garden created by Hortas Cariocas in that community, she argued that there was no meaningful relationship with the residents and that the organization was overprotective of the garden. She also said that this garden is considered a showcase for the program, which is why resources are still made available for its upkeep compared to other cases that are not considered successful, and that this is a business model. Finally, she suggested that an attempt be made to deconstruct the project so that the garden could be made available for the collective use of the local residents and not be considered the property of Hortas Cariocas or the individuals working in the garden.

350 Hearn, "Beanstalks," 102.

351 Hearn, "Beanstalks," 104.

352 Personal communication, Manguinhos, December 17, 2018.

353 Rekow, "Fighting Insecurity."

354 Nally, "Green Revolution."

355 Nally and Taylor, "Politics of Self-Help," 52.

356 Cullather, *Hungry World*, 80.

357 Nally and Taylor, "Politics of Self-Help," 52.

358 Dardot and Laval, *New Way*, 264.

359 Nally and Taylor "Politics of Self-Help," 52.

360 Nally, "Green Revolution."

361 See summary in Rutherford, "Environmentality."

BIBLIOGRAPHY

"Afghan Money Pit and The Pacification of Rio." Vice, September 12, 2016. Video, 28:48, https://video.vice.com/en_us/video/afghan-money-pit-and-the-pacification-of-rio/578426c19e5b33a85b4cd8a2.

Agamben, Giorgio. *Homo Sacer: Sovereign Power and Bare Life*. Translated by Daniel Heller-Roazen. Stanford: Stanford University Press, 1998.

———. *State of Exception*. Translated by Kevin Attell. Chicago: University of Chicago Press, 2005.

Albertus, Michael, Thomas Brambor, and Ricardo Ceneviva. "Land Inequality and Rural Unrest: Theory and Evidence from Brazil." *Journal of Conflict Resolution* 62, no. 3 (2018): 557–96.

Almeida, Thamyris F.T. "Araguaia: Maoist Uprising and Military Counterinsurgency in the Brazilian Amazon, 1967–1975." Postgraduate thesis, University of Massachusetts Amherst, 2015. https://scholarworks.umass.edu/cgi/viewcontent.cgi?article=1241&context=masters_theses_2.

Alves, Lise. "Rio to Remove Half of Police Pacifying Units from Favelas." *Rio Times*, April 27, 2018. https://riotimesonline.com/brazil-news/rio-politics/rio-to-remove-half-of-police-pacifying-units-from-favela-communities.

Alves, Maria Helena Moreira, and Philip Evanson. *Living in the Crossfire: Favela Residents, Drug Dealers, and Police Violence in Rio de Janeiro*. Philadelphia: Temple University Press, 2011.

Anguelovski, Isabelle. "From Toxic Sites to Parks as (Green) LULUs? New Challenges of Inequity, Privilege, Gentrification, and Exclusion for Urban Environmental Justice." *Journal of Planning Literature* 31, no. 1 (2015): 23–36.

Ankober. 2010. "Is Huntington the Source of Our Mess?" De Birhan Media, August 11, 2010.

Arendt, Hannah. *The Human Condition*. Chicago: University of Chicago Press, 1958.

———. *On Revolution*. London: Penguin Books, 1990.

Banerjee, Subhabrata Bobby. "Who Sustains Whose Development? Sustainable Development and the Reinvention of Nature." *Organization Studies* 24, no. 1 (2003): 143–80.

Bankoff, Greg. "A Curtain of Silence: Asia's Fauna in the Cold War." In *Environmental Histories of the Cold War*, edited by J.R. McNeill, and Corinna R. Unger, 203–26. New York: Cambridge University Press, 2010.

Barros, Geraldo. "Brazil: The Challenges in Becoming an Agricultural Superpower." In *Brazil as an Economic Superpower? Understanding Brazil's Changing Role in the Global Economy*, edited by Lael Brainard, and Leonardo Martinez-Diaz, 81–109. Washington, DC: Brookings Institution Press, 2009.

Basildon, Peter. 2015. "Regina Tchelly: A Favela Food Fight." *Fine Dining Lovers*, March 30, 2015. https://www.finedininglovers.com/stories/regina-tchelly-food-in-favelas.

Belcher, Oliver. "The Afterlives of Counterinsurgency: Postcolonialism, Military Social Science, and Afghanistan 2006–2012." PhD diss., University of British Columbia, 2013. https://open.library.ubc.ca/media/download/pdf/24/1.0165663/1.

Benjamin, Walter. "Critique of Violence." In *Walter Benjamin: Selected Writings*, vol. 1: *1913–1926*, translated by Marcus Bullock and Michael Jennings, 277–300. London: Belknap Press, 2002.

Biddle, Wayne. 1984. "Nerve Gases and Pesticides: Links Are Close." *New York Times*, March 30, 1984. https://www.nytimes.com/1984/03/30/world/nerve-gases-and-pesticides-links-are-close.html.

Biller, David. "Brazil's Army Will Need More than Guns to Fix Rio de Janeiro Crime." *Bloomberg*, February 20, 2018. https://www.bloomberg.com/news/articles/2018-02-20/brazil-army-will-need-more-than-guns-to-fix-rio-de-janeiro-crime.

Birtle, Andrew J. *US Army Counterinsurgency and Contingency Operations Doctrine 1860–1941.* Washington, DC: US Army Center for Military History, 2009.

———. *US Army Counterinsurgency and Contingency Operations Doctrine 1942–1976.* Washington, DC: US Army Center for Military History, 2006.

Bittencourt, Naiara, and Alessandra Jacobovski. "Agrotóxicos como arma química: a permanente guerra agrária no Brasil." MST, December 9, 2017 https://terradedireitos.org.br/acervo/artigos/artigo-agrotoxicos-como-arma-quimica-a-permanente-guerra-agraria-no-brasil/22695.

Brasil de Fato. 2019. "Bolsonaro Administration Approves 197 Pesticides in Five Months." May 22, 2019. https://www.brasildefato.com.br/2019/05/22/bolsonaro-administration-approves-169-pesticides-in-five-months.

BrasilWire. "David Rockefeller and a Dark Legacy in Brasil—A Critical Obituary." March 20, 2017. http://www.brasilwire.com/david-rockefeller-legacy-in-brasil.

Brito, Fausto. "The Displacement of the Brazilian Population to the Metropolitan Areas." *Estudos Avançados* 20, no. 57 (2006): 221–36.

Cabral, Sergio. "Decreto nº 42.787 de 06/01/2011." Normas Brasil, January 7, 2011. https://www.normasbrasil.com.br/norma/decreto-42787-2011-rj_158962.html.

Catalytic Communities. "Growth Acceleration Program (PAC)." Accessed March 12, 2020, https://catcomm.org/pac.

Carneiro, Júlia Dias. "Violence in Rio: Public Security Expert Warns of a 'Retreat from Rights,' Return to Old Policies of Confrontation." *Rio on Watch*, March 29, 2019. http://www.rioonwatch.org/?p=52373.

Carneiro, Sandro. "Regina Tchelly: The Affective Gastronomy of the Slum." *Believe Earth*, accessed March 13, 2020. https://believe.earth/en/regina-tchelly-the-affective-gastronomy-of-the-slum.

Cay, Cristóbal. "Latin America's Exclusionary Rural Development in a Neo-Liberal World." Paper presented at the meeting of the Latin American Studies Association (LASA), Guadalajara, Mexico, April 17–19, 1997. http://biblioteca.clacso.edu.ar/ar/libros/lasa97/kay.pdf.

Cesar, Julio. "Hortas Cariocas." *Towards the Human City*, accessed March 13, 2020. https://towardsthehumancity.org/initiatives/hortas-cariocas-rio-de-janeiro.

"Children of Agent Orange." Al Jazeera, September 28, 2011. Video, 23:58, https://www.aljazeera.com/programmes/peopleandpower/2011/09/201192811920665336.html.

Christou, Maria. "I Eat therefore I Am: An Essay on Human and Animal Mutuality." *Angelaki* 18, no. 4 (2013): 63–79.

Cipolla, Carla, Patricia Mello, and Ezio Manzini. "Collaborative Services in Informal Settlements: Social Innovation in a Pacified Favela in Rio de Janeiro." In *New Frontiers in Social Innovation Research*, edited by Alex Nicholls, Julie Simon, and Madeleine Gabriel, 128–142. New York: Palgrave Macmillan, 2015.

Cipolla, Carla, Rita Afonso, Bonno Pel, Roberto Bartholo, Édison Renato Silva, and Domício Proença Júnior. "Coproduced Game-Changing in Transformative Social Innovation: Reconnecting the 'Broken City' of Rio de Janeiro." *Ecology and Society* 22, no. 3 (2017): 3–11.

Clausewitz, Carl von. *On War.* Translated by Michael Howard and Peter Paret. Oxford: Oxford University Press, 2007.

Collier, Paul. "The Politics of Hunger: How Illusion and Greed Fan the Food Crisis." *Foreign Affairs* 87, no. 6 (2008): 67–79.

Craig, Alan S. "The Internal Enemy: Insurgency in Brazil." GlobalSecurity.org, March 8, 1985. https://www.globalsecurity.org/military/library/report/1986/CAS.htm.

Crimmins, John Hugh. "Document 97: Telegram 1850 from the Embassy in Brazil to the Department of State." In *Foreign Relations of the United States, 1969–1976, Volume E–11, Part 2, Documents on South America, 1973–1976*, edited by Adam M. Howard, Sara Berndt, Halbert Jones, and James Siekmeier. Washington, DC: USGPO, 2015. https://history.state.gov/historicaldocuments/frus1969-76ve11p2/d97.

Cullather, Nick. "Development Doctrine and Modernization Theory: The Decline of Modernization Theory." Accessed March 13, 2020. https://www. americanforeignrelations.com/A-D/Development-Doctrine-and-Modernization-Theory-The-decline-of-modernization-theory.html.

———. *The Hungry World: America's Cold War Battle Against Poverty in Asia*. Cambridge, MA: Harvard University Press, 2010.

———. "'The Target Is the People': Representations of the Village in Modernization and U.S. National Security Doctrine." *Cultural Politics* 2, no. 1 (2006): 29–48.

Dardot, Pierre, and Christian Laval. *The New Way of the World: On Neoliberal Society*. New York: Verso, 2013.

Davis, Mike. *Planet of Slums*. New York: Verso, 2006.

Dobbins, James, Seth G. Jones, Keith Crane, and Beth Cole Degrasse. *The Beginner's Guide to Nation-Building*. Santa Monica: RAND Corporation, 2007. https://www. rand.org/pubs/monographs/MG557.html.

Donley, Patrick. "Economic Development in Counterinsurgency: Building a Stable Second Pillar." *Joint Force Quarterly*, no. 81, (2016): 102–11.

Duffield, Mark. *Development, Security and Unending War: Governing the World of Peoples*. Malden: Polity Press, 2007.

———. "Global Civil War: The Non-Insured, International Containment and Post-Interventionary Society." *Journal of Refugee Studies* 21, no. 2 (2008): 145–65.

———. "The Liberal Way of Development and the Development-Security Impasse: Exploring the Global Life-Chance Divide." *Security Dialogue* 41, no. 1 (2010): 53–76.

Durand, Etienne de, and Octavian Manea. "Reflections on the French School of Counter-Rebellion: An Interview with Etienne de Durand by Octavian Manea." *Small Wars Journal*, March 3, 2011. https://smallwarsjournal.com/blog/journal/docs-temp/686-manea.pdf.

Evans, Brad, and Julian Reid. *Resilient Life: The Art of Living Dangerously*. Malden: Polity Press, 2014.

Everts, Sarah. "The Nazi Origins of Deadly Nerve Gases." *Chemical & Engineering News* 94, no. 41 (2016): 26–28. https://cen.acs.org/articles/94/i41/Nazi-origins-deadly-nerve-gases.html.

Felbab-Brown, Vanda. *Shooting Up: Counterinsurgency and the War on Drugs*. Washington DC: Brookings Institution Press, 2010.

Fearnside, Philip. "Why Brazil's New President Poses an Unprecedented Threat to the Amazon." *Yale Environment 360*, November 8, 2018. https://e360.yale.edu/features/why-brazils-new-president-poses-an-unprecedented-threat-to-the-amazon.

Ferreira, Isadora. "From Famine to Feast in Brazil." In "A New Model to Feed the World." Special issue, *Frontlines* (November/December, 2011): 4–7. https://2012-2017.usaid.gov/sites/default/files/frontlines/FL_NOVDEC11%20%281%29.pdf.

Food Security Information Network. "Global Report on Food Crises 2018." FSIN, 2018. https://www.fao.org/fileadmin/user_upload/fsin/docs/global_report/2018/GRFC_2018_Full_report_EN.pdf.

Foucault, Michel. *Security, Territory, Population: Lectures at the Collège de France, 1977–78*. Translated by Graham Burchell. New York: Palgrave Macmillan, 2007.

———. *Society Must Be Defended: Lectures at the Collège de France 1975–76*. Translated by David Macey. New York: Picador, 2003.

Freedman, Paul. "Spices: How the Search for Flavors Influenced Our World." *YaleGlobal Online*, March 11, 2003.

Freeman, Michael, and Hy Rothstein. Introduction to *Gangs and Guerrillas: Ideas from Counterinsurgency and Counterterrorism*, edited by Michael Freeman and Hy Rothstein, 1. Monterey: Naval Postgraduate School, 2011. https://www.hsdl.org/?view&did=6229.

Galula, David. *Counterinsurgency Warfare: Theory and Practice*. London: Praeger Security International, 2006.

———. *Pacification in Algeria, 1956–1958*. Santa Monica: RAND Corporation, 2006. https://www.rand.org/content/dam/rand/pubs/monographs/2006/RAND_MG478-1.pdf.

Game, Ibrahim, and Richaela Primus. "Urban Agriculture." *GSDR 2015 Brief*. https://sustainabledevelopment.un.org/content/documents/5764Urban%20Agriculture.pdf.

Glenn, Russell W., Christopher Paul, Todd C. Helmus, and Paul Steinberg. "'People Make the City,' Executive Summary: Joint Urban Operations Observations and Insights from Afghanistan and Iraq." Santa Monica: RAND Corporation, 2007. https://www.rand.org/pubs/monographs/MG428z2.html.

GlobalSecurity.org. "Favela War." Accessed March 13, 2020. https://www.globalsecurity.org/military/world/war/favela-war.htm.

Global Witness. "At What Cost? Irresponsible Business and the Murder of Land and Environmental Defenders in 2017." July 24, 2018. https://www.globalwitness.org/en/campaigns/environmental-activists/at-what-cost.

Gödecke, Theda, Alexander J. Stein, and Matin Qaim. "The Global Burden of Chronic and Hidden Hunger: Trends and Determinants." *Global Food Security* 17 (2018): 21–29.

Gomes, Juliana Cesario Alvim, and Andrés del Río. "Military Justice, Intervention and Human Rights in Brazil." *openDemocracy*, July 5, 2018. https://www.opendemocracy.net/en/democraciaabierta/military-justice-intervention-and-human/.

Gompert, David C., John Gordon IV, Adam Grissom, David R. Frelinger, Seth G. Jones, Martin C. Libicki, Edward O'Connell, Brooke K. Stearns, and Robert E. Hunter. *War by Other Means: Building Complete and Balanced Capabilities for Counterinsurgency*, Santa Monica: RAND Corporation, 2008. https://www.rand.org/pubs/monographs/MG595z2.html.

González, Roberto J. "Embedded: Information Warfare and the 'Human Terrain.'" In *The Counter-Counterinsurgency Manual or, Notes on Demilitarizing American Society*, edited by the Network of Concerned Anthropologists, 97–113. Chicago: Prickly Paradigm Press, 2009.

González, Roberto, Hugh Gusterson, and David Price. "Introduction: War, Culture, and Counterinsurgency." In Network of Concerned Anthropologists. The Counter-counterinsurgency Manual or, Notes on Demilitarizing American Society, 1–20. Chicago: Prickly Paradigm Press, 2009.

Gould, Kenneth A., and Tammy L. Lewis. *Green Gentrification: Urban Sustainability and the Struggle for Environmental Justice*. New York: Routledge, 2017.

Gros, Frédéric. *The Security Principle: From Serenity to Regulation*. New York: Verso, 2019.

Gupta, Gauri Shankar. "The Paradox of Sustainable Development: A Critical Overview of the Term and the Institutionalization Process." *Periodica Polytechnica Social and Management Sciences* 25, no. 1 (2017): 1–7.

Haase, Dagmar, Sigrun Kabisch, Annegret Haase, Erik Andersson, Ellen Banzhaf, Francesc Baro, Miriam Brenck, Leonie K. Fischer, Niki Frantzeskaki, Nadja Kabisch, Kerstin Krellenberg, Peleg Kremer, Jakub Kronenberg, Neele Larondelle, Juliane Mathey, Stephan Pauleit, Irene Ring, Dieter Rink, Nina Schwarz, and Manuel Wolff. "Greening Cities—To Be Socially Inclusive? About the Alleged Paradox of Society and Ecology in Cities." *Habitat International* 64 (June 2017): 41–48.

Hazen, Jennifer M. "Understanding Gangs as Armed Groups." *International Review of the Red Cross* 92, no. 878 (2010): 369–86.

Healy, Meg. "Brazil's Political Crisis Threatens Essential Upgrading Works in Rocinha." *Rio on Watch*, June 8, 2016. https://www.rioonwatch.org/?p=28887.

Hearn, Adrian H. "Beanstalks and Trust in Chinese and Brazilian Food Systems." *Journal of Latin American Geography* 17, no. 2 (2018): 84–112.

Huber, Joseph. "Towards Industrial Ecology: Sustainable Development as a Concept of Ecological Modernization." *Journal of Environmental Policy & Planning* 2, no. 4 (2000): 269–85.

Human Rights Watch. "'You Don't Want to Breathe Poison Anymore': The Failing Response to Pesticide Drift in Brazil's Rural Communities." *Human Rights Watch*, 2018. https://www.hrw.org/sites/default/files/report_pdf/brazil0718_web.pdf.

Huntington, Samuel. "The Bases of Accommodation." *Foreign Affairs* 46, no. 4 (1968): 642–56.

———. "How Countries Democratize." *Political Science Quarterly* 106, no. 4 (1991–92): 579–616.

Jacobs, Andrew, and Matt Richtel. 2017. "How Big Business Got Brazil Hooked on Junk Food." *New York Times*, September 16, 2017. https://www.nytimes.com.

Janvry, Alain de, and Eisabeth Sadoulet. "A Study in Resistance to Institutional Change: The Lost Game of Latin American Land Reform." *World Development* 17, no. 9 (1989): 1397–1407.

Jones, Gareth A., and Dennis Rodgers. "The World Bank's World Development Report 2011 on Conflict, Security and Development: A Critique through Five Vignettes." *Journal of International Development* 23 (7) (2011): 980–95. http://eprints.lse.ac.uk/38462.

Kaika, Maria. "'Don't Call Me Resilient Again!': The New Urban Agenda as Immunology … or … What Happens when Communities Refuse to Be Vaccinated with 'Smart Cities' and Indicators." *Environment and Urbanization* 29, no. 1 (2017): 89–102.

Kaiser, Anna Jean. "Rio Governor Confirms Plans for Shoot-to-Kill Policing Policy." *The Guardian*, January 4, 2019. https://www.theguardian.com/world/2019/jan/04/wilson-witzel-rio-police-security-shoot-to-kill.

Khoury, Colin K., Anne D. Bjorkman, Hannes Dempewolf, Julian Ramirez-Villegas, Luigi Guarino, Andy Jarvis, Loren H. Rieseberg, and Paul C. Struik. "Increasing Homogeneity in Global Food Supplies and the Implications for Food Security." *PNAS* 111, no. 11 (2014): 4001–4006. https://doi.org/10.1073/pnas.1313490111.

Kilcullen, David J. *Counterinsurgency*. New York: Oxford University Press, 2010.

———. *Out of the Mountains: The Coming Age of the Urban Guerrilla*. New York: Oxford University Press, 2013.

Kitson, Frank. *Low Intensity Operations: Subversion, Insurgency, Peace-Keeping*. Dehra Dun: Natraj Publishers, 1992.

Krueger, Rob, and David Gibbs. "Introduction: Problematizing the Politics of Sustainability." In *The Sustainable Development Paradox: Urban Political Economy in the United States and Europe*, edited by Rob Krueger, and David Gibbs, 1–11. New York: Guilford Press, 2007.

Lamb, Robert. "Ungoverned Areas and Threats from Safe Havens: Final Report of the Ungoverned Areas Project." Washington, DC: Office of the Under Secretary of Defense for Policy, 2008. https://cissm.umd.edu/sites/default/files/2019-07/ugash_report_final.pdf.

Langan, Mark. *Neo-Colonialism and the Poverty of 'Development' in Africa*. Cham, CH: Palgrave Macmillan, 2018.

Larkins, Erika Robb. "A Different Kind of Security: The Need for Appropriate Healthcare Policies in Rio de Janeiro's Favelas." LSE Research Online, April 8, 2015. http://eprints.lse.ac.uk/63051.

———. *The Spectacular Favela: Violence in Modern Brazil*. Oakland: University of California Press, 2015.

La Rocque, Eduarda de, and Petras Shelton-Zumpano. 2014. "The Sustainable Development Strategy of the Municipal Government of Rio de Janeiro." Paper presented at the "Citizen Security in Brazil: Progress and Challenges" seminar at the Woodrow Wilson International Center for Scholars, Washington, DC, March 28, 2014.

Larsen, Marcus Ferreira. "Pacifying Maré: The Militarisation of Urban Policing in Rio de Janeiro." MA thesis, University of Copenhagen, 2016. https://www.academia.edu/29889400/Pacifying_Mar%C3%A9_The_Militarisation_of_Urban_Policing_in_Rio_de_Janeiro.

Latouche, Serge. "Sustainable Development as a Paradox." Paper presented at the Baltic Sea Symposium of the Religion, Science and the Environmental Movement, 2003. http://www.rsesymposia.org/themedia/File/1151679499-Plenary2_Latouche.pdf.

Lazzarato, Maurizio. *The Making of the Indebted Man: An Essay on the Neoliberal Condition*. Los Angeles: Semiotexte, 2012.

Leeds, Elizabeth. "What Can Be Learned from Brazil's 'Pacification' Police Model?" *WOLA*, March 11, 2016. https://www.wola.org/analysis/what-can-be-learned-from-brazils-pacification-police-model.

Long, Austin. *On "Other War": Lessons from Five Decades of RAND Counterinsurgency Research*. Santa Monica: RAND Corporation, 2006. https://www.rand.org/content/dam/rand/pubs/monographs/2006/RAND_MG482.pdf.

Malleret, Constance. "'The End of 'Pacification': What Next for Rio de Janeiro's Favelas?" PhD diss., University of Essex, 2018. https://repository.essex.ac.uk/26930/1/1807428_Dissertation.pdf.

Martine, George, and Gordon McGranahan. 2010. "Brazil's Early Urban Transition: What Can It Teach Urbanizing Countries?" London: IIED, 2010. https://pubs.iied.org/pdfs/10585IIED.pdf.

McClintock, Nathan. "Cultivating (a) Sustainability Capital: Urban Agriculture, Eco-gentrification, and the Uneven Valorization of Social Reproduction." *Annals of the American Association of Geographers* 108, no. 2 (2017): 579–90.

McClintock, Nathan, Jason Sauer, and Marissa Matsler. "Green Gentrification and Urban Agriculture," January 1, 2018, *Future Cities*, podcast, MP3 audio, 46:56. https://sustainability.asu.edu/urbanresilience/news/archive/future-cities-podcast-episode-5-green-gentrification-urban-agriculture.

Medby, Jamison Jo, and Russell W. Glenn. "Streetsmart: Intelligence Preparation of the Battlefield for Urban Operations." Santa Monica: RAND Corporation, 2002. https://www.rand.org/pubs/monograph_reports/MR1287.html.

Miklos, Manoela, and Tomaz Paoliello. "Militarization of Public Security in Rio, and Around the World." *openDemocracy*, October 4, 2017. https://www.opendemocracy.net/en/democraciaabierta/militarization-of-public-security-in-rio-and-around.

Miller, Sergio. "The Simple Truth? Securing the Population as a Recent Invention." *Small Wars Journal*, May 30, 2012. https://smallwarsjournal.com/jrnl/art/the-simple-truth-securing-the-population-as-a-recent-invention.

Mintz, Sidney W. *Sweetness and Power: The Place of Sugar in Modern History*. New York: Penguin Books, 1986.

Motta, Rodrigo Patto Sá. "Modernizing Repression: USAID and the Brazilian Police." *Revista Brasileira de História* 30, no. 59 (2010): 235–62.

Muggah, Robert. "A Manifesto for the Fragile City." *Journal for International Affairs* 68, no. 2 (2015): 19–36.

———. "The State of Security and Justice in Brazil: Reviewing the Evidence." Working Paper Series No.4, Brazil Initiative, Elliott School of International Affairs, 2016. https://pdfs.semanticscholar.org/8d6e/2d4e331bd0db37713411bb8f086e00116b14.pdf.

Muggah, Robert, and Albert Souza Mulli. "Rio Tries Counterinsurgency." *Current History* 111, no. 742 (2012): 62–66.

Mueller, Bernardo, and Charles Mueller. "The Political Economy of the Brazilian Model of Agricultural Development: Institutions versus Sectoral Policy." *Quarterly Review of Economics and Finance*, no. 62 (2016): 12–20.

Nagl, John. Foreword to *Counterinsurgency Warfare: Theory and Practice*, by David Galula, vii–x. London: Praeger Security International, 2006.

Nally, David. "The Green Revolution as Philanthropy." *HistPhil*, April 18, 2016. https://histphil.org/2016/04/18/the-green-revolution-as-philanthropy.

Nally, David, and Stephen Taylor. "The Politics of Self-Help: The Rockefeller Foundation, Philanthropy and the 'Long' Green Revolution." *Political Geography*, no. 59 (2015): 51–63.

Neocleous, Mark. "A Brighter and Nicer New Life: Security as Pacification." *Social & Legal Studies* 20, no. 2 (2011): 191–208.

———. *Critique of Security*. Edinburgh: Edinburgh University Press, 2008.

———. "Resisting Resilience." *Radical Philosophy*, no. 178, (2013): 1–7.

———. *War Power, Police Power*. Edinburgh: Edinburgh University Press, 2014.

Neocleous, Mark, George Rigakos, and Tyler Wall. "On Pacification: Introduction to the Special Issue." *Socialist Studies* 9, no. 2 (2013): 1–6.

Norton, Richard. "Feral Cities." *Naval War College Review* LVI, no. 4 (2003): 97–106.

NutriCities. "Community Brief #1, May 2018: Contextualising Food (In)Security—Nutritional Urgencies of the Urban Periphery as Studied in Rio de Janeiro." https://www.thebritishacademy.ac.uk/sites/default/files/Nutricities-Community-Brief-1-EN.pdf.

Oliveira, Gustavo de L.T. "The Geopolitics of Brazilian Soybeans." *Journal of Peasant Studies* 43, no. 1 (2016).

Oliver, Mark. "The Banana Wars: How the US Plundered Central America on Behalf of Corporations." Edited by John Kuroski. AllThatsInteresting.com, updated February 12, 2018. https://allthatsinteresting.com/banana-wars.

O'Reilly, Érika de Mattos. "Agricultura Urbana: Um Estudo de Caso do Projeto Hortas Cariocas em Manguinhos, Rio de Janeiro." Graduation project, Federal University of Rio de Janeiro, February 2014. http://monografias.poli.ufrj.br/monografias/monopoli10009377.pdf.

Owens, Patricia. *Economy of Force: Counterinsurgency and the Historical Rise of the Social.* Cambridge: Cambridge University Press, 2015.

———. "From Bismarck to Petraeus: The Question of the Social and the Social Question in Counterinsurgency." *European Journal of International Relations* 19, no. 1 (2011): 139–61.

Parnell, John. "Sustainability in the Favelas: Swapping Guns for Gardens." *Climate Home News,* June 13, 2012. http://www.climatechangenews.com/2012/06/13/sustainability-in-the-favelas-swapping-guns-for-gardens.

Patel, Raj. "The Long Green Revolution." *Journal of Peasant Studies* 40, no. 1 (2013): 1–63.

Paulino, Eliane Tomiasi. "The Agricultural, Environmental and Socio-Political Repercussions of Brazil's Land Governance System." *Land Use Policy* 36 (2014): 134–44.

Pellow, David Naguib. *Resisting Global Toxics: Transnational Movements for Environmental Justice.* Cambridge, MA: MIT Press, 2007.

Pereira, Anthony W. "Samuel Huntington and 'Decompression' in Brazil." *Journal of Latin American Studies* 53, no. 2 (2021): 349–71. doi:10.1017/S0022216X21000250.

Pereira, Isabella Nunes, Roberto Bartholo, Édison Renato Silva, and Domício Proença. "Entrepreneurship in the Favela of Rocinha, Rio de Janeiro: A Critical Approach." *Latin American Research Review* 52, no. 1 (2017): 79–93.

Perkins, John. *Geopolitics and Green Revolution: Wheat, Genes, and the Cold War.* Oxford: Oxford University Press, 1997.

———. "The Rockefeller Foundation and the Green Revolution." *Agriculture and Human Values* 7, no. 3–4 (1990): 6–18.

Perlman, Janice. *Favela: Four Decades of Living on the Edge in Rio de Janeiro.* New York: Oxford University Press, 2010.

Peters, Ralph. "The Human Terrain of Urban Operations." *Parameters* 30, no. 1 (2000): 4–12. https://ssi.armywarcollege.edu/pubs/Parameters/articles/00spring/peters.htm.

Petraeus, David H. "Reflections on the 'Counterinsurgency Decade': *Small Wars Journal* Interview with General David H. Petraeus, by Octavian Manea," *Small Wars Journal,* September 1, 2013. https://smallwarsjournal.com/jrnl/art/reflections-on-the-counterinsurgency-decade-small-wars-journal-interview-with-general-david.

Pfrimer, Matheus Hoffman, and Ricardo César Barbosa Jr. "Neo-Agro-Colonialism, Control over Life, and Imposed Spatio-Temporalities." *Contexto Internacional* 39, no. 1 (2017): 3–33.

Pilsch, Thomas D., "Operation Ranch Hand." Accessed March 13, 2020. https://www.cc.gatech.edu/~tpilsch/AirOps/ranch.html.

Power, Marcus. *Geopolitics and Development.* New York: Routledge, 2019.

Prada, Paulo. 2015. "Fateful Harvest: Why Brazil Has a Big Appetite for Risky Pesticides." Reuters, April 2, 2015. https://www.reuters.com/investigates/special-report/brazil-pesticides.

Ramos da Cruz, Claudio, and David H. Ucko. "Beyond the Unidades de Polícia Pacificadora: Countering Comando Vermelho's Criminal Insurgency." *Small Wars & Insurgencies* 29, no. 1 (2018): 38–67.

Randale! Bambule! Hamburger Schule! *Dérive,* no. 11 (2003), 25–27.

Rekow, Lea. "Fighting Insecurity: Experiments in Urban Agriculture in the Favelas of

Rio de Janeiro." *Field Actions Science Reports* 8 (2015). http://factsreports.revues.org/4009.

———. "On Unstable Ground: Issues Involved in Greening Space in the Rocinha Favela of Rio de Janeiro." *Journal of Human Security* 12, no. 1 (2016): 52–73. https://doi.org/10.12924/johs2016.12010052.

Rieff, David. "Where Hunger Goes: On the Green Revolution." *The Nation*, February 17, 2011. https://www.thenation.com/article/where-hunger-goes-green-revolution.

Rio+20. *The Future We Want: Outcome Document of the United Nations Conference on Sustainable Development*. United Nations, 2012. https://sustainabledevelopment.un.org/content/documents/733FutureWeWant.pdf.

Robinson, Corey. "Order and Progress? The Evolution of Brazilian Defense Strategy." Postgraduate thesis, Naval Postgraduate School, 2014.

Royte, Elizabeth. "Urban Farming Is Booming, but what Does It Really Yield?" *Ensia*, April 27, 2015. https://ensia.com/features/urban-agriculture-is-booming-but-what-does-it-really-yield.

Ruiz, Carmelo. "Wycliffe and the CIA: The Summer Institute of Linguistic Connection SIL and the CIA," accessed March 14, 2020. http://www.akha.org/content/missiondocuments/wycliffecia.html.

Russell, Ruby. 2016. "Going for Green: No Medals for the Rio Olympics' Environmental Legacy." *Deutsche Welle*, August 23, 2016. https://www.dw.com/en/going-for-green-no-medals-for-the-rio-olympics-environmental-legacy/a-19495318.

Rutherford, Stephanie. "Environmentality and Green Governmentality." In *The International Encyclopedia of Geography*, edited by Douglas Richardson, Noel Castree, Michael F. Goodchild, Audrey Kobayashi, Weidong Liu, and Richard A. Marston. Hoboken, NJ: John Wiley & Sons, 2017.

———. "Green Governmentality: Insights and Opportunities in the Study of Nature's Rule." *Progress in Human Geography* 31, no. 3 (2007): 291–307.

Saborio, Sebastian. "The Pacification of the Favelas: Mega Events, Global Competitiveness, and the Neutralization of Marginality." *Socialist Studies* 9, no. 2 (2013): 130–45.

Salem, Tomas. "Security and Policing in Rio de Janeiro: An Ethnography of the Pacifying Police Units." Postgraduate thesis, UiT Arctic University of Norway, 2016. https://www.researchgate.net/publication/315669322_Security_and_Policing_in_Rio_de_Janeiro_An_Ethnography_of_the_Pacifying_Police_Units.

Sassen, Saskia. "When the City Itself Becomes a Technology of War." *Theory, Culture & Society* 27, no. 6 (2010): 33–50.

Schouten, P. "Theory Talk #38: James Scott on Agriculture as Politics, the Danger of Standardization and Not Being Governed." *Theory Talks*, May 15, 2010. https://www.files.ethz.ch/isn/155099/Theory%20Talk38_Scott.pdf.

Scott, Felicity D. *Outlaw Territories: Environments of Insecurity / Architectures of Counterinsurgency*. New York: Zone Books, 2016.

Siman, Maíra, and Victória Santos. "Interrogating the Security-Development Nexus in Brazil's Domestic and Foreign Pacification Engagements." *Conflict, Security & Development* 18, no. 1 (2018): 61–83.

Sims, Shannon. "Regina Tchelly: Bringing Good Food to Rio's Hilltop Favelas." *Ozzy*, October 2, 2014.

Sörensen, Stilhoff Jens, and Fredrik Söderbaum. "Introduction: The End of the Development-Security Nexus?" *Development Dialogue*, no. 58 (2012): 7–19.

Souza, Sabrina de Cássia Mariano de, Niemeyer Almeida Filho, and Henrique Dantas Neder. "Food Security in Brazil: An Analysis of the Effects of the Bolsa Família Programme." *Review of Agrarian Studies* 5, no. 2 (2015): 1–32.

Spanne, Autumn. "Brazil World Cup Fails to Score Environmental Goals." *Scientific American*, June 19, 2014. https://www.scientificamerican.com/article/brazil-world-cup-fails-to-score-environmental-goals.

Strobl, Tyler. "Inexplicable Sky High Electric Bills Threaten Rio das Pedras, Escalate Fear of Eviction." *Rio on Watch*, January 25, 2018. https://www.rioonwatch.org/?p=41384.

Sunderland, Riley. *Resettlement and Food Control in Malaya*. Santa Monica: RAND Corporation, 1964. https://www.rand.org/pubs/research_memoranda/RM4173.html.

Sustainable Development Solutions Network. *An Action Agenda for Sustainable Development: Report for the UN Secretary General*. SDSN, June 6, 2013. https://unstats.un.org/unsd/broaderprogress/pdf/130613-SDSN-An-Action-Agenda-for-Sustainable-Development-FINAL.pdf.

Tarlock, A. Dan. "Ideas Without Institutions: The Paradox of Sustainable Development." *Indiana Journal of Global Legal Studies* 9, no. 1 (2001): 35–49.

Tidball, Keith G., and Marianne E. Krasny. "From Risk to Resilience: What Role for Community Greening and Civic Ecology in Cities?" In *Social Learning towards a Sustainable World: Principles, Perspectives, and Praxis*, edited by Arjen E.J. Wals, 149–164. Wageningen: Wageningen Academic Publishers, 2007.

Tidball, Keith G., and Marianne E. Krasny, eds. *Greening in the Red Zone: Disaster, Resilience and Community Greening*. London: Springer, 2014.

Trinquier, Roger. *Modern Warfare: A French View of Counterinsurgency*. Translated by Daniel Lee. London: Praeger Security International, 2006.

Tudobeleza. "End of the UPP Is Nigh." *Deep Rio*, December 18, 2017.

Tulloch, Lynley, and Neilson David. "The Neoliberalisation of Sustainability." *Citizenship, Social and Economics Education* 13, no. 1 (2014): 26–38.

United Nations, Department of Economic and Social Affairs, Population Division. "World Urbanization Prospects: The 2018 Revision, Key Facts." United Nations, 2018. https://population.un.org/wup/Publications/Files/WUP2018-KeyFacts.pdf.

UN-Habitat. "Urbanization and Development: Emerging Futures." Nairobi, KE: UN-Habitat, 2016. https://unhabitat.org/sites/default/files/download-manager-files/WCR-2016-WEB.pdf.

USAID. *USAID's Legacy in Agricultural Development: Fifty Years of Progress*. Washington, DC: USAID, 2016. https://www.usaid.gov/agriculture-and-food-security/document/usaids-legacy-agricultural-development-50-years-progress.

US Department of the Army. *Counterinsurgency*. FM 3-24/MCWP 3-33.5. Washington, DC: Department of the Army, 2006. https://www.thenewatlantis.com/wp-content/uploads/legacy-pdfs/20090202_COINFieldManual2006.pdf.

———. *Insurgencies and Countering Insurgencies*. FM 3-24/MCWP 3-33.5. Washington, DC: Department of the Army, 2014. https://fas.org/irp/doddir/army/fm3-24.pdf.

———. *Urban Operations*. FM 3-06. Washington, DC: Department of the Army, 2006. https://fas.org/irp/doddir/army/fm3-06.pdf.

Watts, Jonathan. "The Rio Favela Transformed into Prime Real Estate." *The Guardian*, January 23, 2013. https://www.theguardian.com/world/2013/jan/23/rio-favela-real-estate.

Welch, Clifford A. "Rockefeller and the Origins of Agribusiness in Brazil: A Research Report." Rockefeller Archive Center, 2014. https://www.issuelab.org/resources/27973/27973.pdf.

Werling, Esther. "Rio's Pacification: Paradigm Shift or Paradigm Maintenance?" Humanitarian Action in Situations Other than War (HASOW) Discussion

Paper 11, August 2014. https://igarape.org.br/wp-content/uploads/2016/04/Rio%E2%80%99s-Pacification-.pdf.

Williams, Kristian. "The Other Side of the COIN: Counterinsurgency and Community Policing." In *Life During Wartime: Resisting Counterinsurgency*. Edited by Kristian Williams, Will Munger, and Lara Messersmith-Glavin, 83–110. Edinburgh: AK Press, 2013.

World Bank. "Bringing the State Back into the Favelas of Rio de Janeiro: Understanding Changes in Community Life after the UPP Pacification Process." October, 2012. http://documents.worldbank.org/curated/en/255231468230108733/pdf/760110ES WoP12300RioodeoJaneiroo2013.pdf.

Young, James Armour. "Rio Has Broken Its Promise of an Environment-Friendly Olympics." VICE, August 1, 2016. https://news.vice.com/en_us/article/kz99wz/rio-has-broken-its-promise-of-an-environment-friendly-olympics.

Zambri, John. "Counterinsurgency and Community Policing: More Alike than Meets the Eye." *Small Wars Journal*, July 8, 2014. https://smallwarsjournal.com/jrnl/art/counterinsurgency-and-community-policing-more-alike-than-meets-the-eye.

———. "Peasant Roles in Insurgency and Counterinsurgency: A Brief Historical Analysis." *Small Wars Journal*, June 17, 2017. https://smallwarsjournal.com/jrnl/art/peasant-roles-in-insurgency-and-counterinsurgency-a-brief-historical-analysis.

Zierler, David. "Against Protocol: Ecocide, Détente, and the Question of Chemical Warfare in Vietnam, 1969–1975." In *Environmental Histories of the Cold War*, edited by J.R. McNeill and Corinna R. Unger, 227–56. New York: Cambridge University Press, 2010.

Index

"Passim" (literally "scattered") indicates intermittent discussion of a topic over a cluster of pages.

About the Contributors

Timo Bartholl engages in local grassroots work and has lived in the Maré favela in Rio de Janeiro since 2008. He works at the interface of university and community, is a geography professor at the Fluminense Federal University (UFF) in Niterói, Brazil, and a founding member of the Roça! Collective. Geographies in movement(s), militant investigation, favela resistance, urban struggles related to food sovereignty/food autonomy, collective economies, and geopolitics from a Global South perspective are his key fields of interest.

Christos Filippidis is an independent researcher living in Athens.

Antonis Vradis is an urban geographer based at the University of St Andrews, Scotland. He is the director of the university's Radical Urban Lab, a new research unit that tries to cut across hierarchies and to research, in a more egalitarian manner, some of the most pressing urban questions of today.

Minhocas Urbanas was the Maré-based community action research group of *Favela Resistance*. It consisted of Maré residents Geandra Nobre do Nascimento, Alessandra de Lima, Bruna Pierroux, and local coordinator Timo Bartholl, at the time all members of Minhocas Urbanas's local research partner the Roça! Collective; Joelma Nobre do Nascimento de Oliveira, a local market vendor; Amanda Mendonça, a social assistant and public health specialist; Jamylle Andrade, a nutritionist; Naldinho Lourenço, a community media activist; and Juliana de Medeiros Diniz, an agroecological farmer from the periurban area of Magé.

Raj Patel is an award-winning author, filmmaker, and academic. He is a research professor at the Lyndon B. Johnson School of Public Affairs at the University of Texas, Austin. He is the author of *Stuffed and Starved* and *The Value of Nothing*.

ABOUT PM PRESS

PM Press is an independent, radical publisher of critically necessary books for our tumultuous times. Our aim is to deliver bold political ideas and vital stories to all walks of life and arm the dreamers to demand the impossible. Founded in 2007 by a small group of people with decades of publishing, media, and organizing experience, we have sold millions of copies of our books, most often one at a time, face to face. We're old enough to know what we're doing and young enough to know what's at stake. Join us to create a better world.

PM Press
PO Box 23912
Oakland, CA 94623
www.pmpress.org

PM Press in Europe
europe@pmpress.org
www.pmpress.org.uk

FRIENDS OF PM PRESS

These are indisputably momentous times—the financial system is melting down globally and the Empire is stumbling. Now more than ever there is a vital need for radical ideas.

In the many years since its founding—and on a mere shoestring—PM Press has risen to the formidable challenge of publishing and distributing knowledge and entertainment for the struggles ahead. With hundreds of releases to date, we have published an impressive and stimulating array of literature, art, music, politics, and culture. Using every available medium, we've succeeded in connecting those hungry for ideas and information to those putting them into practice.

Friends of PM allows you to directly help impact, amplify, and revitalize the discourse and actions of radical writers, filmmakers, and artists. It provides us with a stable foundation from which we can build upon our early successes and provides a much-needed subsidy for the materials that can't necessarily pay their own way. You can help make that happen—and receive every new title automatically delivered to your door once a month—by joining as a Friend of PM Press. And, we'll throw in a free T-shirt when you sign up.

Here are your options:

- **$30 a month** Get all books and pamphlets plus a 50% discount on all webstore purchases

- **$40 a month** Get all PM Press releases (including CDs and DVDs) plus a 50% discount on all webstore purchases

- **$100 a month** Superstar—Everything plus PM merchandise, free downloads, and a 50% discount on all webstore purchases

For those who can't afford $30 or more a month, we have **Sustainer Rates** at $15, $10, and $5. Sustainers get a free PM Press T-shirt and a 50% discount on all purchases from our website.

Your Visa or Mastercard will be billed once a month, until you tell us to stop. Or until our efforts succeed in bringing the revolution around. Or the financial meltdown of Capital makes plastic redundant. Whichever comes first.

Nourishing Resistance: Stories of Food, Protest, and Mutual Aid

Edited by Wren Awry with a Foreword by Cindy Barukh Milstein

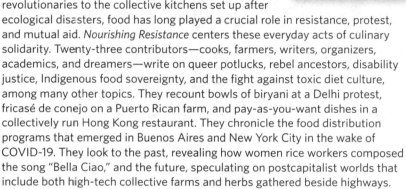

ISBN: 978-1-62963-992-5
$20.00   192 pages

From the cooks who have fed rebels and revolutionaries to the collective kitchens set up after ecological disasters, food has long played a crucial role in resistance, protest, and mutual aid. *Nourishing Resistance* centers these everyday acts of culinary solidarity. Twenty-three contributors—cooks, farmers, writers, organizers, academics, and dreamers—write on queer potlucks, rebel ancestors, disability justice, Indigenous food sovereignty, and the fight against toxic diet culture, among many other topics. They recount bowls of biryani at a Delhi protest, fricasé de conejo on a Puerto Rican farm, and pay-as-you-want dishes in a collectively run Hong Kong restaurant. They chronicle the food distribution programs that emerged in Buenos Aires and New York City in the wake of COVID-19. They look to the past, revealing how women rice workers composed the song "Bella Ciao," and the future, speculating on postcapitalist worlds that include both high-tech collective farms and herbs gathered beside highways.

Through essays, articles, poems, and stories, *Nourishing Resistance* argues that food is a central, intrinsic part of global struggles for autonomy and collective liberation.

"This collection of essays offers invaluable frameworks and inspirational models on how to get food out of capitalist markets and into the hands and stomachs of all. They fiercely demonstrate how the harvesting, growing, preparing, cooking, sharing, and eating of food has shaped and reshaped our cultures, created the social conditions for conviviality, and helped to break the seclusion and alienation that racist capitalist patriarchies organize. A must read for all who dream of keeping practices of commoning alive."
—Silvia Federici, author of *Re-enchanting the World: Feminism and the Politics of the Commons*

"A thoughtfully assembled, refreshingly global collection of radical voices who urge us to reimagine the meaning of the phrase 'food is political.'"
—Mayukh Sen, author of *Taste Makers: Seven Immigrant Women Who Revolutionized Food in America*

Cultivating a Revolutionary Spirit: Stories of Solidarity, Solar Cooking, and Women's Leadership in Central America

Laura Snyder Brown & William Fleet Lankford

ISBN: 979-8-88744-021-7
$21.95   208 pages

An exemplary story of solidarity in action, Cultivating a Revolutionary Spirit conveys the exhilarating experience of being part of paradigm-changing revolut ons.

Bill Lankford visited Nicaragua in 1984 to see the Sandinista revolution for himself. What he found led this physics professor to volunteer his skills teaching at the National Autonomous University of Nicaragua. There, he and his students developed a solar cooking project which took on a life of its own, spreading throughout the five countries of Central America.

In *Cultivating a Revolutionary Spirit*, Bill describes how local women used the tools of carpentry to build solar cvens and how they used the tools of feminism to take more control over their own lives and their communities. Bill leveraged his personal resources as a white North American man—professionally educated, fluent in English, with access to money and connections—to facilitate the work of Central American women who started by building ovens and went on to create an array of projects to meet basic needs, improve health, and increase access to educational and leadership opportunities for women.

"This is a story of extraordinary commitment, deep solidarity, uncommon integrity, and humility—of learning about struggle and transformation from strong and courageous Central American women. Beautifully told. Hopeful. Rooted in reality."
—Marie Dennis, senior adv ser, and co-president (2007-19) of Pax Christi International, program chair of the Catholic Nonviolence Initiative, prolific author, most recently *Choosing Peace: The Catholic Church Returns to Gospel Nonviolence*

"This is a story of women learning to cook with the sun during a time of revolution and social change. It takes us deep into the kitchens, lives, struggles and dreams of the women of Central America who harnessed the power of their solar ovens to cook, organize and empower themselves and their communities. It is the story of accompaniment and solidarity at its best; of walking with, listening, learning, and letting the women lead the way. Thank you for sharing this extraordinary journey—it shines!"
—Jennifer Atlee, Friendship Office of the Americas, author of *Red Thread: A Spiritual Journal of Accompaniment, Trauma and Healing*

Other Avenues Are Possible: Legacy of the People's Food System of the San Francisco Bay Area

Shanta Nimbark Sacharoff

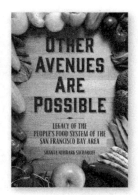

ISBN: 978-1-62963-232-2
$14.95   200 pages

Other Avenues Are Possible offers a vivid account of the dramatic rise and fall of the San Francisco People's Food System of the 1970s.

Weaving new interviews, historical research, and the author's personal story as a longstanding co-op member, the book captures the excitement of a growing radical social movement along with the struggles, heartbreaking defeats, and eventual resurgence of today's thriving network of Bay Area cooperatives, the greatest concentration of co-ops anywhere in the country.

Integral to the early natural foods movement, with a radical vision of "Food for People, Not for Profit," the People's Food System challenged agribusiness and supermarkets, and quickly grew into a powerful local network with nationwide influence before flaming out, often in dramatic fashion. *Other Avenues Are Possible* documents how food co-ops sprouted from grassroots organizations with a growing political awareness of global environmental dilapidation and unequal distribution of healthy foods to proactively serve their local communities. The book explores both the surviving businesses and a new network of support organizations that is currently expanding.

"In this book, Shanta Nimbark Sacharoff inspires us all by recounting how cooperation created other avenues for workers and consumers by developing a food system that not only promoted healthy food but wove within it practices that respect workers and the environment."
—E. Kim Coontz, executive director, California Center for Cooperative Development

"I have been waiting more than twenty years for this book! Shanta Nimbark Sacharoff's Other Avenues Are Possible *details the history of the People's Food System, a grand experiment in combining good food and workplace democracy.* Other Avenues *answers many of my questions about how the food politics of the Bay Area developed and points the way towards a better—and more cooperative— future. A must-read for anyone who eats food."*
—Gordon Edgar, author of *Cheesemonger: A Life on the Wedge* and a worker owner of Rainbow Grocery Cooperative

Against Urbanism

Franco La Cecla
Translated by Mairin O'Mahony

ISBN: 978-1-62963-235-3
$14.95   144 pages

After demolishing the myth of the rock star architect with his book *Against Architecture*, Franco La Cecla now explores the decisive challenges that cities are going to have to confront in the near future. Urban planning and development has become increasingly inadequate in response to the daily realities of life in our cities. Human, economic, ethnic, and environmental factors are systematically overlooked in city planning and housing development, and anachronistic, sterile, and formalistic architecture almost invariably prevails. Meanwhile, our cities grow out of internal impulses, not only in slums and favelas but through the pressing needs for public spaces which have sprung forth in great events and movements such as Istanbul's Gezi Park and Occupy Wall Street. Never more than today has democracy played itself out in public spaces, sidewalks, and streets. Urban planners and developers, however, are still prisoners of an obsolete vision of passivity which betrays actual city needs and demands. A new urban science is required which can, first of all, guarantee a civil, dignified life for all—urban development which ensures the right to a humane mode of daily living, which has been and still is completely ignored.

"Accustomed as we are to thinking that changes take place online or on a global scale, we sense that they are not made of human bodies in urban spaces and that the mere presence in the square of people claiming their right to the city is a political fact, explosive in nature." —Franco La Cecla (from *Against Urbanism*)

"La Cecla's tract against urbanism is a eulogy for the city."
—Renzo Piano

Stop, Thief!
The Commons, Enclosures, and Resistance

Peter Linebaugh

ISBN: 978-1-60486-747-3
$21.95   304 pages

In this majestic tour de force, celebrated historian Peter Linebaugh takes aim at the thieves of land, the polluters of the seas, the ravagers of the forests, the despoilers of rivers, and the removers of mountaintops. Scarcely a society has existed on the face of the earth that has not had commoning at its heart. "Neither the state nor the market," say the planetary commoners. These essays kindle the embers of memory to ignite our future commons.

From Thomas Paine to the Luddites, from Karl Marx—who concluded his great study of capitalism with the enclosure of commons—to the practical dreamer William Morris—who made communism into a verb and advocated communizing industry and agriculture—to the 20th-century communist historian E.P. Thompson, Linebaugh brings to life the vital commonist tradition. He traces the red thread from the great revolt of commoners in 1381 to the enclosures of Ireland, and the American commons, where European immigrants who had been expelled from their commons met the immense commons of the native peoples and the underground African-American urban commons. Illuminating these struggles in this indispensable collection, Linebaugh reignites the ancient cry, "STOP, THIEF!"

"There is not a more important historian living today. Period."
—Robin D.G. Kelley, author of *Freedom Dreams: The Black Radical Imagination*

"E.P. Thompson, you may rest now. Linebaugh restores the dignity of the despised luddites with a poetic grace worthy of the master . . . [A] commonist manifesto for the 21st century."
—Mike Davis, author of *Planet of Slums*

"Peter Linebaugh's great act of historical imagination . . . takes the cliché of 'globalization' and makes it live. The local and the global are once again shown to be inseparable—as they are, at present, for the machine-breakers of the new world crisis."
—T.J. Clark, author of *Farewell to an Idea*

Abolishing Fossil Fuels: Lessons from Movements That Won

Kevin A. Young

ISBN: 979-8-88744-033-0
$22.95   264 pages

Climate destruction is a problem of political power.

We have the resources for a green transition, but how can we neutralize the influence of Exxon and Shell? *Abolishing Fossil Fuels* argues that the climate movement has started to turn the tide against fossil fuels, just too gradually. The movement's partial victories show us how the industry can be further undermined and eventually abolished. Activists have been most successful when they've targeted the industry's enablers: the banks, insurers, and big investors that finance its operations, the companies and universities that purchase fossil fuels, and the regulators and judges who make life-and-death rulings about pipelines, power plants, and drilling sites. This approach has jeopardized investor confidence in fossil fuels, leading the industry to lash out in increasingly desperate ways. The fossil fuel industry's financial and legal enablers are also its Achilles heel.

The most powerful movements in US history succeeded in similar ways. The book also includes an in-depth analysis of four classic victories: the abolition of slavery, battles for workers' rights in the 1930s, Black freedom struggles of the 1950s and 1960s, and the fight for clean air. Those movements inflicted costs on economic elites through strikes, boycotts, and other mass disruption. They forced some sectors of the ruling class to confront others, which paved the way for victory. Electing and pressuring politicians was rarely the movements' primary focus. Rather, gains in the electoral and legislative realms were usually the byproducts of great upsurges in the fields, factories, and streets.

Those historic movements show that it's very possible to defeat capitalist sectors that may seem invulnerable. They also show us how it can be done. They offer lessons for building a multiracial, working-class climate movement that can win a global green transition that's both rapid and equitable.

"Of the many present crises facing the future of humanity, climate change and its threat of mass extinction appears to be the most daunting. Kevin Young argues compellingly, however, that electoral strategies to fight climate change are a dead end. Rather, his study of past successful movements suggests that radical upsurges, the building of disruptive mass movements, including demonstrations, civil disobedience, and large strikes, are more compelling alternatives for stemming the tide, while ultimately only the end of capitalism will save us. A tour de force! "
—Michael Goldfield, author of *The Southern Key: Class, Race, and Radicalism in the 1930s and 1940s*

Autonomy Is in Our Hearts: Zapatista Autonomous Government through the Lens of the Tsotsil Language

Dylan Eldredge Fitzwater
with a Foreword by John P. Clark

ISBN: 978-1-62963-580-4
$19.95   224 pages

Following the Zapatista uprising on New Year's Day 1994, the EZLN communities of Chiapas began the slow process of creating a system of autonomous government that would bring their call for freedom, justice, and democracy from word to reality. *Autonomy Is in Our Hearts* analyzes this long and arduous process on its own terms, using the conceptual language of Tsotsil, a Mayan language indigenous to the highland Zapatista communities of Chiapas.

The words "Freedom," "Justice," and "Democracy" emblazoned on the Zapatista flags are only approximations of the aspirations articulated in the six indigenous languages spoken by the Zapatista communities. They are rough translations of concepts such as *ichbail ta muk'* or "mutual recognition and respect among equal persons or peoples," *a'mtel* or "collective work done for the good of a community" and *lekil kuxlejal* or "the life that is good for everyone." *Autonomy Is in Our Hearts* provides a fresh perspective on the Zapatistas and a deep engagement with the daily realities of Zapatista autonomous government. Simultaneously an exposition of Tsotsil philosophy and a detailed account of Zapatista governance structures, this book is an indispensable commentary on the Zapatista movement of today.

"This is a refreshing book. Written with the humility of the learner, or the absence of the arrogant knower, the Zapatista dictum to 'command obeying' becomes to 'know learning.'"
—Marisol de la Cadena, author of *Earth Beings: Ecologies of Practice across Andean Worlds*

"Autonomy Is in Our Hearts is perhaps the most important book you can read on the Zapatista movement in Chiapas today. It stands out from the rest of the Anglophone literature in that it demonstrates, with great sensitivity, how a dialectic between traditional culture and institutions and emerging revolutionary and regenerative forces can play a crucial role in liberatory social transformation. It shows us what we can learn from the indigenous people of Chiapas about a politics of community, care, and mutual aid, and—to use a word that they themselves use so much—about a politics of heart. A great strength of the work is that the author is a very good listener. He allows the people of Chiapas to tell their own story largely in their own words, and with their own distinctive voice."
—John P. Clark, from the Foreword

Zapatista Stories for Dreaming Another World

Subcomandante Marcos
Edited and translated by Colectivo
Relámpago/Lightning Collective with a
Foreword by JoAnn Wypijewski

ISBN: 978-1-62963-970-3
$16.95   160 pages

In this gorgeous collection of allegorical stories, Subcomandante Marcos, idiosyncratic spokesperson of the Zapatistas, has provided "an accidental archive" of a revolutionary group's struggle against neoliberalism. For thirty years, the Zapatistas have influenced and inspired movements worldwide, showing that another world is possible. They have infused left politics with a distinct imaginary—and an imaginative, literary, or poetic dimension—organizing horizontally, outside and against the state, and with a profound respect for difference as a source of political insight, not division. With commentaries that illuminate their historical, political, and literary contexts and an introduction by the translators, this timeless, elegiac volume is perfect for lovers of literature and lovers of revolution.

"From the beating heart of Mesoamerica the old gods speak to Old Antonio, a glasses-wearing, pipe-smoking beetle who studies neoliberalism, and both tell their tales to Subcomandante Marcos who passes them on to us: the stories of the Zapatistas' revolutionary struggles from below and to the left. The Colectivo Relámpago (Lightning Collective), based in Amherst, Massachusetts, translates and comments with bolts of illumination zigzagging across cultures and nations, bringing bursts of laughter and sudden charges of hot-wired political energy. It seems like child's play, yet it's almost divine!"
—Peter Linebaugh, author of Red Round Globe Hot Burning

"This is a beautiful, inspired project. In a joyful Zapatista gesture readers will welcome, this volume invites us to play, to walk on different, and even contrary paths through smooth and crystalline translations that bring these 'other stories' to life. The translators' commentaries preserve a delicate balance of expertise and autonomy as they illuminate the historical, political, and cultural forces that provoked the stories' creation. Among these forces are Zapatista women, whom the translators rightly dignify in their meticulous and provocative introduction. This volume is a gift to so many of us as we (attempt to) bring the Zapatista imagination to our students and organizing communities."
—Michelle Joffroy, associate professor of Spanish and Latin American & Latino Studies, Smith College and co-director of Domestic Workers Make History

Between Earth and Empire: From the Necrocene to the Beloved Community

John P. Clark
with a Foreword by Peter Marshall

ISBN: 978-1-62963-648-1
$22.95   352 pages

Between Earth and Empire focuses on the crucial position of humanity at the present moment in Earth History. We have left the Cenozoic, the "new period of life," and are now in the midst of the Necrocene, a period of mass extinction and reversal of the course of evolution of life on Earth. We are now nearing the end of the long history of Empire and domination, faced with the alternatives of either continuing the path of social and ecological disintegration or initiating a new era of social and ecological regeneration.

The book shows that conventional approaches to global crisis on both the right and the left have succumbed to processes of denial and disavowal, either rejecting the reality of crisis entirely or substituting ineffectual but comforting gestures and images for deep, systemic social transformation. It is argued that an effective response to global crisis requires attention to all major spheres of social determination, including the social institutional structure, the social ideology, the social imaginary, and the social ethos. Large-scale social and ecological regeneration must be rooted in communities of liberation and solidarity, in which personal and group transformation take place in all these spheres, so that a culture of awakening and care can emerge.

Between Earth and Empire explores examples of significant progress in this direction, including the Zapatista movement in Chiapas, the Democratic Autonomy Movement in Rojava, indigenous movements in defense of the commons, the solidarity economy movement, and efforts to create liberated base communities and affinity groups within anarchism and other radical social movements. In the end, the book presents a vision of hope for social and ecological regeneration through the rebirth of a libertarian and communitarian social imaginary, and the flourishing of a free cooperative community globally.

"Whether in Rojava where women are fighting for their people's survival, or in the loss and terror of New Orleans after the Katrina flood, Clark finds models of communality, care, and hope. Finely reasoned and integrative, tracing the dialectical play of institution and ethos, ideology and imaginary, this book will speak to philosophers and activists alike."
—Ariel Salleh, author of *Ecofeminism as Politics*